Socio-Economic Changes in a Religious Complex: A Case Study of Tarakeswar (1729 - 1952)

Socio-Economic Changes in a Religious Complex: A Case Study of Tarakeswar (1729 - 1952)

Soumyajyoti Chakrabarty

MOTILAL BANARSIDASS INTERNATIONAL
DELHI

First Edition : Delhi, 2026

ISBN : 978-93-47683-85-5

Also available at :

MOTILAL BANARSIDASS INTERNATIONAL

41 U.A. Bungalow Road, (Back Lane) Jawahar Nagar, Delhi-110007
4261/3 (Basement), Ansari Road, Darya Ganj, New Delhi-110002
Shop#. 6, 241, Luz Ginza Complex, Luz Corner, Mylapore, Chennai - 600004
12/1A, 2nd Floor, Bankim Chatterjee Street, Kolkata - 700073

Stockist : Motilal Books, Ashok Rajpath, Near Kali Mandir, Patna-800004

Printed in India by
MOTILAL BANARSIDASS INTERNATIONAL

To

My wife

Mrs. Mala Chakrabarty

Acknowledgement

During my teaching tenure at Ramakrishna Mission Vidyamandira, Belur Math, I became interested in Tarakeswar *'Saiva Tirtha'* as a backdrop for studying regional history in relation to my advancement of learning. My research focused on the "*Math*" system's evolution from 1729 to 1952.

My journey was greatly supported by Professor Shri Upendra Narayan Chakrabarty, who introduced me to Professor Shri Ramakanta Chakrabarty of Burdwan University, whose guidance and assistance were invaluable in directing my research towards successful results. I am deeply grateful to both of them as well as, to all those well-wishers, who supported me towards achieving my goal in my academic journey.

Above all, the supportive family environment played a significant role in reaching my objectives. My wife's support was a crucial factor throughout the process.

I acknowledge that the outcome of the entire effort is attributable to my actions, and I take full responsibility for any inadvertent errors or deviations.

Preface

This compilation encompasses the history of the evolution of Tarakeswar as a place of pilgrimage with reference to the cult of Lord *Taraknath* from 1729 to 1952. The presiding deity remains all through the sheet-anchor of the socio-economic evolution of this place of pilgrimage. The process of evolution had begun following the participation of a member of the *Gopa* caste and the Chhatri zamindar of Baligari, not far-off from this pilgrim centre. The subsequent addition to this process was a *Dashnami Giri Sannyasi* who led to the establishment of the monastic system under the patronage of the aforesaid *Chhatri zamindar*, that lasted for over two centuries at Tarakeswar.

Tarakeswar has also been studied in retrospect with reference to the existing geography of the region in which this place of pilgrimage is situated. Besides the *Kaibarttas* and the *Gopas*, all were found to have been outsiders to this place of pilgrimage.

Noticeably, the age-old rituals and beliefs of the original inhabitants came easily to terms with the *Mohanta* culture resulting in popular form of *Saivism* with its bearing of fairs and festivals.

It has been emphasised that the evolution of the pilgrim town owes greatly to the evolution of the monastic system put forward by the *Dashnami Giri* Sannyasis with preceptor-disciple lineage. Hence, the *Tarakeswar Math* was the nucleus, around which the temple-zamindari evolved in due course.

With an overall commitment to keep a good hold on the twin institutions up to the end of the 18th century, the *Giri Mohantas* overcame the forces of destabilisation often threatened the *Tarakeswar Math* during this period under review.

The evolution of the monastic system during the 19th century witnessed the same process of extension as well as consolidation of the *temple-zamindari* by dint of the perseverance of the *Giri Mohantas*. The gradual development of this pilgrim centre in this phase owed much to the extension of the railway network that happened during the tenures of the last two *Giri Mohantas*. Despite these, the diminishing trend in the monastic system became conspicuous that led to the overthrow of the said regime.

The verdict given by the District Judge on 6.11.29 in connection with the Title Suit 28/1922, brought about the overthrow of the *Giri* regime.

Actually, the *Satyagraha* movement at Tarakeswar facilitated the removal of the *Giri* regime in the given perspective. This was resorted to on 20 May, 1924 and came to an end on 22 Sept. 1924 simply because of the lack of human as well as material resources.

The interregnum between the passing of the *Giri* regime into oblivion and the advent of the *Ashram* order of the *Dashnami Sannyasis* in the administration of the twin institutions, witnessed the tenures of two Receivers Amulya Chandra Bhaduri and Rashbehari Mukherjee.

The appointment of the new *Mohanta* coincided with the setting up of a new administrative hierarchy in accordance with the order passed on 29.8.34 by the Calcutta

High Court. However, his disenchantment with the litigation strengthened his determination to resign in favour of his trusted disciple, Hrishikesh Ashram in 1952 (1358 B.S.).

However, Tarakeswar is a celebrated place of fairs and festivals of different types from the month of *Baisakh* to that of *Chaitra* of the Bengali calendar year. In fact, casteism plays an important role in almost all the sacred performances except during the time of fairs and festivals which are held at frequent intervals. The rituals performed within the temple conform to sanskritised prescription while folk-rites are mostly found to have been performed during the gajan festival. The proof of compromise with the *Lokayata* (popular) culture on the part of the upholders of Brahminical religion remains all through spectacular in this place of pilgrimage.

The exposure of this temple-town by virtue of the improvement in the communication system resulted in the development of this pilgrim-town as also a commercial centre. Hence, Tarakeswar always remains like other places of pilgrimage a refuge for those seeking fulfilment of material and psychological needs as well as spiritual satisfaction in ever changing socio-economic scenario.

Content

Introduction

I

The process of secularisation of the present-day intellectual community does not hinder intellectuals from understanding the motivation behind the practice of religion. Historians as well as social analysts agree that people belonging to different societies have always been swayed by their religious inclinations. Therefore, one discovers that histories of societies have often been compiled in terms of the rise of different types of religious sects from different theological standpoints.

In fact, an understanding of religious activity in this perspective seems crucial for an understanding of the present-day society, for in many countries religious activity appears to be yet viable and of considerable scope at least on the surface. Religious behaviour, indeed, has immense consequences that affect the various aspects of socio-economic life. In his famous essay, 'The Protestant Ethic and the Spirit of Capitalism', Max Weber puts forward the hypothesis that religious beliefs and behaviour do have a major impact on economic development. Incidentally, arguments about the impact of religion on socio-economic development have frequently been applied to India by Western scholars like Burton Stein, Bernard S. Cohn, Carl Gustav Diehl and others as well as Indian scholars, among whom L.P. Vidyarthi and N.K. Bose, were the earliest.

Although a few historical descriptions of Hindu places of pilgrimage by Indologists, Orientalists and travellers provide one with valuable information about the utility of these institutions over the last century and a half, it was not until the early fifties that cultural analyses of these places began to appear. From time immemorial, ascetics, wayfarers, merchants, rulers and even ordinary householders have been drawn towards the various centres of pilgrimage that fall within the domain of this land of unity in diversity, with a sense of inherent compulsion. This perennial flow of pilgrims from all walks of life speaks much for the socio-economic evolution centred on a religious complex.

Hinduism, like all other religions, refers to certain places as sacred. The Hindus visit periodically or earnestly cherish the desire to visit those places at least once in their lives. In fact, Hinduism does in no way lay down rigorous instructions to its followers to visit those holy places sanctified by tradition at regular intervals. The holy scriptures, however, bear ample references to the process of feeling the presence of the Almighty God in oneself through meditation[1]. In spite of that, a devout Hindu takes pleasure in visiting holy places like Amarnath and Badrinath in the Himalayan region, Somnath on the shore of the Arabian Sea, Sriksetra in Orissa, Gaya and Deoghar in Bihar, Kalighat and Tarakeswar in West Bengal, Kamrup in Assam, Kanyakumari in the Southern part of India as well as innumerable places of pilgrimage in and around India as and when possible.

Buddhists all over the world likewise take pleasure in visiting Sarnath, Bodhgaya and other holy places celebrated for their association with the life and works of Lord Buddha. In the same way, the disciples of Lord Mahabira find religiosity in visiting Ajmer and Pabapuri. This behaviourism is evident even in the case of the Jews and the Christians when they look with emotion towards Jerusalem and Bethlehem.

Similarly, devout Muslims nourish lifelong desires to visit Mecca and Madina at least once in their lives. Besides, the tombs and graves of reputed Muslim saints elsewhere infuse them also with an earnest desire to take recourse to pilgrimages.

Hindu pilgrims are generally interested in visualising the manifestations of the divinities of deities in places of pilgrimage, identified in the holy scriptures as sacred. There are, in fact, innumerable sacred places associated with the many religions that exist in India, among which those associated with Hinduism form the greatest number. The incessant flow of pilgrims to these places of pilgrimage is an evidence of the impact of these sacred centres on Indian society. No doubt that the urge for spiritual and metaphysical satisfaction, to some extent, goads an individual to visit a place of pilgrimage, but more often material interests dominate.

It has already been noted that during the second half of the twentieth century, a great deal of attention has been paid to the institution of pilgrimage, especially its impact on socio-economic evolution within a given context. Gaya was perhaps the first to draw the attention of a renowned anthropologist like L.P. Vidyarthi and Bhubaneswar, another famous pilgrimage centre of ancient origin, was also taken up by N.K. Bose in the first phase of the anthropological study of holy places in India.[2] Both the studies were inspired in many ways by Prof. Robert Redfield who was of opinion that the study of the complexities of a civilisation along with the traditional social organization is in some manner dependent on the study of traditional centres of pilgrimage. His concept of civilisation as a complex structure of great as well as little traditions has generated keen interest for studying temples and other places of pilgrimage in this context.[3]

Moreover, reference can be made to a commendable work about Sriksetra, a famous pilgrim centre in Eastern India by Sundarananda Vidyavinod. Besides, a comprehensive work on 'The Cult of Jagannath and the Regional Tradition of Orissa', has also been brought out under the purview of the South Asia Inter-disciplinary Regional Research Programme. This work, however, approaches the subject from a historical as well as an anthropological standpoint.[4]

The importance of the places of pilgrimage has been conceived from various viewpoints by different scholars. Milton Singer's definition of 'cultural centre', 'cultural specialists' and 'cultural performance' as well as Mckim Marriot and B.S. Cohn's concept of the pilgrim centres as 'networks and centres' in the process of the integration of Indian civilisation offer useful guidelines for this study.[5] In fact, the places of pilgrimage are worth studying from the point of view of the Indian tradition. Not only European scholars but also their Indian counterparts have seriously attempted to study the places of Hindu pilgrimage in their given perspectives. Prof. L.P. Vidyarthi had also made an attempt to approach a Hindu place of pilgrimage i.e. Kashi as a dimension of Indian civilisation and analysed the structure incidentally in terms of three analytical tools i.e. the sacred geography, the sacred performances and the sacred specialists. However, a large number of publications have been brought out in this sphere since the publication of his 'Sacred Complex in Hindu Gaya' in 1961.[6]

But scholars seldom remain satisfied with merely the structural analyses of the places of Hindu pilgrimage.

This is somewhat clear from Burton Stein's essay on 'The Economic Function of a Medieval South Indian Temple', where he emphasised the economic network of the Tirupati temple.[7] Here he has elaborated how the temple of Lord *Tirupati*, as a sacred institution, caters to the secular functions of society.

Moreover, the references to different types of religious groups taking keen interest in extending their influences as and when possible, on the economic network around the religious complex, have been made amply clear in the writings of Bernard S. Cohn's 'The Role of the Gosains in the Economy of Eighteenth and Nineteenth Century Upper India.[8] Therefore, it must be conceded that the temple as a sacred complex can obviously initiate functions of secular types within the network of society.

Besides, pilgrim centres usually become nuclear areas of intensive Hinduisation and this process can be perceived during the periods of fairs and festivals. In fact, temple promotion in a certain place speaks much for the steady growth of the Hindu population around the sacred complex. The fascinating study about the 'Organisation of Services in the Temple of Lingaraj in Bhubaneswar' by N.K. Bose with special emphasis on the participation of castes as well as service pattern in connection with ritual deliberations within the temple also points to the phenomenon of a caste hierarchy within the given social context. Besides, S. Sinha's study of the Kali temple at Kalighat enumerates too the role played by the Kali temple in regional as well as national integration and the role of present day media in the spread of the cult of the Kali temple at Calcutta.[9] Prafulla Chakrabarty's 'Social Profile of Tarakeswar' is also a commendable contribution in this perspective.

However, the aforesaid references to the studies about the centres of pilgrimage by different erudite scholars make it clear that most of the important places of pilgrimage are conspicuously traceable to puranic origins, thus representing traditional aspects of puranic holy places. Therefore, it is not clearly understood whether the patterns developed in their hypotheses are applicable to those places of pilgrimage with somewhat regional bias. Moreover, different groups of people living at important places of pilgrimage with different commitments towards the deities seem to have been under-represented in the studies by these scholars. They entertain only superficial treatment. Even when the pilgrims as the consumers of the sacred centres receive attention, they are hardly ever viewed in the context of their socio-economic characteristics.

Most of the scholars have started from the common premise that the sacred complex of a Hindu place of pilgrimage reflects a level of continuity, compromise and combination between great and little traditions. Secondly, the sacred specialists like the *Mohantas, Sebayets* or the priests of a place of pilgrimage maintain distinct life styles. Usually, they endeavour to transmit certain elements of the great traditions to the rural population of India through the popularisation of certain texts as well as the organisation of pilgrimages within the scope of their hallowed role as religious functionaries. Thirdly, the sacred complex in general and the sacred specialists in particular have usually participated in the process of modification as well as transformation over the years. This, however, leads to a general development in the larger spectrum of Hindu civilisation, of which they form an integral part.

II

The temple of Lord *Taraknath* at Tarakeswar is a major place of pilgrimage for Hindus in Eastern India.[10] For over two centuries or more, the presiding deity remains the main attraction for the pilgrims visiting this place from the farthest as well as nearest corners of this subcontinent. This place of pilgrimage has undergone gradual development over the years solely owing to the patronage of the cult of Lord *Taraknath*.

However, the primary objective of this study will be to put forward an accurate profile of the socio-economic and religious perspectives of this pilgrim centre at Tarakeswar. An earnest endeavour has also been made in this connection to highlight the change that took place in and around this pilgrim town over the years.

The present study initially intends to classify the salient features of *Svayambhulingam* which are felt to resemble the cult of Lord *Taraknath*. An effort has also been made to throw adequate light on certain qualities of the cult that correspond to the mythological cult of *Siva* elsewhere. It is, however remarkable that the cult of Lord *Taraknath* bears scanty references to the holy texts. Moreover, a serious attempt has been made to study the revelation of the cult against a historical background. But the mythological background has not been ignored.

An intensive study has been initiated to clarify the positional perspective and topographic features of the region in which Tarakeswar is situated, in terms of its history. The socio-economic and cultural background of the original inhabitants has consequently been brought within the purview of discussion.

The revelation of the cult of Lord *Taraknath* coincided with the evolution of the monastery system under the aegis of the *Mohantas*, the principal religious functionaries of the sacred complex. This pilgrim town owes much to the *Mohantas* for its initial growth, consequent development and fame. This monastery was established at the behest of the *Giri* subsect of the *Dashnami Sannyasis* which adhered to 'Guru-Sisya parampara' or the preceptor-disciple lineage. Therefore, an extensive study of the role of the *Mohantas* has been undertaken not only in the sphere of religious orientation but also in the temporal arena of this pilgrim-town. Incidentally, emphasis has been put on the commercial endeavours of the *Mohantas* as well as on their functions as landlords with different implications for the *debutter* property in general and the *debutter* land in particular, in the context of *Tarakeswar Math*.

This study does not concentrate itself exclusively on the socio-economic orientation of this place of pilgrimage. Therefore, attention has been paid to the capacity of religion in the mobilisation of mass activity around the religious complex. The outbreak of Tarakeswar *Satyagraha*, in fact, created political convulsions not only in this region but also had its immediate fallout on the broader political arena. This eventful *Satyagraha* movement deserves adequate space in the discussion because of its impact on the transformation of this pilgrim town into a modern one, as also on the system of management employed by the twin institutions - the temple and the monastery.

Any discussion about the aspects of a place of pilgrimage remains incomplete until and unless its pilgrim component is taken into account. Therefore, a careful study of the pilgrims with their seasonal characteristics round the year has carefully been undertaken along with associated matters in relation to this place of pilgrimage. The incessant flow of pilgrims along with inherent impact of this on the lifestyle of the pilgrim-town has only incidentally found deserving place in the present study. Moreover, emphasis has been laid on the discussion about the socio-cultural background of the pilgrims along with the change in their motives and behaviour vis-a-vis the sacred specialists and others associated with the temple for livelihood. In short, this study seeks to demonstrate how this pilgrim-town has undergone a change over the years in the socio-economic context as a result of its dependence on the temple and its pilgrims.

However, careful analyses of the characteristics of the fairs and festivals held in this pilgrim-town reveal clearly the nature of the festivals as also of those associated with them. The cult of Lord *Taraknath* seems to have been associated somehow or the other with almost all types of Hindu festivals arranged in accordance with the Hindu almanac in and around the place of pilgrimage. Therefore, the interaction among diverse groups of people from far and wide with the consequent fallout on the residents of this pilgrim centre has also been brought within the purview of discussion.

The present work also tends to elucidate various factors operating in this minor regional centre of pilgrimage with special reference to the role of the sacred specialists. There has evolved here an ordered system of relationships depending largely on the bond of religion. Therefore, an assessment has been made of the service of religion both from the practical as well as the divine perspectives in association with the role of the *Mohanta*, the *Sebayets* and others belonging to the sacred complex. Moreover, this study seeks to clarify the gradual change in the attitude of the sacred specialists in relation to their profession in the present context.

The compilation also takes into account the importance of the cult of Lord *Taraknath* and the sacred complex which is in no way exclusively confined to the religious aspect alone. It has been noted that the economy of the pilgrim-town depends to a large extent on the orientation of the temple and various occupational groups, who earn their livelihood by rendering service to the deity. Therefore, this study seeks to determine the prevalent context that helped the orientation of the economy of this place of pilgrimage. In fact, this orientation of economy revolving round the cult of Lord *Taraknath* makes an interesting study in the given context.

That the structural analysis of a sacred complex alone will not serve the purpose to the desired extent has well been emphasised in the ensuing discussion. This results in a detailed discussion about the hinterland of the pilgrim-town which is definitely and symbiotically linked economically, culturally as well as socially to Tarakeswar.

Besides, an earnest endeavour has also been made to establish the overwhelming presence of the traditional aspects of this pilgrim centre with its adaptability to the forces of change in the given context. It is, indeed, an attempt to establish a link between the researches done by eminent scholars about the famous centres of Hindu pilgrimage and a systematic and rigorous study of a regional pilgrim centre. This study endeavours to encompass almost all perspectives and aspects of this religious complex from a detached standpoint. It also highlights the fact that religious activities with their ramifications require not only religious sentiments but also organisations which contain forces that are independent of the religious sentiments involved.

No study, of course, can satisfactorily answer all the glaring questions one might face about the religious activities of the participants in and around the sacred complex. Therefore, the study undertaken also attempts to answer a few of these questions so far as possible within the scope of an all-round evolution of a religious complex i.e. Tarakeswar.

Note

1. "Idam tirtham idam tirtham bhramanti tamasajanah.
   Atmatirtham na Jananti katham moksah baranane"
   Jnanasankuli Tantra. Ramtosan Vidyalankar (ed.)- Prantosani Tantra. p. - 177. (Oh beloved! the laymen travel holy places elsewhere being unaware of the fact that way to salvation lies in themselves.)

2. L.P. Vidyarthi - Origin and Development of the Gayawal : A Priestly Community. Journal of Bihar Research Society. 1954. XI, Part. 2.
   Also,
   N.K. Bose - Organisation of Services in the Temple of Lingaraj, Bhubaneswar. Culture and Society in India. Chap.-7. Asia Publishing House. Cal. 1967. PP - 105-168.

3. Robert Redfield and Milton Singer - The Cultural Role of Cities. Economic Development and Cultural Change. 3. PP-53-73. 1954.
   Also,
   Robert Redfield - The Social Organisation of Traditions. Far Eastern Quarterly. 15(1) : PP-13-21.

4. Sundarananda Vidyavinod - Sriksetra. Calcutta. Gaudiya Mission. 2nd ed. 1951.
   Also,
   A Eschmann., H. Kulke and G. C. Tripathi - The Cult of Jangannath and the Regional Tradition of Orissa. South Asia Inter-disciplinary Regional Research Programme. Orissa Research Project, South Asia Institute, New Delhi, Monohar Publications. (1978).

5. Milton Singer - The Great Tradition in a Metropolitan Centre: Madras, in Milton Singer (ed.) Traditional India : Structure and Change. 1959. PP.- 207-215.

Also,

Mckim Marriot and B. S. Cohn - Networks and Centres in the Integration of Indian Civilisation. Journal of Social Research 1.(1). PP-1-9. 1958.

6. L.P. Vidyarthi, B. N. Saraswati and Makhan Jha - The Sacred Complex of Kashi : a Microcosm of Indian Civilisation. Delhi. Concept Publishing Co. 1979. Also, L. P. Vidyarthi - Sacred Complex in Hindu Gaya. 1961. Asia Publishing House. Bombay.

7. Burton Stein - The Economic Function of a Medieval South Indian Temple. Journal of Asian Studies. 19(2) : PP- 163-176.1960.

8. Bernard S. Cohn - The Role of the Gosains in the Economy of Eighteenth and Nineteenth Century Upper India. Also, L. P. Vidyarthi and Makhan Jha (ed.) - Symposium on the Sacred Complex in India. Ranchi. Council of Social and Cultural Research. PP.- 88-95. 1974.

9. S. Sinha - Kali Temple at Kalighat and the city of Calcutta. S. Sinha (ed.) - Cultural Profile of Calcutta. The Indian Anthropological Society. PP.-61-72.

10. A. K. Banerjee - West Bengal District Gazetteers. Hooghly. P.-665.

Chapter - I

The revelation of the cult of Lord Taraknath and the consequent evolution of Tarakeswar as a place of pilgrimage

I

The evolution of Tarakeswar as a place of pilgrimage, is linked to history and legend. This holy centre for pilgrimage owes its name and fame to the hallowed cult of Lord *Taraknath*. There was no human endeavour behind the initiation of this cult of *Siva* at Tarakeswar. Hence, the self-manifested cult of Lord *Taraknath* is of *Svayambhulingam* type.[1] This can be asserted with reference to *Svayambhulingadi laksanam* in the *Prantosani Tantra*. The description given in it of the salient features of a *Svayambhulingam*, indeed, relates to the hallowed revelation of Lord *Taraknath*, the presiding deity of this place of pilgrimage in Eastern India.[2]

In this context, one may take into account ample references to the twelve *Jyotirlingams* along with the other *Sivalingams* in the *Satarudra Samhita* and the *Kotirudra Samhita* of the *Siva Purana*. But no allusion has been made in these, either to Lord *Taraknath* as an important *Sivalingam* or to Tarakeswar as a *Sivaksetra* of puranic origin. This seems surprising given the reference to Lord *Baidyanath* of Deoghar in Bihar.[3] This is also the case in the

Dvadas Jyotirlinga Stotram in the *Stavakavacamala* by Satish Chandra Mukherjee.[4]

Metaphysically, *Siva* is pure consciousness, perfect enlightenment and the symbol of pure intelligence (*Visuddha Sattva*). The white colour of the Lord bears a subtle harmony with his metaphysical nature.[5] As Lord *Siva* is worshipped as the origin of everything of this universe (*Visvabijam*), it is in fact difficult to imagine *Siva* in his original form. Therefore, he can best be conceived through a symbol which conveniently corresponds to the *Lingam*.[6] Besides, there is an explicit reference to the derivation of the term *Lingam* in the *Skandapurana* which belittles the idea of conceiving it as merely a symbol of generative power.[7] He, indeed, is symbolised with his inherent characteristics through the *Lingam* which corresponds in no way to the cult of *Siva* in a primordial form of phallic worship.[8] In fact, this degeneration in the conception of the holy manifestation of *Siva* through *Lingam* owes much to the lucid description of the authors of the *Puranas*. *Rudra* with his inherent traits as depicted in the *Rigveda* and *Yajurveda* is totally absent with his all-encompassing dimensions in the *Puranas*. This use of mean connotation no doubt betrays the poverty of the philosophical outlook of the authors of the *Puranas*.

The *Svayambhulingam* at Tarkeswar in the Southern *Rarh* region is worshipped from the initial phase of the revelation as *Anadilingam* by devotees in general. It is interesting to note that the *Svayambhulingam* (*Anadilingam*) at this place of pilgrimage resembles the spectacular type of *Sivalingam* as depicted in the chapter entitled *Brahmakhanda* in the *Bhavisya Purana* (7/8). An allusion can be found in the same compilation to a region with the name of *Rarhi-Khanda-Jangal* which happens to have fallen within the periphery of Northern *Rarh*. The neighbourhood of the

Rarhi-Khanda-Jangal included the places like Bakreswar, Birbhumi, Baidyanath as well as rivulets like the Ajay and also some rivers. It seems that the Kandi subdivision of present-day Murshidabad district along with the whole of Birbhum district as well as the northern part of the Katwa subdivision of Burdwan district comprised the regional entity of Northern *Rarh*.

The earliest reference to Southern *Rarh* may be found in the inscription of Vakpati Munj or Vakpatiraja II (A.D. 972-A.D. 993) , the most powerful ruler of the Paramara dynasty as well as in the *Nayakandali* compiled by Sridharacharya (991-992). The *Nayakandali* refers to Bhurisrsti as an important village in the Southern *Rarh* inhabited mostly by well-versed *Brahmins* as well as wealthy merchants. The reference bears,

"Asiddaksinaradhayam dvijanam bhurikarmanam/
Bhurisrstiriti gramo bhurisresthijanasrayah"//

Moreover, the reference to Southern *Rarh* also occurs in the *Pravodhacandrodaya* (Act II), a drama compiled by Krishna Misra presumably in either the 11th or the 12th century. Both Sridharacharya and Krishna Misra had referred to Bhurisresthik or Bhurisrsti and Nabagram as two important villages in the Southern *Rarh*. Moreover, an allusion had also been made to *Rarha* or *Rarhapuri* as well as Bhurisresthik or Bhurisrsti in the *Pravodhacandrodaya* by Krishna Misra. This *Rarha* or *Rarhapuri* happened to have fallen within the geographical perspective of *Gaudha* which included the region surrounding the present districts of Malda, Murshidabad, Birbhum and Burdwan. Besides, references to Southern *Rarh* are also explicit in the *Chandimangal* (1593-94) compiled by Kabikankan Mukundaram. He was born in the village of Damunya on the South bank of the river Damodar which is now in the district of Burdwan. However, Bhurisresthik or Bhurisrsti is at present in the district of Howrah while Nabagram as well as Damunya are in the districts of Hooghly and Burdwan respectively now-a-days. Therefore, it can safely be argued in the light of the above discussion that the present geographical entity of Howrah, Hooghly and several parts of Burdwan did fall within the region known as Southern *Rarh*.[9]

It is remarkable that Kabikankan had given a vivid account of almost all the important as well as holy places in and around Damunya. But he made no allusion to the cult of Lord *Taraknath* at Tarakeswar which, indeed, fell within the regional entity of Southern *Rarh*. Moreover, Damunya was not far from Tarakeswar. Although Kabikankan was oblivious to the revelation of the cult of Lord *Taraknath* in the district of Hooghly of Southern *Rarh*, reference can be had of Tarakeswar with obvious implication to the cult in the *Sri Mahalingesvara Tantra*.[10] He could not have missed the opportunity of referring to the cult of Lord *Taraknath* at Tarakeswar had it come within his purview, although he referred to even *Chakraditya Siva* of his native village. Perhaps, the people at large in and around this place of pilgrimage were in the dark about the charismatic cult of Lord *Taraknath* prior to or even during the period of the poet of the *Chandimangal*. But it was probable that the *Svayambhulingam* had been there, at Tarakeswar, from time immemorial along with *Baidyanath*, *Bakresvar*, *Siddhinath*, *Ghantesvar* and the other *Sivalingams* in and around Bengal. Therefore, it seems that the growth of this place of pilgrimage in association with the cult is, indeed, a recent phenomenon.[11] Despite aforesaid assertions, we should also consider the historical probability that the places associated with *Saiva* worship were mentioned in certain texts only after the worship had been introduced. Such texts were composed, indeed, in mythological style by the priests and their patrons with a view to disseminating the cult.

II

The place is not shown in Rennell's Atlas (1779-1781), but it appears in the survey maps of 1830-1845 as *Taressure*.[12] This place of pilgrimage gradually flourished along with the initiation of the monastery system after the revelation of the cult.[13] *Taressure* has also been considered the ancient name of this famous pilgrim town of Tarakeswar in the *Tarakeswar Sivatattva*.[14] The compilation of this book was the result of an earnest endeavour by Satishchandra Giri, the last *Mohanta* of the *Giri* order at *Tarakeswar Math*. Despite its lack of commitment to the chronological perspective of history, this book seems to be an important one so far as it represents the viewpoint of the establishment with regard to the antecedents of this place of pilgrimage, during the process of evolution, at the behest of the *Giri Mohantas*.

That the place was little known owing to relative inaccessibility, can also be corroborated with reference to the *Tarakeswar Bandana* compiled by Dwija Sahadeb in form of a hand written *Punthi* (manuscript) in 1244 B.S. (1837 A.D.). This manuscript has been kept at present in the custody of the Asiatic Society of Bengal. He stressed the point unequivocally that the place was not inhabitable for a long time simply because of its being covered with dense reeds and *Ulu* (Imperata Arundinacea) grass that grew on swampy land.[15] The poet was a resident of the village Nandanbati of Baligari *Paragana* in the vicinity of Tarakeswar. In fact, the lyrical exposition of the place and the cult leads us to no definite conclusion regarding the possible time of the revelation of the *Sivalingam* at Tarakeswar. Therefore, local myths and ballads guide us up to a certain point, but not beyond that.

There is no denying that the region in which Tarakeswar was situated remained scarcely populated prior to and even immediately after the revelation of the cult of Lord *Taraknath*. But it is amazing that Khanakul-Krishnanagar, which is not far from Tarakeswar, was densely populated in the first half of the sixteenth century. This place was famous for the *Sripata* of Gopala Abhirama Krishnadasa, an important follower of Nityananda. In fact, Tarakeswar was almost uninhabitable primarily because of its deterring geographical perspective. This proposition can easily be substantiated with reference to O'Malley's description of the region in which Tarakeswar is situated. "Further inland between the Damodar and the Dwarakeswar there is a tract of low lying land, which, unless protected by embankments, is more or less liable to constant floods, as the boundary rivers with their connected streams, are gradually raising their beds by annual deposits of silt and sand. In the rains this tract becomes a sheet of water, from which the village sites stand out like small islands. Owing to its liability to submersion, cultivation is precarious".[16] The Damodar has been much more harmful than the Hooghly, and there are records of its ravages for over the last hundred years.[17] Naturally, "the over flooding of embankments, frequent change of courses, total blockade of drainage systems giving rise to swamps and marshes" made this region almost uninhabitable.[18]

The place finds mention in the *Sivayana* of Ramakrishna Das, who, according to Dinesh Chandra Bhattacharya, flourished in the first half of the 17th century.[19] This book, published at the behest of Bangiya Sahitya Parishad, makes it quite clear that the *Svayambhulingam* at Tarakeswar was in rather inaccessible place even before its hallowed manifestation and the corresponding growth of the pilgrim town along with the initiation of the monastery system. Dinesh Chandra Bhattacharya emphatically opined that the poet of the *Sivayana* was fully aware of the manifestation of the cult in its primordial shape.[20]

In spite of O'Malley's assertion that "the village is not old, nor is the shrine", the fact remains that the *Svayambhulingam* in its primordial shape was known at least to the local people.[21] This proposition becomes amply clear also from the engraving, "*Suvamastu Sakabda - 1543*" on a stone-slab in the frontal part of the dome-shaped shrine at Tarakeswar. In fact, "*Sakabda - 1543*" corresponds to 1621 A.D. This, however, gives credence to the familiarity of the place as holy before its formal inception.

The case filed against the monastery at Tarakeswar by the Government of Bengal in 1838 and the verdict of the Collector of Hooghly seem quite important in this context for ascertaining the period of the gradual emergence of Tarakewswar as a place of pilgrimage. According to the verdict, "*Raja* Bharamalla gifted some landed properties for the maintenance of the temple services and regular worship of Lord *Taraknath*. The area of land gifted, spread between the villages *Jote* Saman, (*Jote* Sambhu), Bijpur (Bhanjipur) and Sahapur. As these were insufficient for meeting the expenses of daily services to the deity, the *Maharajas* of Burdwan namely Jagat Roy, Kirti Chandra Roy and Tilak Roy also donated land to one of the predecessors of Mohanchandra Giri, the *Mohanta* of the monastery at Tarakeswar, during the initial phase. The Collector, however, conceded that the ancestors of the *bibadi* (contestant) had been enjoying the landed properties long before the initiation of the British *Raj* in India...."[22]

However, Mohanchandra Giri incidentally produced some *Charpatras* (letters of exemption) before the court which revealed that the landed properties under reference had been shown as rent-free for the services to the deity. Reference can be made to two such *Charpatras* dated as 26 *Chaitra*, 1162 B.S. and 12 *Bhadra*, 1169 B.S. Therefore, these documents, if considered valid, allow us to determine the period of the revelation of the cult along with gradual evolution of Tarakeswar prior to 1162 B.S. or 1755 A.D.[23]

Moahnchandra Giri, the twenty-second *Mohanta* of the monastery at Tarakeswar, had also produced, on requirement, before the court a deed of grant of 1025 *bighas* and 11 *cottahs* of land (342 acres app.) signed by *Raja* Bharamalla on 10 *Chaitra*, 785 B.S. The fact that the year mentioned along with signature on the deed of grant had been forged, was proved beyond doubt. It was upheld on scrutiny that the digit '1' had unscrupulously been deleted with an obvious motive to push back the date of establishment of twin institutions - the temple as well as the monastery. The Collector was against the acceptance of the deed as genuine simply because it would amount to pushing back the year of emergence of the twin institutions purposely a few hundred years. Therefore, it was clearly held that the monastery at Tarakeswar was institutionalised in 1785 *Sambat* or 1729 A.D. at the behest of the *Giri Mohantas*.[24] In one of the oldest compilations, Kedarnath Sarkar put forward more or less the same date regarding the origin of the shrine of Lord *Taraknath*.[25]

It will not be out of context to point out that the information regarding the measurement of the land - 1023 *bighas* gifted through the deed of grand - as put forward by

Sudhir Kumar Mitra in his '*Hooghly Jelar Itihas O Bangasamaj*', is at variance with the version of Satishchandra Giri, the last *Giri Mohanta* at *Tarakeswar Math*. Satishchandra Giri's reference to the claim of Mohanchandra Giri, the twenty-second *Mohanta* in succession, regarding 1025 *bighas* and 11 *cottahs* of land in the possession of the monastery as valid *lakheraj* definitely contradicts the proposition of the author of the aforesaid compilation. This claim had incidentally been put forward while the East India Company was on the prowl for resuming *lakheraj* lands. As a matter of fact, "508 *bighas* were resumed by the government and about 517 *bighas* were released after a great deal of litigation..."[26]

This earnest endeavour of the administration of the company towards resuming the *lakheraj* lands can be corroborated with reference to the 'Historical Introduction to the Bengal Portion of the Fifth Report'. The Government made it unequivocally clear that "the holders of *taluks, jagirs* and *lakheraj* lands were to be given a reasonable time in which to display their title deeds; forfeiture of the lands to Government was to be the penalty for undue delay; and transfers of *taluks* unconfirmed by deeds signed by the *Nawab*, were to be regarded as void and the lands forfeited to Government."[27]

That Tarakeswar had evolved as a religious centre for the Hindus during the early part of the 18th Century can also be corroborated with reference to Lt. Col. D.G. Crawford who opined that Bishnudas, the *Raja* of Ramnagar, probably came to Bengal during the first quarter of the 18th century.[28] It is also noteworthy to mention about what had been recorded by virtue of a statement given by Dharanidhar Sinharoy, one of the plaintiffs in the Title Suit No. 28/1922, on 30 July, 1926. The statement as follows; "We originally came to Bengal from the west. Our ancestor who came to Bengal first, was

Keshab Hazari. He had two sons-- *Rao* Bharamalla and *Raja* Bishnudas. We are the direct descendants of *Raja* Bishnudas. I am tenth in succession from him". If three generations conform to a century, the period marked for the initiation of the twin institutions is pushed back accordingly to the first half of the 17th century, which seems quite absurd.

Moreover, '*Brihat Tarakeswar Mahatmya*' compiled by *Pundit* Nibaranchandra *Smrititirtha* points to the gradual development of this place of pilgrimage immediately after the migration of this *Rajput Kshatriya* family to Bengal from Northern India. The descendants of Bishnudas scattered in and around the district of Hooghly take pride in tracing their lineage to him. The ruins of Bishnudas's palace at Ramnagar and also at Bahirgarh where he shifted his residence afterwards are visible even at present. Ramnagar lies about 12.8 kms. to the south-east off Tarakeswar while Bahirgarh lies about 4 kms. to the south-west off this place of pilgrimage. *Swami* Vishnusivananda Giri also refers to the fact of migration of this family to this part of Bengal around 1740 A.D.[29]

On the basis of above discussion, it can be propounded that the revelation as well as popularity of the cult and the gradual emergence of this place of pilgrimage had definitely begun not earlier than the late twenties of the eighteenth century. But here is no denying that the cult of Lord *Taraknath* was here at Tarakeswar long before its revelation as *Svayambhulingam* or *Anadilingam*.

III

However, the legendary perspective of *Svayambhulingam* at Tarakeswar strikingly corresponds to similar legends associated with almost all the places of Hindu pilgrimage.[30] The legend common all over India, of cows shedding their milk secretively in unfrequented parts of forest, leading to the discovery of godheads is also told about the revelation of the *Sivalingam* at Tarakeswar. The discoverer in the present case was one Mukunda Ghosh a member of the *Gopa* (milkman) caste and cattle keeper of *Raja* Bishnudas, the *Chhatri zamindar* of Baligari, not far-off from Tarakeswar.[31] L. S. S. O'Malley seems to be wrong in his opinion that *Raja* Bharamalla discovered the "sacred stone" while wandering about the neighbourhood as a "religious mendicant".[32] The last *Giri Mohanta* was, in fact, opposed to these assertions. He was emphatic in his proposition that Mayagiri *Dhumrapan*, the first *Mohanta* of the *Tarakeswar Math*, was the first witness to the revelation of the *Sivalingam*.[33] But the deed of grant given to Mayagiri by *Raja* Bharamalla contradicts not only the statement of O'Malley but also that of the last *Giri Mohanta*.

According to popular legend, the unmanifested *Anadilingam* in the forest covered with dense reeds and surrounded on all sides by swampy lands, was used for grinding paddy by the village women. This resulted in the creation of a cavity on the surface of the unassuming chunk of stone. Apart from being used as a favourite haunt for the village kids, this place was also considered as a lucrative pasture for cattle.[34] Mukunda Ghosh, the chief cowherd of *Raja* Bishnudas and a resident of Ghurebhata village not far-off from Tarakeswar, also used to graze the cattle in this pasture.[35] While temporarily residing in the woods of Tarakeswar, then known by the name of *Jote Savaram*, he observed that many cows entered the jungle with udders full of milk and returned with them empty.[36] Anxious to discover the same, one day he followed a kine and saw her discharging milk on a stone which had a deep hollow in it. He instantly reported this mysterious behaviour of the kine to *Raja* Bharamalla, the brother of *Raja* Bishnudas.

On verification. *Raja* Bharamalla in consultation with his elder brother decided to bring the sacred stone to a deserving place within his domain. The *Koras* or labourers employed to dig up the sacred stone spent a whole day at the work without reaching its underside.[37] The worried *Raja* dreamt at night that the Lord appeared to him and ordered him not to dig up the sacred stone, but to build over it a temple. He related his dream to his brother *Raja* Bishnudas and the two brothers accordingly rendered yeoman service to the erection of the temple of Lord *Taraknath* over the 'sacred stone'. The original temple having fallen in decay, the present structure of the temple was erected by the *Raja* of Burdwan.[38] This legendary perspective is in no way corroborated by citations from ancient texts.

IV

In the 'List of Ancient Monuments of Burdwan District', Lt. Col. D.G. Crawford refers to a *Kshatriya* King Bishnudas living at *Mohaba* Garkalinjar in the province of Oudh early in the 18th century.[39] In fact, he was a big *zamindar* of Hariharpur in the *pergana* of Dobhi of Jaunpur district on the bank of the river Gomati.[40] As he could not sustain the pressure from Balwant Singh, the *Raja* of Benaras at the behest of Sadat Ali, the *Musalman Nawab* of Oduh, he thought it wise to leave the place and emigrate to Bengal along with about five hundred people of his own caste and one hundred *Brahmins* from Kanauj.[41] The fact that the *Rajas* of Benaras carried out extensive military operations from 1732 onwards with full recognition of the *Nawab* of Oudh against all other *Rajas* in their territories as well as against some of the *Rajput Brahmin and Bhumihar* corporate bodies is clearly elaborated in Bernard S. Cohn's essay on the 'Structural Change in Rural Society.'[42]

Probably, the process of giving undue pressure on this *zamindar* family concerned had begun well before 1732 that ultimately forced *Raja* Bishnudas to settle at Ramnagar - a village then in the district of Burdwan and now in Hooghly. It seems more so on the background of institutionalisation of twin institutions at Tarakeswar in 1729 under their patronage. However, "the inhabitants of the neighbourhood suspected them of being robbers and sent word to the *Nawab* of Bengal at Murshidabad that a large gang of marauders, in complete armour and with strange beards and moustaches, had come and settled near Haripal. The *Nawab* having sent for them, the *Raja* presented himself, and said that they were harmless folk who only wanted some land whereon to settle. Tradition states that, to prove his innocence, *Raja* Bishnudas went through the ordeal by fire, holding in his hand a red-hot iron bar without sustaining injury. The *Nawab* was convinced of his honesty and gave him a grant of 500 *bighas* of land (equal to 1,500 *bighas* at the present day) eight miles from Tarakeswar."[43] The *Taidad* (a register containing the description of the boundary of a plot of land), numbered 1931, preserved in the Collectorate of Hooghly shows this grant as rent-free. Despite O'Malley's repeated hesitance in naming the then *Nawab* of Bengal, it seems against the background of these developments that they emigrated to Bengal either during the last years of Murshid Quli's rule over Bengal or in the beginning of Sujauddin's (1727-'39) tenure. Evidently, the legendary perspective does not suffer from concoction and, indeed, bears a definite historical background.

Raja Bishnudas was very happy to settle himself as *zamindar* in the pristine locality of Ramnagar. Thereafter, *Raja* Bharamalla, as the successor to his elder brother made permanent arrangements for regular worship of the deity. Reference has already been made to the deed of grant of 1025 *bighas* and 11 *cottahs* of land gifted by *Raja* Bharamalla in the name of Lord *Taraknath* and also to the consequent appointment of Mayagiri *Dhumrapan*, a *Dashnami Saiva Sannyasi* as the *Mohanta* of the *Tarakeswar Math*.[44] Henceforward, the *Mohanta* was made responsible to look after the twin institution the temple and the *Math*. Meanwhile, *Raja* Bharamalla had been initiated into *Sannyasa* at the behest of Mayagiri *Dhumrapan*.[45] In fact, *Raja* Bharamalla was never the first *Mohanta* as was erroneously believed by O'Malley.[46]

Mukunda Ghosh was not, indeed, denied contextual relevance possibly because of his association with the process of the revelation of the cult at least during the initial phase. H.R. Sanyal's assertion that Mukunda Ghosh was ordered by Lord *Siva* in his dream to dig out the *Anadilingam* and arrange for his worship contradicts the generally held traditional version as well as the version given in the Bengal District Gazetteers (Hooghly).[47] However, he was advised by the *Raja* to take recourse to *Sannyasa* in honour of the cult of Lord *Siva* in the month of *Chaitra* (March-April) each year. Moreover, *Raja* Bharamalla made it a point that until and unless a successor to Mukunda Ghosh was initiated into *Sannyasa* in the beginning of the last month of the Bengali calendar in continued process, none would have the right to initiation thenceforward.[48] This custom is in vogue even in these days. S.K. Mitra was perhaps mistaken in his assertion, as was also Prafulla Chakrabarty, that the mortal remains of Mukunda Ghosh had been buried within the precinct of the sacred complex as a mark of respect to the departed soul.[49] In fact, the *Samadhi Ksetra* (burial space) adjacent to the temple of Lord *Taraknath* in the east was dedicated to one Mukunda Giri at the behest of Mayagiri *Dhumrapan*, the first *Giri Mohanta* of the monastery at Tarakeswar.[50] He is being worshipped to date as the *Bhairab* (incarnation) of the cult of Lord *Siva* at Tarakeswar.

V

Legend apart, Tarakeswar, according to historical evidence, appears to have been a *Saiva* centre prior to Bishnudas's time.[51] Since the establishment of the temple of Lord *Taraknath* in the early 18th century by the immigrant *Kshatriya* king in association with the *Saiva* monk of the *Giri* order of *Dashnami Sannyasis*, it has already passed through several phases. Tarakeswar, at present is a growing town in a rural setting in West Bengal. In fact, the *Dashnami Saivas* assumed control of this centre with subsidiary seats at Guptipara, Nayangarh, Bhotbagan, Baidyabati, Garh Bhawanipur, Santoshpur and Chaipat under the patronage of *Raja* Bharamalla. Incidentally, the *Mohanta* of the *Tarakeswar Math* became the *Mahamandalesvar* (head) of the *Mandali* (assembly) of *Mohantas* stationed at other places.[52]

The primary motive behind taking initiative for the erection of the temple of Lord *Taraknath* at Tarakeswar was possibly that the *Kshatriya zamindar* of Ramnagar desired to uphold his status and dignity among the peasants and artisans constituting the majority around the sacred complex. He could have indulged in this endeavour also with the end in view of making capital of the religious sentiments of the inhabitants. There is no denying the fact that Lord *Siva* with puranic perspective wields special appeal for the people belonging to the lower castes. In fact, Lord *Siva*, as depicted in Bengali literature, is not the same one with whom we are acquainted in Brahminical literature including the *Vedas*. He, indeed, has been transformed into a typical Bengali God.[53] Human interest in the family life of Lord *Siva*, therefore, far outweighs the interest in his divine nature. So it was quite natural that the rural population in and around the sacred complex with mostly low caste ingredients emotionally associated themselves with the endeavour of the *Kshatriya zamindar* for the establishment of the temple complex at Tarakeswar.

"Temple-building was, indeed, a very important form of social service in traditional society. At the same time temples represented the wealth and social power of the founder and were also a medium of spreading and consolidating influence."[54] Therefore, it was only natural for the *Raja* to tread this path with an eye to achieving a permanent place in the history of the evolution of this place of pilgrimage. Apart from the *Chhatri Zamindar*, the *Maharaja* of Burdwan and one Gobardhan Rakshit of Patulsandhipur near Seakhala in the district of Hooghly as well as Chintamani De of Howrah had also probably been guided to some extent with this consideration in mind while taking part in the initiative for the rejuvenation of the temple and *Natyamandira* in due course.[55]

The shrine consists of two parts, the sanctum and the veranda or porch in front of it. The sanctum is plain within, with the *Lingam* in the middle. Its exterior architecturally resembles a Bengali hut. The floor has a marble pavement.

Facing this porch is a large open hall with a roof supported by pillars and a floor paved with marble. The temple is fully surrounded by houses on all sides, so that no good view of it can be obtained from outside.[56]

In order to explore various facets of sacred traditions of Tarakeswar, a few points must also be noted, from where the traditional and mythological pageant of the sacred complex in Tarakeswar can be viewed at a glance. These are : (i) The cult of Lord *Taraknath*; (ii) the cult of Goddess *Kali*; (iii) the cult of Lord *Damodar Narayan* and (iv) the cult of *Dudhpukur*. These cults are intertwined with the principal cult of Lord *Taraknath*.

However, the *Raja* of Ramnagar might not have visualised the wider social relevance of the cult in the context of the incessant inflow of pilgrims at Tarakeswar from almost all over India in the far future. With its potentiality to cater to the socio-religious needs of a large section of the rural population, this sacred complex at present can rival other places of pilgrimage of countrywide repute. In short, this growth and the fame it has earned over the years, owe much to the revelation of the cult of Lord *Taraknath*. Therefore, the evolution of this place of pilgrimage minus the cult of Lord *Taraknath* would become meaningless.

Note

1. Akshoy Kumar Dutta - Bharatbarsiya Upasak Sampradaya. Vol. I and II. P.-283. Pathbhaban. Ashar - 1376.

2. "Lingam hi dvividham proktam krtrimakrtrimanca tat/.Akrtrimam svayambhutam svayambhubanalingadi, krtrimam, nirmitam dhatulingadi".

(The Lingams are of two types - unreal and real. The self-manifested Lingams are real while those made up of metals are unreal.)
Also,
"Nanachidrasusanjuktam nanabarna samanvitam Adrstamulam yallingam karkasam bhuvidrsyate" (Usually the Svayambhulingams are of different colours bearing numerous pores on themselves. Besides, these are coarse in nature and devoid of their ends.)

Ramtosan Vidyalankar (ed.) - Prantosani Tantra. P.-325.

3.   Sri Ram Sarma Acharya (ed.) - Sri Mahasiva Purana. 1966.
     Sanskriti Samsthan. Berily. U.P. 1966.
     Satarudra Samhita. PP.-516-517. Part-X. Slokas. 1-4.
     Kotirudra Samhita. P.-529. Part-I. Slokas -21-23. And
     PP.- 533-537, Part-II, Slokas -1-25.

4.   Satish Chandra Mukherjee (ed.) - Stavakavacamala (in Bengali).
     PP.-82-84. Basumati Sahitya Mandir. Cal. 1928.

5.   Sashibhusan Dasgupta - Obscure Religious Cults. P.-300.

6.   Bholanath Nath - Nathdharma' in Asit Kumar
     Bandopadhyaya (ed.) Bangalir Dharma O Darshanchinta. PP.-223-224.

7.   "Akasam lingamityahuh prthivi tasya pithika, Alayah sarvadevanam,
     layanat lingamucyate."
     (The sky is entitled as Lingam, the earth is its base. It is the abode of the genre of gods where everything meets with an end. Therefore, the sky corresponds to the Lingam.)

Ramtosan Vidyalankar (ed.) Prantosani Tantra. P.-328.

8.   Hansa Narayan Bhattacharya - Hinduder DebDebi : Udbhab O Kramabikash. Vol. 2. P.-120 (in Bengali).

9.   Nihar Ranjan Roy - Bangalir Itihas. PP.-148-154.

10. "Jharkhande Vaidyanatho Bakresvarastathaiva ca, Virabhumau Siddhinatho Rarhe ca Tarakesvara."
     (Baidyanath is in Jharkhanda. Bakresvar and Siddhinath are in Birbhum and Tarakesvar is in the Rarh.)
     Satish Chandra Mukherjee (ed.) - Stavakavacamala. Sivasatanamastotram. P.-62.

11. Sudhir Kumar Mitra - Hooghly Jelar Itihas O Bangasamaj. (in Bengali) vol. II. P. - 1109.

12. Capt. James Rennel - Memoir of a Map of Hindustan. Also, L. S. S. O'Malley and M. M. Chakrabarty - Bengal District azetteers, Hooghly. P.-322.

13. West Bengal District Hand books. Hooghly. 1952. Series -10 - Ancient monuments and fairs. Glossary of the better known ancient monuments in Hooghly District.

14. Satishchandra Giri - Tarakeswar Sivatattva. PP. -6-7.

15. "Bandiba baner madhye khepa Pashupati. charidike Ulu Khagra Benar basati."
(I shall worship the insane Pashupati within the forest strewn with Ulu, Khagra and Bena grasses on all sides.)

16. L. S. S. O'Malley and Monomohan Chakrabarty - Bengal District Gazetteers. Hooghly. P.-3.

17. Ibid - P.-150.

18. A. K. Banerjee - West Bengal District Gazetteers. Hooghly. P.-246.

19. Ibid. - P.-726

20. Masik Basumati. Bhadra. 1362 B.S. PP. - 800-801.

21. L. S. S. O'Malley and M. M. Chakrabarty - Bengal District Gazetteers, Hooghly. P.-322.

22. Pramathanath Sanyal - Tarakeswar.

23. Prafulla Chakrabarty - Social Profile of Tarakeswar. PP.-15-16.

24. Sudhir Kumar Mitra - Hooghly Jelar Itihas O Bangasamaj. (in Bengali) vol. II. P. - 1115.

25. Kedarnath Sarkar - Tarakmangal (in Bengali). 'Introduction'.

26. Title Suit No. 28/1922. D. Sinharoy and others Vs. Satishchandra Giri. Suit Under Sec. 92; Civil Procedure Code. Para.-16.

27. W. K. Firminger - Historical Introduction to the Bengal Portion of the Fifth Report. Cal. 1917. P.-192.

28. Lt. Col. D. G. Crawford - A Brief History of the Hugli District.

29. Swami Vishnusivananda Giri - Tarakeswar Math O Sadhu Bharamalla. (in Bengali).

30. Ashok Mitra (ed.) - Paschim Banger Puja Parban O Mela. vol. II., P.-49 and P.-479.

31. A. K. Banerjee - West Bengal District Gazetteers. Hooghly. PP. - 725-726.

32. L. S. S. O'Malley and M. M. Chakrabarty - Bengal District Gazetteers, Hooghly. P.-322.

33. Title Suit No. 28/1922. Suit Under Sec. 92. Civil Procedure Code. Para-16.

34. Satishchandra Giri - Tarakeswar Sivatattva. P.-58.

35. Sudhir Kumar Mitra - Tarakeswarer Itikatha. P.-7.

36. L. S. S. O'Malley and M. M. Chakrabarty - Bengal District Gazetteers, Hooghly. P.-322.

37. Satishchandra Giri - Tarakeswar Sivatattva. P.-64.

38. L. S. S. O'Malley and M. M. Chakrabarty - Bengal District Gazetteers, Hooghly. P.-322.

39. Lt. Col. D. G. Crawford - A Brief History of the Hugli District.

40. Ashok Mitra (ed.) - Paschim Banger Puja Parban O Mela. vol. II., P.-603.

41. L. S. S. O'Malley and M. M. Chakrabarty - Bengal District Gazetteers, Hooghly. P.-322.

42. R. E. Frykenberg (ed.) - Land Control and Social Structure in Indian History. PP.-58-59.

43. L. S. S. O'Malley and M. M. Chakrabarty - Bengal District Gazetteers, Hooghly. P.-322. Also, S.K. Mitra - Tarakeswarer Itikatha. PP.-3-7.

44. A. K. Banerjee - West Bengal District Gazetteers. Hooghly. P. - 726.

45. Satishchandra Giri - Tarakeswar Sivatattva. P.-70.

46. L. S. S. O'Malley and M. M. Chakrabarty - Bengal District Gazetteers, Hooghly. P.-322.

47. H. R. Sanyal - Social Mobility in Bengal. P.-87.

48. Satishchandra Giri - Tarakeswar Sivatattva. P.-82.

49. S. K. Mitra - Hooghly Jelar Itihas O Bangasamaj. Vol. II. P.-1113. Also, Prafulla Chakrabarty - Social Profile of Tarakeswar. P.-53.

50. Satishchandra Giri - Tarakeswar Sivatattva. P.- 79.

51. A. K. Banerjee - West Bengal District Gazetteers. Hooghly. P.-726.

52. Ibid. - P.-726.

53. Sashibhusan Dasgupta - Obscure Religious Cults. 'Introduction'.

54. H. R. Sanyal - Social Mobility in Bengal. PP.-67-68.

55. A. K. Banerjee - West Bengal District Gazetteers. Hooghly. P.-725.

56. L. S. S. O'Malley and M. M. Chakrabarty - Bengal District Gazetteers. Hooghly. P.-321.

Chapter - II

Tarakeswar in retrospect

I

Tarakeswar, the renowned pilgrim town of Eastern India is situated in the district of Hooghly.[1] Initially, this greatest centre of the *Saiva* sect in West Bengal was within the district of Burdwan prior to 1795 A.D. Under the regulation XXXVI of 1795, the district of Burdwan was divided into two parts, each under a separate officer. The present Hooghly district was one of the six constituent units of the Burdwan division.[2] Previously, the district of Hooghly was divided into two subdivisions-Hooghly Sadar and Sreerampur. Tarakeswar fell within the Sreerampur subdivision as "an important village *in thana* Haripal situated in 22°53′ north and 88°2′ east".[3] Again on 2 October, 1954; Chandernagore subdivision was created with five Police Stations of which Tarakeswar was an important one.[4] However, Tarakeswar had been classified as a town in the Census of 1961, for its pronounced urban characteristics.[5] This erstwhile rural trade centre came to be regarded "as a non-municipal town for the purpose of the 1961 Census."[6] Tarakeswar became a municipal town in 1975 which gave it a considerable advantage in the present context.

In fact, the topographic features of the region, in which Tarakeswar was situated, remained unfavourable to its civic evolutionary process prior to and also long after the revelation of the cult of Lord *Taraknath*. It was, in fact, "a flat alluvial plain intersected by a number of sluggish rivers and streams..... Another topographic feature of this region consisted of the relatively high riparian strips and the extensive depressions in between them."[7] The Dwarakeswar-Damodar inter riverine plain, in which this place of pilgrimage was situated, became liable to floods during the rainy season. Except where protected by an embankment, this region was susceptible to constant floods. The crops being liable to sudden and unpredictable submersion, cultivation in this area was precarious. Besides, the Mundeswari played havoc with this region because of its constantly shifting banks which were neither embanked nor covered with perennial plants "to prevent soil erosion and consequent increase in the load of the streams."[8] This baneful geographical condition was, therefore, the principal cause for this region being a backward segment of the district.

The Damodar surpassed all other rivers in this region with its power to play havoc with the inhabitants of the surrounding region. The record of the Damodar dates back to October 1787 when the "river of sorrow", having burst its banks, swept away "*hats*, temples, *ganjes* and *golahs*."[9] As a result, "no upland crops such as jute, aus rice or vegetables could safely be grown and roads could not be properly kept up." The same was repeated with vengeance in 1823.[10] The Damodar rose again in high flood in 1885-'86 as well as in 1903 causing immense sufferings to the inhabitants of both banks. In 1903, the flood waters reached the well-known Tarakeswar temple and for a time fears were entertained about its safety.[11] The fury with which the Damodar seasonally flooded this place of pilgrimage even long after the establishment of the monastery at Tarakeswar had also been noted in the *Tarakeswar Sivatattva*.[12] The above mentioned references are ample to establish the notoriety of the Damodar, as a cause behind the retarded process of civic evolution of the region surrounding Tarakeswar, for more than a century.

The incessant floods of the Damodar must have an adverse impact on the landed properties of the region surrounding Tarakeswar prior to and also long after the initiation of the cult of Lord *Taraknath*. The flood waters of the Damodar had long been a source of terror to the *zamindars* and cultivators of land on its banks, and of trouble and expense to the Government.[13] This must have reduced the income of the proprietors of landed estates and consequently their worth. Meanwhile, the resumption laws involving difficulties of identification and of procedures also diminished popular confidence in landed property, not excluding rent-free tenures.[14] Given this background, it can be assumed that the sketch of the region surrounding this place of pilgrimage might not have been a different one at least prior to and also long after the initiation of the cult of *Siva*. Besides, the inaccessibility of this region surrounding Tarakeswar around the same time should have also had an adverse impact on landed properties, thus reducing their market values during this period.

The mortal diseases were the aftermath of the seasonal floods in this region encompassing Tarakeswar. In the nine years following the Census of 1872, the population decreased owing mainly to the terrible epidemic of malarial fever, known as Burdwan fever.[15] It appears from the Census Report of 1901 that as far back as in 1872 Tarakeswar was a populous village along with Haripal and Singur. As the drainage system in general was defective, "the flood waters remained stagnant in depressions choked with weeds, which foster the propagation of fever-bearing mosquitoes."[16] With the excavation of the Eden Canal and the construction of the Sheoraphuli-Tarakeswar Branch of the Eastern Railway, both in 1885, agriculture and trade got a boost. This resulted in the corresponding growth in population in these areas. The Census Report of 1931 makes it clear that Tarakeswar, however, registered a little growth despite these developments.[17] These socio-geographic features of the region in which Tarakeswar was situated remained, possibly, a vital reason for this place being underpopulated prior to or even long after the initiation of the cult of *Siva*.

II

The topographic features of the region, in which Tarakeswar was situated, presumably had an adverse impact on the lifestyles of the inhabitants prior to or at least immediately after the revelation of the cult of Lord *Taraknath*. In fact, the original inhabitants of this place did belong to the peasant community and were, therefore, from the lower stratum of society. This, indeed, becomes clear from the familiarity of the site of the revelation of the cult to the men and women belonging to the peasant community long before its initiation.[18] In fact these people, known as *Rarhs*, were the original inhabitants of the *Rarh* region of Bengal.[19]

The *Kaibarttas* congregated chiefly in the southern part of this district, where Tarakeswar was situated. L. S. S. O'Malley noted that next to the *Bagdis*, the *Kaibarttas* were the most numerous caste in Hooghly.[20] It was found in the first Census of 1872, that the numerical strength of the caste *Kaibarttas* and caste *Bagdis* was considerable in comparison with even those of the *Kayasthas* and *Tilis*. The

Brahmins, Sadgopas and *Gopas* were placed in between these two extremes. However, the *Kaibarttas* traditionally were fishermen. But the dissidents among them, had in course of time, abandoned their traditional occupation to take to agriculture.[21] The caste *Bagdis* were, indeed, from the lowest strata of the caste hierarchy.[22]

However, there was also the preponderance of the *Gopa* community in and around the place where the revelation of the cult occurred. This becomes amply clear from the fact of association of the cowherds in general as well as of one Mukunda Ghosh in particular belonging to the *Gopa* community with the revelation of the cult.[23] Besides, the special status accorded to Mukunda Ghosh, in relation to the service to the deity, implied much for the importance of this community in and around this place. The pastoral *Gopas* appear to have an important role in spreading the cult of Lord *Siva*.[24] Incidentally, Kabikankan Mukunda in his *Chandimangal* indicates that the *Gopas* engaged in cultivation enjoyed better social position than the pastoral section of the caste.[25]

Besides these original inhabitants, all those who were associated with the revelation as well as the manifestation of the cult were outsiders to this place of pilgrimage. It has already been noted that the rise of the *Raja* of Ramnagar and the first *Mohanta* of the *Giri* order at the *Tarakeswar Math* coincided with the revelation of the cult. Besides, the *Brahmins* who came in due course after the revelation of the cult and were given various organisational responsibilities with regard to the worship of the deity, were similarly outsiders to this religious complex. This process began with the arrangements for the worship being made the responsibility of one Chaturbhuj Ganguly, a *Brahmin* from Singti-Sibpur.[26] This development, in the regional perspective of the pilgrim town, also substantiates the proposition that the lower-caste people were possibly the original inhabitants of this region. Most of these original inhabitants were usually dependent on agriculture although it failed to keep them above the basic subsistence level as was evident from the varied topographical nature of this region. But those who were alien to this region were not, in fact, averse to the idea of coming to terms with the original inhabitants. Their interaction with the original inhabitants belonging to the peasant as well as the *Gopa* communities prior to and even after the revelation of the cult makes this proposition stronger. However, the caste composition of this place of pilgrimage remained unchanged prior to and also long after the revelation of the cult.

The association of these local inhabitants in the process of the revelation of the cult and the participation of the *Gopa* community in particular in the organisation of service at the behest of the *Raja* of Ramnagar obviously stood for their religious inclination. It is well-known that the influence of *Saivism* was deep-rooted in the *Rarh* region of Bengal. This tradition continues to exist. The *Mangalakavyas* of medieval Bengal refer to the popularity of Lord *Siva* among the people of rural Bengal, especially among the lower castes. The conventional narratives of the *Mangalakavyas* constitute the bulk of the literary products during the sixteenth, seventeenth and eighteenth centuries. It is significant that such *kavyas* were composed in large numbers and those earned great popularity all over Bengal. In fact, the popularity of Lord *Siva* among the *Sudras*, members of the lowest caste, in rural bengal reinforces the theory that *Rudra* of the *Vedas* was gradually transformed over the years to become a god popularly worshipped among the non-*Aryans*.[27] The popular myths regarding Lord *Siva* have taken shape as a result of the influence of non-*Aryan* culture. This was possible simply because of the absorption of the culture of outsiders and the resultant cultural transformation of the castes of the lower rungs. This was, in fact, a continuous process in Hindu society.[28] Moreover, the worship of Lord *Siva* in association with his status as the god of agriculture speaks much for the assimilation of the *Aryan* and non-*Aryan* cultures in rural Bengal.[29]

With this transformation in the theological stature, Lord *Siva* also lost his puranic identity in rural Bengal. Even the *Sivayana* of Rameswar Bhattacharya places Lord *Siva* in this agricultural perspective. This elucidation makes it clear that, although the *Saivaistic* cult was very popular in the *Rarh* region, the presence of its followers as a sect was not conspicuous.[30] This was, indeed, true of the lower-caste people who inhabited this place of pilgrimage within the entity of the *Rarh* region. Although they were not organised as a sect, they were never averse to come to terms with this *Mohanta* culture along with the superimposed monastery system.

III

This pilgrim town, indeed, has achieved its radiant modern face with its traditional soul placed within the cult of Lord *Taraknath*. The revelation of the cult of Lord *Siva* at Tarakeswar was followed by the steady process of initiation of the monastery system at the behest of the *Dashnami Sannyasis* of the *Giri* order. The *Saivas* in Bengal were never familiar with the organisation of the monastery system which, however, was conspicuously present in the culture of the *Saivas* of Northern India prior to the advent of these non-Bengali *Dashnami Sannyasis*.[31] In addition to this outstanding development in the religious history of Tarakeswar, this place of pilgrimage has assumed an ever increasing stature over the years in popular Bengali culture. "It is worthy of note that almost all the *Dashnami Maths* in Bengal were founded by *Brahmins* who came from the North-West provinces and not by *Brahmins* domiciled in Bengal, and the persons who are now connected with these *Maths* either as *Mohantas* or *Chelas* are fresh arrivals from the North-West."[32] They were no doubt the upholders of the Brahminical culture. But they were very wise from the initial phase in not antagonising the intrusion of age-old *lokayata* (popular) rituals into the general religious functions although they had the ability to do that if they so wished. In fact, this attitude of forbearance in the upholders of the Brahminical religion towards popular rituals possibly began to change after he compilation of the *Bishnupurana*, *Matsyapurana* and the *Agnipurana*. However, the popular religious practices have stood the test of time in rural Bengal despite the overwhelming existence of the Brahminical religious context.[33]

The *Dashnami Sannyasis* of the *Giri* order never endeavoured to even minimally influence the local religious tradition and beliefs. On the whole, the *Giri Mohantas* kept themselves satisfied with the establishment of the *Math* as their bastion at Tarakeswar in perpetuity as well as with the supervisory authority over the *debutter* property in the name of Lord *Taraknath*. They never took any interest in raising barriers against the forceful existence of *lokayata* (popular) beliefs and rites. Thereafter, they took an earnest interest in popularising the monasteries at Tarakeswar and elsewhere to enhance their influence. They knew well that if they opposed the popular culture, it would jeopardise their long-term plans. Naturally, the worship of the cult of Lord *Siva* along with his consort and the associated festivals as well as other important popular religious rites (*lokacharas*) continue to exist alongside each other over the years at Tarakeswar under the supervision of the *Math*.[34] The case was almost the same with other *Maths* established by the *Dashnami Sannayasis* elsewhere in Bengal. These *Maths* which were the elements of the *Tarakesvar Mandali* were organised mostly in the districts of Hooghly. Howrah, Midnapur and 24 Parganas. The *Mohantas* of these *Maths* always belonged to one of the ten orders of the *Dashnami Sannyasis*.[35]

In course of time Tarakeswar developed into the confluence of various types of religious rites and festivals with local as well as classical traditions. These *lokayata* or popular rites outside the orbit of classical religious performances give birth usually to die hard customs that transcend geographical boundaries. Therefore, the orientation of this pilgrim town has no direct link to the history of the evolution of the *Mohanta* culture as well as consequent evolution of the monastery system headed by the *Mohantas*. Moreover, there was no direct link between the revelation of the cult and the organisation of *lokayata* rituals of a variegated religious background.[36]

The overwhelming influence of *lokadharma* or popular religion in the districts of Southern *Rarh* is also an interesting phenomenon. Tarakeswar which fell within the entity of Southen *Rarh* was no exception to this general trend. The practice of popular religion or *lokadharma* with reference to gods and goddesses like *Sitala*, *Sasthi* revolves here round the cult of Lord *Taraknath*, the presiding deity of this place of pilgrimage. This vivacious trend is as strong today as it was, over a hundred years ago. Usually, the alien *Giri Sannyasis* never thought of taking on this popular and traditional Bengali religious culture. This resulted in the gradual assimilation of Brahminical rituals with popular religious rites or *lokacharas*. This, indeed, facilitated the development of the *lokayata* form of *Saivism* in which the worship of Lord *Siva* as well as that of *Dharmathakur* could be performed together.

An attempt to discover the possible influence of the *Nathpanthis* on the religious history of Tarakeswar prior to or after the advent of the *Giri Sannyasis* will in no way be out of context in the discussion. The suffix *nath* appended to the deity's name suggests some connections with the *Nathpanthi Saivites* who once flourished in adjacent areas. Lord *Siva*, the supreme *natha* (lord) and the source of *nad*, the primordial sound, became their principal divinity. The religious beliefs of the *Nathpanthis* were the assimilation of the earlier *Saivism* which flourished at the place adjacent to Tarakeswar and the *Tantrik* form of Buddhism prevalent during the *Pala-Sena* period.[37] The *Nathpanthi Yogis* felt the power of the Almighty God in themselves through meditation. They believed in the principle-'what is in the macrocosm, is in the microcosm.' In fact, the *Nathpanthis* had an important role in the containment of the influence of Buddhism and this they did under the able leadership of *Yogiguru* Gorakshanath. His zeal in this context was comparable to that of Shankaracharya who had also done the same during the 8th century A.D.[38]

The proximity between Tarakeswar and Mahanad, an ancient place administratively situated between Pandua and Polba, within the district of Hooghly as an important centre of the *Natha* sect, gives rise to such speculation. Moreover, the existence of the not too famous but age-old temple of Lord *Loknath* in the vicinity of this pilgrim town also strengthens the speculation of the influence of the *Nathpanthis* in and around Tarakeswar possibly prior to the advent of the *Giri Sannyasis*. There is no denying the fact that the influence of the *Nathpanthis* was immense across West Bengal, particularly in the districts of Hooghly and Howrah.[39]

Another notable development in the religious perspective of this place of pilgrimage is the prevailing trend of adherence to popular *Tantrik* rites in and around the religious complex. In fact, the initiation of the cult of the Goddess *Kali*, the variform of the consort of Lord *Taraknath*, at the behest of Kamalnath Giri, the second *Mohanta* of the *Tarakeswar Math* and the consequent erection of the temple of the Goddess as a result of the endeavours of Mohanchandra Giri, the twenty-second *Mohanta* in succession within the sacred complex, speak much for the creation of an ambience favourable to the sustenance of *Tantrik* culture.[40] There is no denying the fact that the presence of the cult of *Siva* without his *Sakti* and vice versa is considered to have been quite unnatural.[41] Thereafter, the worship of the Goddess began to be performed under the direct supervision of the *Giri Mohantas*. Whether the *Giri Sannyasis* were accustomed to *Tantrik* rites remains controversial. The *Giri Mohantas* might have preferred *Tantrik* rites as the worship of the Goddess *Kali* could not have properly been done without such preference. Moreover, the sacrifice of items alternative to animals as is in vogue at present on auspicious occasions within the sacred complex, must have been a follow up process of an earlier tradition. Satishchandra Giri, the last *Mohanta* of the *Giri* order incidentally claimed in the Title Suit in the Court of the District Judge of Hooghly that "the defendant does not belong to *Brahmacharya Ashram* but belongs to the *Giri* sect of *Dashnama Sannyasis* and this defendant observes all such rites and ceremonies and performs all such duties as are enjoined by the *Shastras* and long established custom of the *Mandali* to be performed by that class of *Sannyasis* and to which as aforesaid the defendant belongs."[42] But the verdict of the District Judge of Hooghly must be taken note of in this context in which he stated that "the *Dashnami Sannyasis* are *Vedic Sannyasis* ... and that the *Mathdhari Sannyasis* belonging to the school of Shankaracharya are *Vedic* not *Tantrik Sannyasis*, that the *Tarakeswar Math* is governed by the Shankaracharya school of thought, that the *Mohunt* of the *Tarakeswar Math* ... is a *Mathdhari Dashnami Sannyasi*."[43]

Whatever the case may be, the adherence to *Tantrik* rites remains usual in and around the sacred complex even at present despite the general changes in the twin institutions-- the *Math* and the temple. This becomes possible primarily owing to the adherence to *Tantrik* rites on the part of a large number of sacred specialists directly attached to the responsibility of rendering service to the cult of Lord *Taraknath*. The *Sakta Tantriks* of this pilgrim town with their inclination to highly esoteric *Tantrik* practices, attach utmost importance to the female principle despite their indisputable commitment to the cult of *Siva*.

Despite this socio-cultural and economic background prior to the revelation of the cult, this non-puranic place of pilgrimage always absorbed newer traits over the years. Moreover, Tarakeswar has also displayed its capacity to adjust and get attuned to new developments which sway society at large. This process had certainly begun with the erection of the temple of Lord *Taraknath* in the early eighteenth century by an immigrant *Kshatriya* king, and a *Dashnami* monastery later on by a *Saiva* monk of the *Giri* order. Since then Tarakeswar has become an important *Saiva* centre in Eastern India through several developmental phases. Despite the prevalent features of Tarakeswar with its heterogeneous population in recent years, this place of pilgrimage also exhibits a rural character in the low-caste people who are dependent generally on agricultural occupations. Somehow, the influence of the deity upon the socio-cultural and economic life of the dwellers of this place of pilgrimage seems all-pervasive in spite of the general changes which threaten our society.

Note

1. A. K. Banerjee - West Bengal District Gazetteers. Hooghly. P.-724.

2. Ibid - P.-3

3. L. S. S. O'Malley and M. M. Chakrabarty - Bengal District Gazetteers, Hooghly. P.-320.
    Also,
    Imperial Gazetteer of India, Povincial Series. Bengal. Vol. I, P.-336.

4. A. K. Banerjee - West Bengal District Gazetteers. Hooghly. P.-663.

5. Census of India, Paper No. 1 of 1962. 1961 Census. Government of India. XXXVII.

6. A. K. Banerjee - West Bengal District Gazetteers. Hooghly. PP.- 175-176.

7. Ibid - P.- 663.

8. Ibid - P.- 11 .

9. The Calcutta Gazettee - 11 October, 1787.

10. L. S. S. O'Malley and M. M. Chakrabarty - Bengal District Gazetteers, Hooghly. P.-3 and P. -150.

11. A. K. Banerjee - West Bengal District Gazetteers. Hooghly. P.-280.

12. Satishchandra Giri - Tarakeswar Sivatattva. P-120.

13. W. W. Hunter - A Statistical Account of Bengal. Vol. III. District of Midnapur and Hugli (including Howrah). P.- 254.

14. G. Toynbee - A Sketch of the Administration of the Hooghly District. (1795-1845). PP. - 63-64.

15. L. S. S. O'Malley and M. M. Chakrabarty - Bengal District Gazetteers, Hooghly. P.- 92.
    Also,

C.E. Buckland - Bengal Under the Lieutenant Governors. Vol. II. P. - 612.

16. West Bengal District Census Hand Book. Census : 1961. P.-XXVII.

17. A.K. Banerjee - West Bengal District Gazetteers. Hooghly. P.-165.

18. Satishchandra Giri - Tarakeswar Sivatattva. P.- 58.

19. S. K. Mitra - Hooghly Jelar Itihas O Bangasamaj. Vol. I, P.-35. 20. L. S. S. O'Malley and M. M. Chakrabarty - Bengal District Gazetteers, Hooghly. P.-102.

21. H.R. Sanyal - Social Mobility in Bengal. P. - 41.

22. Nihar Ranjan Roy - Bangalir Itihas. (in Bengali). P.-310.

23. Satishchandra Giri - Tarakeswar Sivatattva. P.- 58.

24. H. R. Sanyal - Social Mobility in Bengal. P. - 46.

25. Kabikankan Mukunda - Chandimangal. P.- 80.

26. Nibaran Chandra Smrititirtha - Brihat Tarakeswar Mahatmya. P.- 38.

27. Hansa Narayan Bhattacharya - Hinduder Deb Debi : Udbhab O Kramabikash. Vol. II. PP. - 73-74.

28. Nihar Ranjan Roy - Bangalir Itihas. (in Bengali), P.-575.

29. Asit Kumar Bandyopadhyaya - Bangla Sahityer Itibritta. Vol. III. P.-88.

30. A. K. Banerjee - West Bengal District Gazetteers. Hooghly. PP.- 207-208.

31. Benoy Ghosh - Paschim Banger Sanskriti. Vol II. P.-367.

32. Judgement of the Calcutta High Court in F.A. No. I of 1930; 6 July 1934 and 24 August 1934.

33. Nihar Ranjan Roy - Bangalir Itihas. (in Bengali). P.-583.

34. Benoy Ghosh - Paschim Banger Sanskriti. P.-376.

35. Appendix to the Judgement in F.A. No. 255 of 1930. Dated-1.8.1934.

36. Benoy Ghosh - Paschim Banger Sanskriti. Vol. II. P.-369.

37. A. K. Banerjee - West Bengal District Gazetteers. Hooghly. P.- 206 and P.-705.

38. Bholanath Nath - 'Nathdharma' in Asit Kumar Bandopadhyaya (ed.) "Bangalir Dharma O Darshanchinta". PP.-216-223.

39. Benoy Ghosh - Paschim Banger Sanskriti. (in Bengali). Vol.-II, P.-373.

40. Satishchandra Giri - Tarakeswar Sivatattva - 'Preface' and P.-126.

41. Shibchandra Vidyarnab - Tantratattva. 'Introduction'. P.- 47.

42. Title Suit No. 28/1922. Suit Under Sec. 92. Civil Procedure Code. Para - 15.

43. Judgement of Mr. Justice K. C. Nag, District Judge of Hooghly, in the Title Suit No. 28/1922. Dated 6 November 1929.

Chapter - III

The evolution of the monastic system at Tarakeswar up to the end of the 18th Century

I

The evolution of the pilgrim town owes to a great extent to the simultaneous growth and development of the monastery system. The fame, the pilgrim town has earned so far, is no doubt the result of the service rendered by some of the illustrious *Mohantas* of the *Tarakeswar Math*. However, the evolution of the monastery at Tarakeswar and the consequent growth of the pilgrim town in due course had begun immediately with the initiation of the cult of Lord *Taraknath*. The embodiment of the religious complex at Tarakeswar is the *Math* administered by the *Mohantas*, the principal religious functionaries of the sacred complex.

The monastic system at Tarakeswar had been put into order in course of time by the *Giri* subsect of the *Dashnami Sannyasis* with obvious adherence to the *Guru-Sisya Parampara* or the preceptor-disciple lineage. The reference to *Dashnami* or ten names can be had in the *Mahanirvanatantram* along with those of four important *Maths* or monasteries.[1] Shankaracharya, the great Hindu revivalist, organised his *Advaita* School of *Saivism* and set out to establish four *Maths* or monasteries in four corners of India. He established *Shringagiri Math* at Shringagiri, *Sarada Math* at Dwaraka, *Gobardhan Math* at Puri and *Joshi Math* at Badrikasram. All these monasteries at four important religious centres in India, were placed under his four famous disciples-Padmapada, Hastamalaka, Sureswara and Totaka. They, in turn, took ten acolytes who, during the prescribed ceremony of renouncement of the world of senses, took the names of : (i) *Puri* (city), (ii) *Bharati* (learning), (iii) *Saraswati* (perfect knowledge), (iv) *Tirtha* (temple), (v) *Ashram* (heritage), (vi) *Ban* (wood), (vii) *Aranya* (forest), (viii) *Giri* (hill), (ix) *Parbat* (mountain) and (x) *Sagar* (ocean).[2]

These ten pupils were, as their successors now are, the heads of the ten sects of Hindu monks or *Sannyasis* in India. Usually, the ascetics of the *Advaita* school of *Saivism* are given, and have to bear one of the aforesaid ten names at the time of and ever after their *diksa* or initiation.[3]

Of these four monasteries, the *Shringagiri Math* at Shringagiri holds sway over the *Puri, Bharati* and *Saraswati* categories of the *Dashnami Sannyasis*. The *Tirtha* and *Ashram* categories among these *Dashnami Sannyasis* owe their allegiance to the monastery at Dwaraka. Accordingly, the *Giri, Parbat* and *Sagar* categories of the *Dashnamis* comply with the *Joshi Math* at Badarikasram while the *Ban* and *Aranya* categories sustain themselves at the behest of the *Gobardhan Math* at Puri. In fact, the *Aranya, Sagar* and *Parbat* categories among the *Dashnami Sannyasis* are now extinct.[4]

Besides these four important monasteries, the subsects of the *Dashnami Sannyasis* organised innumerable monasteries elsewhere in India in the shadows of those established by Shankaracharya. He who is supposed to be in charge of such a monastery is known as a *Mohanta*. He enjoys full control over the financial resources of the *Math* with the associated administrative power at regional level.

However, the original disciples of Shankaracharya had learnt to bear arms to fight their rivals. Long after the institutionalisation of the *Advaita* School of *Saivism*, it became gradually clear that both the *Giri* and the *Puri* sects were more militant in their outlook. It is interesting to note that at a certain stage these two sects indulged in internecine squabbles over trifles. As early as in 1567, the Emperor Akbar witnessed a fight between the armed *Sannyasis* of the *Giri* and the *Puri* suborders at Thaneswar.[5] But in course of time, their military character practically disappeared although some of them continued to bear arms.

The real ascetics never indulged in such unsocial activities. That the early Britishers confused the real ascetics and saints with the 'vagrants and erratic beggars' of the more or less gipsy tribes becomes clear from a description by H. H. Wilson. Wilson writes, "*Sannyasi* is a generic term and equally applicable to any of the erratic beggars of the Hindoos be they of what religious order they may. It signifies in fact nothing more than a man who has abandoned the world or has overcome its passions and, therefore, equally suitable to any of the religious vagrants we meet in Hindoostan...."[6]

In fact, the inroads made by the *Sannyasis* on Bengal through the ages began principally with their intention to participate in the bathing ceremonies at the Karatoya, Brahmaputra, Ganges or in the *Ganga-Sagar-* where the Ganges meets the sea. The *Ganga-Sagar-* an important place of ancient pilgrimage for the mendicants lies in the district of South 24 Paraganas at present. It is considered very auspicious to bathe there on the last day of the Bengali month of *Paus* which, according to the English calendar, falls sometime around the middle of January. They came from the west and "after passing through the territory of the *Nawab* of Oudh, they followed a route generally through the north of Bihar and the borders of the Nepal terai."[7] Whatever their intentions might have been, the *Sannyasis* were no more than beggars and bandits in the eyes of the officials of the English East India Company during this period. During the latter half of the 18th century, a constantly recurring theme in the correspondence of the East India Company's officials was that the *Sannyasis* or the mendicants who "have long infested these countries and under the pretence of religious pilgrimage, haven been accustomed to traverse the chief parts of Bengal, begging, stealing and plundering wherever they go, and as it best suits their convenience to practice."[8]

The *Bargis*, indeed, showed the way for the organised loot of Bengal and Bihar to the Upper India robber bands who called themselves *Sannyasis*.[9] Here is no denying the fact that they had taken advantage of the tumultuous situation of rural Bengal and were naturally very enthusiastic to fish in troubled waters. Their determination was strengthened by the belief that the people of Bengal were so timid and enervated that they would not resist.[10]

Whatever the case might be with the *Sannyasis* elsewhere in Bengal, the *Dashnami Giri Sannyasis* were there at Tarakeswar to try their luck long before the Battle of Plassey. In fact, the presence of these *Giri Sannyasis* was felt a few years before the *Bargis* invaded Bengal to perpetrate wanton destruction. The fact that the monastery at Tarakeswar was established in 1785 *Sambat* or 1729A.D. at the behest of the *Giri Mohantas* bears the proof of their presence around this sacred complex. Despite their incidental response to the Maratha terror, they were more or less decided right from the initial phases that they would concentrate their influence on this region with the *Math* as their bastion. They perhaps preferred the site on which they built the monastery because of its secluded nature, with low marshy lands as well as thick forests around it. The *Math* was, therefore, the nucleus, around which the big temple-*zamindari* evolved in due course. The *Tarakeswar Sivatattva* edited by the last *Giri Mohanta* gives vivid descriptions of the reactions of the *Giri Sannyasis* to the Maratha invasions, the first of which occurred in Bengal in April, 1742.[11] Besides, their reactions to the *Sannyasi* rebellion that raged across East as well as North Bengal from 1763 to 1800, had also been clearly put in this compilation.[12] Nonetheless, the establishment of the monastic system certainly brought about a complete transformation in their outlook which had definite implications for the future.

II

It has already been mentioned that the *Giri* sub sect of the *Dashnami Sannyasis* took keen interest in putting the monastery at Tarakeswar into order in the district of Hooghly. Numerous *Sannyasis*, generally belonging to the *Giri* community, settled also in Mymensingh and other districts of East Bengal during this period under review. Innumerable *Maths* were organised in those districts which usually became the nodes of a powerful network.[13] As soon as they transformed themselves into resident monks, they endeavoured earnestly to develop the *Math* at Tarakeswar with any an eye to defending themselves against possible adversaries.

It has already been emphasised that the advent of these *Giri Sannyasis* almost coincided with the advent of the

Kshatriya Rajputs who had already established themselves as *zamindars* of Ramnagar in the vicinity of this place of pilgrimage. Although this had happened towards the end of the second decade of the eighteenth century, information about the periods attributable to successive *Mohantas* suffers from the lack of chronological accuracy. The information in this regard can only be had in the *Tarakeswar Sivatattva* compiled at the behest of the last *Giri Mohanta* of the *Tarakeswar Math*.

The genealogical order of succession in accordance with the *Guru-Sisya Parampara* or the preceptor-disciple lineage cannot be ascertained at ease without taking recourse to the *Kurshinama* (genealogical table) put forward in the preface of the *Tarakeswar Sivatattva*. This chronological order of succession cannot be authenticated in the absence of any other document in this regard. There were altogether twenty-five *Giri Mohantas* including the last *Giri Mohanta*, Satishchandra Giri who had administered the monastery as well as the temple over the years. However, the information about the succession of the *Mohantas* cannot be taken for granted.

If the information is taken for granted, it will be observed that the first *Mohanta* of the *Tarakeswar Math* assumed office sometime in 855 *Sambat* or 799 A.D.[14] This is somewhat absurd since we know that the monastery at Tarakeswar was institutionalised in 1785 *Sambat* or 1729 A.D. Incidentally, this *Kurshinama* puts forward two lists of names of the *Giri Mohantas*, of which the correct one includes twenty-five names. The other which is considered as incorrect, includes nineteen names. Besides these two lists, there is also a third list with five names in it who were elevated to the office as temporary *Mohantas* of the *Tarakeswar Math*.

The incorrect list names of the *Giri Mohantas* given on the left side of the '*Kurshinama*' includes :-	The correct list of names of the *Giri Mohantas* who took over the office of the *Mohanta* in succession given in the middle space includes :-	Similarly, the list of names of the temporary *Mohantas* given on the extreme right side of the '*Kurshinama*' includes :-
1. Dhumrapan Giri	1. Mayagiri Dhumrapan	1. Shibnath Giri
2. Kamalnath Giri	2. Kamalnath Giri	2. Mahendranath Giri
3. Mukteswar Giri	3. Balgiri Balkhandi	3. Bilas Giri
4. Yogeswar Giri	4. Amarnath Giri	4. jagannath Giri
5. Gournath Giri	5. Keshabnath Giri	5. Shyamchandra Giri
6. Nirmalnath Giri	6. Golabnath Giri	
7. Shibnath Giri	7. Jawahirnath Giri	
8. Samudranath Giri	8. Rajendranath Giri	
9. Bilas Giri	9. Suratnath Giri	
10. Arunachal Giri	10. Kumudnath Giri	
11. Balbhadra Giri	11. Balkrishna Giri	
12. Prasad Giri	12. Gaurnath Giri	
13.Jagannath Giri	13. Nirmalnath Giri	
14.Parasuram Giri	14. Mukteswarnath Giri	
15. Mohanchandra Giri	15. Balbhadranath Giri	
16. Raghuchandra Giri	16. Birbhadranath Giri	
17. Madhabchandra Giri	17. Mahendranath Giri	
18. Shyamchandra Giri	18. Samudranath Giri	
19. Satishchandra Giri	19. Arunachal Giri	
	20. Prasad Giri	
	21. Parasuram Giri	
	22. Mohanchandra Giri	
	23. Raghuchandra Giri	
	24. Madhabchandra Giri	
	25. Satishchandra Giri	

It is interesting to note that both the incorrect as well as the correct lists accept *Dhumrapan* Giri or Mayagiri *Dhumrapan* as the first *Mohanta* and Satishchandra Giri as the last one of the *Giri* sub sect of *Dashnami Sannyasis* at the *Tarakeswar Math*. Differences, in fact, crop up only with those who are named in between the first and the last one. The

Taidad No. 1931 mentioned in the Court Register, however, names Mayagiri *Dhumrapan*, Balbhadra Giri, Shibchandra Giri, Arunachal Giri, Prasad Giri and Parasuram Giri prior to Mohanchandra Giri, the twenty-second *Mohanta* as the heads of the religious estate at Tarakeswar. Another striking feature is that a few names of the *Giri Mohantas* in the *Kurshinama* are common to all the three consecutive lists.

So far as the major activities of these *Giri Mohantas* at the *Tarakeswar Math* were concerned, it appears that they usually spent their time in pursuit of religious activities. The successive *Giri Mohantas* generally possessed hordes of disciples who engaged themselves in learning the holy scriptures and other religious practices. Although Prafulla Chakrabarty does not carry out a definitive study of the diverse roles of the ascetics of the *Tarakeswar Math*, there are in fact ample references to the various activities of these *Giri Sannyasis* which were strikingly similar to those of their counterparts in Northern India.[15]

Notwithstanding their continuous struggle for survival, these *Giri Sannyasis* at the *Tarakeswar Math* often indulged in commercial transactions that were common among the *Giri* section of the *Gosains* in Northern India during the eighteenth and early nineteenth centuries.[16] The *Giri Mohantas* who were involved in commercial transactions, were generally called the *Dangli Sannyasis*.[17] The Title Suit Under Sec. 92, Civil Procedure Code also bears ample references to the temporal activities of the *Mohantas* at the *Tarakeswar Math*.

The last *Giri Mohanta* was very emphatic in his assertion that no legal or scriptural barriers could debar a *Mohanta* of the *Tarakeswar Math* from acquiring properties accruing from the *pranamis* given to him personally and "from the profits of the money lending business and trade and from the income of those properties". Besides, he pointed out that this practice at the *Tarakeswar Math* of the *Mohantas* acquiring properties and holding the same over the years was in keeping with the *Mohantas* of similar *Maths* elsewhere.[18]

III

It has already been pointed out in the previous chapter that Mayagiri *Dhumrapan* owed his allegiance to the *Giri* order of the *Dashnami Sannyasis* and had become the first *Mohanta* at the *Tarakeswar Math* at the behest of *Raja* Bharamalla, the *zamindar* of Ramnagar. Lt. Col. D.G. Crawford, however, opined that Bharamalla was the first *Mohanta*, and thereafter, the office of the head of the order continued through the *Guru-Sisya Parampara* or the preceptor - disciple lineage.[19] It is erroneous to consider Bharamalla as the first *Mohanta* of the *Tarakeswar Math* as he had already been initiated into *Sannyasa* by Mayagiri *Dhumrapan* and he practised meditation to discover the manifestation of divinity in himself.[20] Mayagiri had incidentally achieved the title of *Dhumrapan* simply because of his addiction to tobacco. He smoked throughout the day, and so he was almost veiled by smoke.[21] Thus the name.

Mayagiri *Dhumrapan*, the first *Mohanta* of the *Tarakeswar Math* was the disciple of one Sri Nispan Giri, the *Mohanta* of *Joshi Math* at Badarikasram. This *Joshi Math* was the original as well as principal *Math* of the *Giri* order of the *Dashnami Sannyasis* of Northern India.[22] After visiting Nepal, Bundelkhand, Varanasi, Deoghar and other places, he appeared at Ramnagar, the village in the vicinity of this place of pilgrimage. He was believed to have mesmerised *Raja*

Bharamalla by virtue of his power to perform miracles.[23] This resulted ultimately in his appointment as the first *Mohanta* of the *Saiva Math* at Tarakeswar.

Reference has already been made to the grant of 1025 *bighas* and 11 *cottahs* of land by *Raja* Bharamalla for the worship of Lord *Taraknath* and the subsequent appointment of Mayagiri, an ascetic of the *Giri* order of the *Dashnami Sannyasis* as an administrator of the temple and the religious endowment. Besides this gift from the *Raja*, "the *Maharaja* of Burdwan from time to time made gifts of some jungles and waste lands to the then *Mohanta*." This formed the nucleus of the *Saiva Math* at Tarakeswar, under the administration of Mayagiri *Dhumrapan* who "established the *Math* with the assistance of his numerous disciples". They "cleared jungle and took possession of the neighbouring lands and obtained as gifts some rent-free lands from the above mentioned pious rich men....."[24]

This ascetic along with his disciples established more than sixteen *Maths* all over Bengal in due course. These were constituted under the holding body called the *Tarakesvar Mandali*. Of these, the *Tarakeswar Math*, *Guptipara Math*, *Puri Math*, *Dewan math*, *Nainagarh Math* and the *Bhadrakali Math* are in the district of Hooghly. The *Bhotbagan Math* is in the district of Howrah. The *Chaipat Math* and *Reyapara Math* are in Midnapur district. However, the *Maths* at Barasi or Hatiagarh, Garh Bhawanipur, Rayan or Raina, Amra, Khamarpara and Par Bagnan no longer exist. The *Math* at Amdanga is now under the management of the *Bhotbagan Math*.[25] All these he did after the propagation of the cult of Lord *Taraknath*.

Some say that one Jagannath Giri, an ascetic of the *Giri* order was the first *Mohanta* of the *Saiva Math* at Tarakeswar.

On his way to Chattagram, now in Bangladesh, to worship the *Siva* cult of *Chandranath*, he heard of the revelation of the cult of Lord *Taraknath* at Tarakeswar and, therefore, stopped at Tarakeswar. Mukundaram Ghosh who had already been given the responsibility of arranging for the daily services to Lord *Taraknath* breathed his last just prior to the arrival of Jagannath Giri at Tarakeswar. Consequently, he was appointed as the principal *Sebayet* of the Lord by order of *Raja* Bharamalla. Thenceforth, he put into effect the process of worshipping the Lord which, in some manner, is still followed today.[26] However, Pramathanath Sanyal argues that Jagannath Giri and Mayagiri *Dhumrapan* were one and the same person.[27] But it is noteworthy that neither the Title Suit No. 28/1922 Under Sec. 92, Civil Procedure Code nor the *Taidad* No. 1931 bear the name of Jagannath Giri as the first *Giri Mohanta* of the *Tarakeswar Math*. Only the *Tarakeswar Sivatattva* edited by the last *Giri Mohanta* of the *Tarakeswar Math* refers to one Jagannath Giri, both in the incorrect list as well as in the list of the *Mohantas* appointed temporarily.

Despite this controversy regarding the identity of the first *Mohanta* of the *Tarakeswar Math*, the fact remains that Mayagiri *Dhumrapan* institutionalised the *Tarakeswar Math* and established the temple-*zamindari* under the administration of the *Giri Sannyasis*. Besides, the establishment of the satellite *Maths* at his behest all over Bengal, which were incorporated into the *Tarakesvar Mandali*, speaks highly of his foresight. Above all, he set the example, following which the succeeding *Giri Mohantas* endeavoured to serve faithfully the cult of Lord *Siva* at Tarakeswar, being fully aware of their religious and temporal responsibilities.

IV

The second *Giri Mohanta* of the *Tarakeswar Math* was Kamal nath Giri, who succeeded Mayagiri *Dhumrapan* in accordance with the preceptor-disciple rule of succession. It is noteworthy that the incumbent *Mohanta* was, indeed, the principal *Chela* (disciple) of his immediate predecessor. This rule was followed with no exception until the assumption of office by the last *Mohanta*. He preferred meditation to administration and, thereby, confined his actions to religious matters only. He installed the Goddess *Kali* within the precinct of the sacred complex as Lord *Siva* devoid of *Sakti* (consort) was thought to be an oddity in the religious context.

Unlike Kamalnath Giri, Balgiri Balkhandi, his close associate, was very active in furthering the interest of the twin institutions as the third *Mohanta*. In order to ensure the security of the sacred complex, he made arrangements for the construction of a fort at Baligari, a village not far from Tarakeswar. He also took the initiative to build a *Cachari* or the replica of a court, to be conducted at the behest of the *Mohantas* of the *Math*.[28] The ruins of these establishments still exist. Activities like those of Balgiri Balkhandi make it clear that the *Giri Mohantas* were equally busy with both spiritual and temporal matters. Knowledge of these activities, indeed, vindicates the standpoint of the last *Giri Mohanta*, that the *Mohantas* of the *Tarakeswar Math* were not required to devote themselves "wholly to the *Seba* (service) of the *Thakur* (deity) and to the *Sadabrata* (hospitality)" within the sacred complex.[29] Hence, there was nothing unusual in their inclination to acquire as well as consolidate considerable property over the years.

Amarnath Giri succeeded the third *Mohanta*. No special reference has been made to him, and also to his five immediate successors. This seems to have been due to the lack of major contributions by them in the evolution of the monastery at Tarakeswar. In fact, the elevation of Keshabnath Giri, Golabnath Giri, Jawahirnath Giri, Rajendranath Giri and Suratnath Giri successively to the office of the *Mohanta* at the *Tarakeswar Math* seems to have had no lasting effect on the administrative policies of the twin institutions.

However, Kumudnath Giri, the tenth *Mohanta* was comparatively more illustrious. He is said to have arranged an *Asvamedha Yajna* at Nadan Ghat on the bank of the Ganges, near Nabadwip Dham, with the obvious aim of popularising the sacred complex at Tarakeswar.[30]

These successive *Mohantas* of the *Tarakeswar Math*, from Mayagiri *Dhumrapan* to Kumudnath Giri, were at the helm of affairs in this place of pilgrimage prior to the beginning of the Maratha invasions. Despite relative differences in their administrative efficiency, the earlier *Mohantas*, from Kamalnath Giri to Kumudnath Giri, were more or less true to their commitment to follow the example set by Mayagiri *Dhumrapan*.

In spite of their commitment to the *Advaita* School of *Saivism*, the inclination of the *Giri Mohantas* to *Tantrik* rites began from the time of the establishment of the deity of the Goddess *Kali* under the direct supervision of the second *Giri Mohanta*. Reference has been made earlier to the impact of this development on the religious ambience of this place of pilgrimage. This inclination to *Tantrik* rites on the part of the *Giri Sanyasis* need not be thought unnatural especially since Shankaracharya, the organiser of the *Advaita* School of *Saivism*, was also a renowned propagator of *Tantrik* religion.

He was incidentally the worshipper of *Srividya*, *Matangi* and *Bhubanesvari* - the three variforms of the consort of Lord *Siva*. Of his famous compilations, the *Prapanchasara* as well as the *Saundaryalahari* are held in high esteem among those inclined to the *Tantrik* religion.[31] Hence, the characterisation of the *Dashnami Giri Sannyasis* "as *Vedic* and not *Tantrik Sannyasis*" as given in the verdict of 6th Nov., 1929 betrays the ignorance of the District Judge.

However, the other salient features in the process of evolution of this sacred complex included endeavours by the *Giri Mohantas* to consolidate the power-structure of the temple-*zamindari*, as was found in the case of Balgiri Balkhandi, and to propagate the popularity of the sacred complex, as was found in the case of Kumudnath Giri.

The *Giri Mohantas* during this period under review dared not to indulge in commerce since that was yet unfeasible. However, the escalation of the Maratha intrusions during the next phase of evolution of the monastery did create a commercially favourable atmosphere.

V

The tumultuous conditions that prevailed in Bengal between 1742 and 1751 because of the incessant Maratha incursions did not affect, initially, the rule of succession of the *Mohantas* at the *Tarakeswar Math*. In fact, five consecutive successors of Kumudnath Giri, the tenth *Mohanta*, witnessed the turmoil in Bengal during this period. The *Tarakeswar Sivatattva* bears ample references to the disturbances created not only out of the Maratha incursions but also of internecine squabbles in the *Math* during this phase of its evolution.[32] Incidentally, Balkrishna Giri, Gournath Giri, Nirmalnath

Giri, Mukteswarnath Giri and Balbhadranath Giri were said to have been the five consecutive successors of the tenth *Mohanta*.[33]

The *Tarakeswar Sivatattva*, indeed, contains vivid description regarding this period of turmoil with special reference to the role played by the *Giri Sannyasis*. It is well-known that the *Sannyasis* were hired in general by the Maratha invaders who used them usually as mercenary soldiers. They were employed also in the armies of the *Rajput Rajas*, as well as in the army of Shujauddaulah, the *Nawab* of Oudh.[34] However that may be, the aforesaid compilation remains repeatedly evasive with regard to chronology. Despite this, the Maratha incursions and the consequent reaction of the *Giri Sannyasis* in general as depicted in the *Tarakeswar Sivatattva*, agrees with the actual historical analysis. The *Giri Sannyasis* generally accompanied the Maratha intruders with twin objectives. While sticking to the primary objective of ensuring the sustenance of their base in and around Tarakeswar and the areas dependent on it, they were also instrumental in enhancing their commercial activities in collusion with the Marathas.[35]

In spite of numerous references to the nature of collusion between the Maratha intruders under Raghuji Bhonsle and the *Giri Sannyasis* in general, the omission of the last *Giri Mohanta* in reporting the nature and conditions of the alliance especially with regard to the activities of the five *Mohantas* of the *Tarakeswar Math* during this period seems incongruous. This becomes glaring when one considers the concentration of the *Giri Sannyasis* around Tarakeswar during this period.[36] In fact, the paucity of corroborative evidence constrains the attempt to fill in this lacuna.

Despite this lacuna in the account of the Maratha incursions and the nature as well as conditions dominating the participation of the *Giri Sannyasis* of the *Tarakeswar Math* in particular, it becomes clear from the *Tarakeswar Sivatattva* that the *Giri Sannyasis* in general did their best to enhance their material interests. They were in collusion with Raghuji Bhonsle, *Raja* of Nagpur, from the beginning of the Maratha incursions.[37] This certainly presupposes their presence in Nagpur which, thereafter, became an important commercial centre for the *Giri Sannyasis*.

The *Giri Mohanta* who encouraged this interest in trade for the first time in this period was Birbhadranath Giri. By then, the storm of the Maratha incursions had blown over. But the consequence of this collusion between the Marathas and the *Giri Sannyasis*, which took the form of establishment of commercial link with Nagpur, remained intact thereafter.

However, Birbhadranath Giri, sixteenth in the line of succession, had taken over the administration of the *Math* accordingly. But he was unable to remain long in the office because of the animosity between him and his *Gurubhrata* (disciple-brother) Mahendranath Giri. Birbhadranath Giri, quiet and peace-loving in nature, was forced out of the *Math* by Mahendranath Giri. This resulted naturally in Mahendranath Giri's taking over of the administration of the monastery as well as the temple at Tarakeswar, as the seventeenth *Mohanta*. More importantly, this also resulted in the interruption in the tradition of the *Guru-Sisya Parampara* for the first time since the process of evolution of the monastery. Birbhadranath Giri left this place of pilgrimage in disguise along with his trusted disciples and moved westward. He and his trusted disciples were thereafter known to have taken up commercial activities in Nagpur.

Mahendranath Giri failed, in the long run, to enjoy the fruit of his success. This facilitated the assumption of the office of the *Mohanta* by Samudranath Giri, the most trusted *Chela* (disciple) of Birbhadranath Giri. The most important cause of Mahendranath Girl's failure was attributed to his acrimonious relationship with the then *Nawab* of Bengal.[38]

A critical analysis of this phase of the evolution of the monastery does not reveal a constructive role on the part of the *Giri Mohantas*, from Balkrishna Giri to BalbhadranathGiri. They were not as illustrious as their predecessors. What was important to them, was their commitment to hold on the gains accumulated over the years.

Moreover, the *Giri Mohantas* of this period, along with their disciples, exploited their collusion with the Marathas in pursuit of the establishment of commercial link with Nagpur. The tradition set by Birbhadranath Giri in this context remained viable till the tenure of Raghuchandra Giri, the twenty-third *Mohanta* of the *Math*.

This phase of evolution was also important, for an unprecedented development that had taken place in the usurpation of power by Mahendranath Giri. This untoward development certainly set an example that was once more followed when Jagannath Giri was the temporary *Mohanta* of the monastery, prior to the taking over of the administration by Parasuram Giri, the twenty-first *Mohanta* of the *Math*. Therefore, this phase of evolution saw the rise of novel trends, which deeply influenced the history of the twin institutions.

VI

In spite of frequent references to the indulgence of the *Giri Mohantas* of the *Tarakeswar Math* in commercial activities, the compilation of the last *Giri Mohanta* seems to have avoided making logical references substantiated with appropriate data in this respect. Besides woollen and cotton goods as well as rice, no other commodities are referred to as items for trade.[39] They also took special interest in money lending, by virtue of which they amassed immense fortunes. However, no statistical data have been provided with reference to either trade or money lending business resorted to by the *Giri Mohantas* particularly from Birbhadranath Giri onwards, in association with their trusted disciples. In fact, the profits from the lending of money as well as trade helped in the long run through the acquisition of property by the *Tarakeswar Math* and its satellites.[40] Besides the book written by the last *Giri Mohanta* and his statement made in the District Court, no other corroborative evidences are available in this context.

Moreover, the reasons behind the selection of far away Nagpur on the part of the *Giri Mohantas* have not been adequately explained. As has been noted earlier, the commercial connection that was created since the Maratha incursions presumably gave rise to this attraction of the *Giri Mohantas* for Nagpur. To prove that they were never at odds with the main stream *Giri Sannyasis* who participated in the Maratha incursions, the *Giri Mohantas* from Birbhadranath onwards not only maintained a viable link with Nagpur over the years but a few of them also returned to Nagpur to indulge in commerce having delegated their authority to their trusted disciples. Therefore, their concern for commercial activities did in no way clash with the common interest of keeping a good hold on the twin institutions at Tarakeswar.

VII

Samudranath Giri, the most trusted disciple of the ousted *Mohanta* Birbhadranath Giri, was informed of the decay in the condition of the twin institutions when he was engaged in business in far-off Nagpur. It has already been pointed out that the internecine quarrels formed a primary cause of this dilapidation, apart from the consequences of the Maratha incursions that had ravaged Bengal for years. In fact, Samudranath Giri appeared at this place of pilgrimage when Mahendranath Giri, the usurper, had failed to exercise his power and ensure the allegiance of the *Giri Sannyasis* in general. Samudranath Giri is said to have amassed meanwhile immense fortunes by virtue of business in Nagpur prior to his initiation as the eighteenth *Mohanta* of the *Tarakeswar Math*.[41]

However, a delegation of the *Giri Sannyasis* along with Samudranath Giri appealed to the then *Nawab*, seeking his permission for the rejuvenation of the temple and the monastery. The tenure of this incumbent *Mohanta* seems to have coincided with the concluding phase of the administration of the *Nawabs* in Bengal, although no *Nawab* has been named. With permission from the *Nawab*, this eighteenth *Mohanta* endeavoured to save the sacred complex from ruin exclusively with the use of his own financial resources. His commendable plan included the digging up of the tank of *Belpukur* adjacent to the temple of Lord *Taraknath*. He was shortly to return to his world of business as his interest in business was very important to him. He authorised one Bilas Giri as the interim *Mohanta* to run the administration on his behalf.[42]

Bilas Giri was always vulnerable to the pressure of circumstances. In fact, the internecine dispute that erupted for the second time during this phase of the evolution of the monastery and the uncertainty about the English East India Company resulted in his decision to sell the twin institutions to one Daman Puri. Thereafter, he left for a distant destination.[43] What is important to note here, is the decision of the interim *Giri Mohanta* to sell the monastery to none but a *Sannyasi* from the *Puri* order of the *Dashnamis*. The East India Company armed with the great of *Diwani* had, by then, become an important player in the changed historical scenario. It had already begun to use coercion to extract money from the *Dashnami Sannyasis* engaged in business elsewhere. That was why he thought of selling the *Math* and the temple at the earliest opportunity.[44]

Samudranath Giri was never heard of again after he returned to his world of business. He died while in Nagpur. Meanwhile, he nominated Arunachal Giri as his favourite disciple, who later became the nineteenth *Mohanta* of the *Tarakeswar Math*. He was then a businessman, following footsteps of his preceptor, and had been busy in transporting goods between Nagpur in Maharastra and Maldaha in Bengal.[45] No details are provided regarding the nature of the commodities. Corroborative data are also unavailable. Presumably, the trade items remained the same with this tradition bound *Giri Sannyasi*. While in Maldaha, in connection with his commercial activities, he heard of this sale and "recovered the *Math* and the temple and all other properties from the purchaser by paying to him the full value thereof."[46] This he did prior to his initiation into the office of the *Mohanta* at the *Tarakeswar Math*. The recovery of the twin institutions usually facilitated the process of his taking over the office of the *Mohanta* by virtue of his having been favourite disciple of Samudranath Giri. Much land along with a vast mango orchard at Sahapur, a village adjacent to

Tarakeswar, was bought during his tenure to raise the income of the estate as well as to make it financially viable.[47]

This historically somewhat well-known *Mohanta* was succeeded by his less illustrious disciple, Prasadchandra Giri, who failed to leave any permanent impression in the history of the evolution of this place of pilgrimage. After his demise, one Jagannath Giri was appointed the temporary *Mohanta* of the *Tarakeswar Math* as Parasuram Giri, the favourite disciple of Prasadchandra Giri was away in Nagpur along with his trusted disciple, Mohanchandra Giri. Meanwhile, one Fatey Giri usurped the office of the *Mohanta* at the *Tarakeswar Math* taking advantage of the senility of Jagannath Giri. This was, in fact, the second incident of usurpation in the history of the *Tarakeswar Math*. Having heard of these developments Parasuram Giri started for Tarakeswar from Nagpur with his coffers already enriched through trade. Immediately after he reached Tarakeswar, he took the decision to file a suit against Fatey Giri at the Judge's Court of Burdwan in 1790. Parasuram Giri won over the case in the long run and ensured his ouster from the *Tarakeswar Math*.[48] The role of Parasuram Giri in this state of affairs bore proof of his efficiency as compared to his *Gurupita* or preceptor, Prasadchandra Giri.

Parasuram Giri was succeeded by Mohanchandra Giri, as the twenty-second *Mohanta* of the *Tarakeswar Math* at the fag end of the eighteenth century.[49] He followed the footsteps of his erstwhile illustrious predecessors. Prior to his initiation into the office of the *Mohanta*, he was also engaged in business in Nagpur along with his *Gurupita*, Parasuram Giri. Initially, he wound up his business in Nagpur and devoted his energy to the increase in the property of the *Math* as well as of the temple in right earnest. He had brought with him about nine *lakhs* of rupees and immense amount of gold, with which he bought tracts of land as *debutter* to the tune of about four hundred *bighas*.[50] Endowed with a humanitarian outlook, he ordered the digging up of two large tanks at Sahapur and Bhimpur-the two adjacent villages on the outskirts of Tarakeswar - in order to relieve the people of the area from the scarcity of water.[51]

His scheme for rejuvenating the sacred complex included the renovation of the dome of the temple of Lord *Taraknath* and the temple of the Goddess *Kali* within the periphery of the sacred complex. Moreover, the *Natyamandira* in front of the temple of the Lord along with the *Gadighar*, the seat of temple administration, was also designed by order of Mohanchandra Giri.[52] This *Natyamandira* had been built with the primary objective of staging mythical as well as puranic plays, particularly during the religious festivals, in front of the *Nataraj* - the figure of Lord *Siva*. But this complex had incidentally begun to be used, almost round the year except at the time of religious festivals, as accommodation for the *dharna* pilgrims. The pilgrims of this type usually perform the ritual of fasting and lying stretched out obstinately in front of the cult of Lord *Siva* for days and nights together, expecting the vision of the Lord in a trance as well as his direction about how to overcome the crises. All these schemes for the renovation of the *Math* along with the temple naturally necessitated a steady inflow of income. Therefore, he, in association with his *Chelas* or disciples began to deal in woollen and cotton goods as well as rice.[53]

Meanwhile, *Lat* Jainabad, *Lat* Ramchandrapur associated with *Lat* Krishnapur, *Lat* Narayanpur and *Lat* Guria were added to the estate during the tenure of Mohanchandra Giri. As *talukdar* of the first two *Lats*, he was bound by agreement to pay land revenue as well as road-cess to the *Habeli Cachari* of the *Rajbati* of Burdwan. For the remaining two *Lats*, he was required to pay the land revenue and road-cess to the *Dewan Daftari Cachari* of the *Rajbati* of Burdwan.[54]

By then, the fame of the pilgrim town spread far and wide and this resulted directly in the steady inflow of pilgrims. Keeping pace with this inflow of pilgrims a few families of the *Sebayet* priests came to settle here from surrounding areas during the period being studied. The descendants of these families claim even at present that their ancestors received free land-grants from the estate by order of the then *Mohanta* of the *Tarakeswar Math*, so that they could settle around the sacred complex.

Mohanchandra Giri was, indeed, the link between the *Mohantas* of the *Tarakeswar Math* during the 18th century as well as those who succeeded him in the 19th century. However, this period of transition, with Mohanchandra Giri at the helm of affairs, witnessed comparative stability in so far as the *Math* as well as the temple were concerned.

However, an overall analysis of this phase of the evolution of Tarakeswar reveals a few interruptions in the process until the end of the 18th century. The primary inclination to trade that had begun with Birbhadranath Giri remained intact until Mohanchandra Giri - the *Mohanta* during whose administration one century gave way to another.

Despite their adherence to the enhancement of commerce, these *Mohantas* of the second half of the 18th century were also concerned with the increase in the temple-*zamindari* and its consolidation. This was specially true in the case of Mohanchandra Giri.

The short-lived interruptions during this phase of the evolution are proofs of the fact that tradition overcame the forces of the destabilisation that often threatened the *Tarakeswar Math*.

Over and above, the illustrious *Mohantas* during this period were at one with their commitment to the principle of making the infra structure of the twin institutions financially strong with the help of the profits, that accrued from their commercial activities especially when crises came into existence.

In addition to their desire to extend and consolidate the temple-*zamindari*, the *Mohantas* during this period were also relatively alert to the necessity of adopting humanitarian measures for those living within the area of the sacred complex.

Note

1. Mihir Kiran Bhattacharya (ed.) Mahanirvanatantram. Vol. I. Chap.-3. PP. -70-72.

2. S. K. Mitra - Hooghly Jelar Itihas O Bangasamaj. Vol-II. P.-1109.

3. S. Sinha and B. N. Saraswati - Ascetics of Kashi. P.-59.

4. Akshoy Kumar Dutta - Bharatbarsiya Upasak Sampradaya. Vol-I and II. P.-208.

5. Anil Chandra Banerjee - Madhya Yuge Bangla O Bangali. P.-214.

6. H. H. Wilson - Hindu Religions. P.-11.

7. J. M. Ghosh - Sannyasi and Fakir Raiders in Bengal. Calcutta. 1930. P.-25.

8. W. W. Hunter - Annals of rural Bengal. P.-77.

9. Sir Jadunath Sarkar - The History of Bengal. (1200-1757). Vol.-II. P.-467.

10. Anil Chandra Banerjee - Madhya Yuge Bangla O Bangali. P.-215

11. Satishchandra Giri - Tarakeswar Sivatattva. PP.-104-109.

12. Ibid - PP. 116-117.

13. A. C. Banerjee - Madhya Yuge Bangla O Bangali. P.-215.

14. Satishchandra Giri - Tarakeswar Sivatattva. P.-100.

15. Prafulla Chakrabarty - Social Profile of Tarakeswar. P-18.

16. Bernard S. Cohn - "The Role of the Gosains in the Economy of Eighteenth and Nineteenth Century Upper India." L. P. Vidyarthi and Makhan Jha (ed.)-Symposium on the Sacred complex in India. Ranchi. Council of Social and Cultural Research. pp. - 88-95.

17. Satishchandra Giri - Tarakeswar Sivatattva. Preface.

18. Title Suit No. 28/1922. D. Sinharoy and others Vs. Satishchandra Giri. Suit Under Sec. 92 C. P. C. Para.-31.

19. Lt. Col. D. G. Crawford - A Brief History of the Hugli District. Bengal Secretariat. Cal. 1902.

20. Satishchandra Giri - Tarakeswar Sivatattva. P.-70.

21. Ibid. - P.-32.

22. Ibid - P.-7.

23. Ibid. PP.-23-37.

24. Title Suit No. 28/1922. D sinharoy and others Vs. Satishchandra Giri, Suit Under Sec. 92. C. P. C. Para.-16 and 17.

25. Appendix to the Judgement in F.A. No. 255 of 1930. Dated -1.8.1934. Also,
Satishchandra Giri - Tarakeswar Sivatattva. P.-70.

26. S. K. Mitra - Hooghly Jelar Itihas O Bangasamaj. Vol-II. P.-1114.

27. Pramathanath Sanyal - Tarakeswar (in Bengal). Dacca. 1936.

28. Satishchandra Giri - Tarakeswar Sivatattva. Preface.

29. Title Suit No. 28/1922. Suit Under Sec. 92. C. P. C. Para.-15.

30. Sri Sri Taraknath Jiu Seba Samiti (ed.) - Sri Sri Tarakeswar Lila. PP. - 11-12.

31. Gopinath Kabiraj - Tantrik Sadhana O Siddhanta. Vol-I. PP.-21-33.

32. Satishchandra Giri - Tarakeswar Sivatattva. 'Preface'.

33. Ibid - 'Footnote'. P.-113.

34. Anilchandra Banerjee - Madhya Yuge Bangla O Bangali. P.-215.

35. Satishchandra Giri - Tarakeswar Sivatattva. P.-109.

36. Ibid. P.-105.

37. Ibid - PP. - 108-109.

38. Ibid - Preface and P.-110.

39. Ibid - P.-126

40. Title Suit No. 28/1922. In the Court of Dist. Judge of Hooghly. Sec. 92. C. P. C. Para.-31.

41. Satishchandra Giri - Tarakeswar Sivatattva. Preface and P.-113.

42. Ibid - PP.-113-115.

43. Plaint Suit No. 4458 of 1790 in the Judge's Court of Burdwan. Parasuram Giri Vs. Fatey Giri.

44. Satishchandra Giri - Tarakeswar Sivatattva. P.-116. Footnote.

45. Ibid - P.-118. Footnote and Preface.

46. Plaint Suit No. 4458 of 1790 in the Judge's Court of Burdwan. Parasuram Giri Vs. Fatey Giri.

47. Prafulla Chakrabarty - Social Profile of Tarakeswar. P.-18.

48. Satishchandra Giri - Tarakeswar Sivatattva. P.-121-122.

49. Prafulla Chakrabarty - Social Profile of Tarakeswar. P.-18.

50. Satishchandra Giri - Tarakeswar Sivatattva. P.-125-126.

51. Prafulla Chakrabarty - Social Profile of Tarakeswar. P.-18.

52. S. K. Mitra - Hooghly Jelar Itihas O Bangasamaj. Vol-II, P.-1131.

53. Satishchandra Giri - Tarakeswar Sivatattva. P.-126.

54. The list of properties submitted by the defendant in the Court of the District Judge, Hooghly. Title Suit No. 28/1922. D. Sinharoy and others Vs. Satishchandra Giri.

Chapter - IV

The Mohantas of the Nineteenth Century : An Overview

I

In fact, the evolution of the twin institutions at this place of pilgrimage, from the initial phase to the end of 18th century, owed more to the illustrious as compared to less illustrious *Giri Mohantas*. Despite the differences in their efficiency, the *Giri Mohantas* in general displayed a primary concern over the years for the retention of their hold over the *Math* as well as the temple. So, along with their endeavours towards trade, they also encouraged an adherence to the *Guru-Sisya Parampara*. Although a series of *Giri Mohantas* succeeded to the helm of affairs in the 18th century, no accurate chronological order can be substantiated on account of the lack of corroborative information. Therefore, no definitive compartmentalisation of the tenures of the *Giri Mohantas* in the 18th Century seems possible in this context.

However, Raghuchandra Giri, the favourite disciple of Mohanchandra Giri, was elevated to the office of the *Mohanta* at the *Tarakeswar Math* after the demise of his *Guru* (preceptor) by virtue of a *Niyampatra* (ordinance) dated 2nd *Aswin* 1249 B.S. (i.e. 1843 A.D.). This *Niyampatra*, prepared at the behest of Mohanchandra Giri, enabled the twenty-third

Mohanta to take over the *Tarakeswar Guddee* along with the *nij* (self) and *debutter* (in the name of the deity) properties which were also bequeathed to him by his preceptor. This, indeed, seems to have created an impression in the minds of successive *Mohantas* that the public in general should have no interest in the administration of the *Tarakeswar Math*.[1]

Raghuchandra Giri's tenure witnessed the inclusion of *Lat* Ramchandrapur associated with *Lat* Naipara within the temple-*zamindari*. He was referred to have been paying land revenue and road cess to the *Habeli Cachari* of the *Rajbati* of Burdwan.[2] This *Mohanta* was very instrumental in convincing the Government of the desirability of making free the property of the temple from tax, and treating it as a religious endowment, under the laws of the British Government.[3] In fact, the *Giri Mohantas* in general took delight in taking the twin institutions to be private religious endowments over the years. The proposition that the shrine was a public religious and charitable endowment, had emphatically been denied by the last *Giri Mohanta* of the *Tarakeswar Math*.[4] But his denial that the gifts of movable as well as immovable properties were made for the entertainment of pilgrims, guests and ascetics did not merit any attention as is evident from the verdict of the District Judge. It upholds that "the *nij* (self) properties have in the past contributed towards the charitable and religious objects and that without such contribution they could never have existed in the past..."[5]

Immediately after Raghuchandra Giri's accession to the office of the *Mohanta* at the *Tarakeswar Math*, the sacred complex along with the surrounding region was flooded by the Damodar.[6] "From the records of the Bengal Government (from 1852) relating to the Damodar floods and embankments, it appears that the inundations of the Damodar could not be controlled because of the lack of detailed knowledge about uncertain monsoon conditions depositing widely varying quantities of water in the upper catchment areas of the Damodar."[7]

Raghuchandra Giri promptly rose to the occasion by taking recourse to the philanthropic activities. He used to help the flood-affected as well as the famine-stricken people living in and around the sacred complex from his own coffers. The so-called *Siva-Ganga* or *Dudhpukur* adjacent to the shrine of Lord *Taraknath* was dug by the order of this *Mohanta*, for the benefit of the pilgrims as well as the residents of the sacred complex.[8] Initially, the cult of *Dudhpukur* achieved considerable dimension with its so-called power of fulfilling the desires of the devotees who took a dip in it.[9]

The main road within the temple-town extending between the compound of the sacred complex and Sahapur, a nearby village, was also constructed during his tenure. Moreover, the repair work of the twenty-one mile long Baidyabati-Tarakeswar road known as the District Board Road in the Sreerampur sub-division, was also undertaken during this period.[10]

This phase of the evolution of the monastery and the temple at Tarakeswar witnessed earnest endeavours on the part of the *Giri Mohantas* to categories the properties acquired over the years using distinct terms- *nij* (self) and *debutter* (in their name of the deity). However, the tradition of playing the role of *talukdar* that had begun during the tenure of Mohanchandra Giri, remained as it was when his disciple Raghuchandra Giri took over. Their proneness to consider the same as a private religious endowment thenceforth seems to have taken shape against this background.

Over and above, this period under consideration witnessed no interruption in the measures adopted traditionally for the upliftment of the image of this place of pilgrimage. This definitely resulted in a steady increase in the inflow of pilgrims since the days of Mohanchandra Giri. This inflow assumed phenomenal proportions with the construction of a main road within the sacred complex as well as the repair of the District Board Road during the tenure of Raghuchandra Giri. In short, this *Mohanta* was witness to the all-round development of the sacred complex in spite of its susceptibility to the ravages of the Damodar.

II

In fact the last two *Mohantas* of the *Giri* order of the *Dashnami Sannyasis* at the *Tarakeswar Math* left permanent marks on the history of this place of pilgrimage. These two *Mohantas* were Madhabchandra Giri and his disciple Satishchandra Giri who became the *Mohantas* successively following the established process. Although Madhabchandra Giri's succession cannot be dated accurately, owing to the lack of evidence, it can be held that he had presumably assumed office with the blessing of his preceptor Raghuchandra Giri sometime in the late sixtieth or early seventieth decade of the 19th century. Prafulla Chakrabarty in his 'Social Profile of Tarakeswar' holds that the tenure of Madhabchandra Giri began in 1867.[11] However, this date remains uncorroborated. Notwithstanding, this difficulty, it is known that he remained the *Mohanta* for about twenty-five years. During this period, he was witness to a number of improvements in the socio-economic and cultural perspectives of the sacred complex.

Reference has already been made to the gradual accumulation of properties at the behest of the *Giri Mohantas* of the *Tarakeswar Math* over the years, which they divided accordingly into two categories - *nij* (self) and *debutter* (in the name of the deity). Madhabchandra Giri, indeed, was no exception in his determined continuation of these policies.

As a matter of fact, Madhabchandra Giri claimed credit for accumulating vast properties in and around the sacred complex amounting to 500 *bighas* of lands along with rent-free *debutter* lands, amounting to 2355 *bighas* during this period. Besides, *lakheraj* lands amounting to over 248 *bighas* in various parts of the district of Hooghly, along with rent-free and *jamai* lands in the districts of Hooghly, 24 parganas and Calcutta were acquired at his behest.[12] Apart from these properties; hard cash, ornaments as well as the other valuables made of gold and silver were procured. However, the references to the rent-free and *jamai* lands as well as the valuables remain unsubstantiated.

Despite his inclination to categorise some properties as *nij* (self) properties, Madhabchandra Giri failed to produce documentary evidences in support of his claim. Moreover, the suit No. 2 of 1878 initiated during his tenure resulted in the judgement that the properties acquired thus far within the purview of the *Tarakeswar Math* were definitely *debutter* in character.

While quantifying the landed properties acquired at the behest of Madhabchandra Giri, the last *Giri Mohanta*, however, admitted that the rent-free lands amounting to 2355 *bighas* along with the *Tarakeswar Bazar* and *Natun Bazar* adjacent to the *Math* were debutter properties. Besides, the *mouza* Bishnubati in the district of Hooghly which was, in fact, the *mokarari* tenure of about 214 *bighas* of lands; was also characterised as *debutter* property. These lands were assigned to the name of the deity of *Gokulchand* of Burdwan during the tenure of Madhabchandra Giri.

That the ornaments, gold and silver articles were included as *debutter* properties of Lord *Taraknath* since the days of Madhabchandra Giri was acknowledged clearly by the last *Giri Mohanta* of the *Tarakeswar Math*.[13]

It is incidentally noteworthy that the gift of a house in Harkatta Lane, Calcutta, by one Tarini Bai, presumably a prostitute, in the name of Lord *Taraknath* was also added to the list of *debutter* properties accumulated during the tenure of Madhabchandra Giri. As this property was considered unprofitable, the *Mohanta* sold it and bought instead rent-free lands measuring over 24 *bighas* at Bishnubati in the district of Hooghly with a view to strengthening the *debutter* estate.[14] In fact, the prostitutes of Calcutta often donated movable and immovable properties for religious causes. A few of such donations are recorded by Ramakanta Chakrabarty in his '*Bange Vaisnava Dharma*.[15]

By then, a close contact had been established with Northern India by virtue of the role of the incumbent *Mohanta* in the development of the link with Benaras. Madhabchandra Giri initiated two idols of Lord *Siva* and Lord *Laksmi-Nrisimgha* respectively at Benaras. The properties that he acquired in the *mouza* of Nachipur along with the *Putni taluk* of *Lat* Belgachia in the district of Hooghly were made *debutter* with reference to aforesaid idols.[16]

The estate-*zamindari* was by then considerable because of the accumulation of *debutter* and the so-called *nij* properties, which the incumbent *Mohanta* claimed to have inherited from his predecessors. In fact, *Lat* Krishnapur, *Lat* Naipara, *Lat* Jainabad, *Lat* Goorea and *Lat* Narayanpur were claimed to have been inherited as his *nij* properties along with the two *mouzas*-Baramba and Vata-in the district of Hooghly. Besides, the aforesaid *lakheraj* lands were also incorporated within the range of his *nij* (self) properties. Satishchandra Giri, his favourite disciple, candidly admitted that from the income of those existing *nij* properties as well as from the *pranamis* and donations given to him personally by his disciples and also from the profits of moneylending business, the incumbent *Mohanta* acquired other *nij* properties during this period.[17]

However, Madhabchandra Giri was very conscious of the *zamindari* held by the *Tarakeswar Math*. The promptness with which he initiated *se-pattani* settlement of the erstwhile *mokarari* lease of properties after its lapse, with one Tirthabasi Sinharoy of Haripal in the Hooghly district deserves mention. While in the other context, a *mokarari* lease of property had been taken in *mouza* Bhata at his behest from one Rakhaldas Laha, a resident of Ala in the district of Hooghly with same end in view.[18]

Irrespective of the nature of properties acquired by the *Tarakeswar Math* during the tenure of the incumbent *Mohanta*, the fact remains that huge properties had been added to the estate-*zamindari* in this period under review. This, in fact, resulted in a major transformation of the sacred complex with the *Mohanta* playing the role of a *zamindar*.

Whether the local merchants and traders had to pay tax to the *Mohanta* for their trade, cannot be ascertained. But it can be assumed that the local merchants and traders were, as tenants, permitted by the *Mohanta* to carry on business following an agreement to pay the amount of land tax imposed on them by the *Mohanta*. Usually, the *Mohanta* as a *zamindar* enjoyed the right to impose any amount of land tax on his tenants by virtue of the *Chandina Sattva* - a Tenancy Act-by which a tenant was entitled to only use the land, but had no right to build permanent structures on it.

Moreover, he was bound to surrender the land concerned when he was asked to do so.[19] Therefore, the local merchants and traders under the jurisdiction of the *Tarakeswar Math* certainly had to pay land tax at par with the other tenants.

In fact, this kind of treatment of the tenants in accordance with the existent patterns followed by the *zamindars*, on the part of the *Mohantas*, had definitely begun during the tenure of Madhabchandra Giri who had by then created a large *zamindari* under the supervision of the *Tarakeswar Math*. It is very interesting to note that the Indian Association organised at the behest of Surendranath Bandyopadhyaya and Anandamohan Basu in 1876 had taken up a programme for organising the tenants against their atrocious *zamindars* particularly in the district of Hooghly when Madhabchandra Giri was at the helm of affairs at Tarakeswar. The Indian Association organised innumerable meetings at different places in the district to build up public opinion in this regard. A meeting had incidentally been arranged at Tarakeswar at which both Surendranath and Anandamohan addressed the audience with a view to inspiring them to stand firm against the atrocious *zamindars*.[20] The treatment meted out to the tenants as *zamindars* gave birth to grievances in the long run and led to the *Satyagraha* movement during the tenure of Satishchandra Giri. In fact, the demand for wiping out the age-old problem of illegal and enforced payments ultimately sounded the death knell so far as the hegemony of the *Giri* order at the *Tarakeswar Math* was concerned.[21]

That the *Mohantas* of the *Tarakeswar Math* were in the habit of subjecting traders, shopkeepers, residents as well as pilgrims to illegal exactions through their agents came into focus immediately prior to the *Satyagraha* movement which was launched against the last *Giri Mohanta* of the *Tarakeswar Math*.[22] Moreover, there was also the *ijaradar* demanding toll, by order of the *Mohanta*, from the people bringing vegetables and fruits by oxen to the market for sale.[23] Although the illegal exactions as well as toll were enthusiastically put into effect during the tenure of Satishchandra Giri, the trend was certainly set during the regime of his predecessor, from whom he had inherited the temple-*zamindari* along with its vices.

III

Like his predecessors, Madhabchandra Giri had taken keen interest in the development of this place of pilgrimage alongside his endeavour to increase the size of the estate-*zamindari*. He was perhaps the first of the *Giri Mohantas* of the *Tarakeswar Math* who worked for the spread of education along traditional as well as modern lines.

The *Tarakeswar Chatuspathi*, an institution for learning Sanskrit, had been established in the vicinity of the *Tarakeswar Math*, under his supervision for imparting knowledge of Sanskrit literature to the residential students with provision for free board and lodging.[24] This practice is still in vogue. O'Malley wrote in the 'Bengal District Gazetteers' about a number of recognised *tols* which imparted advanced education in Sanskrit. He had incidentally referred to several *tols* in the district of Hooghly which were private and were "mostly found in old places such as Tribeni (including Bansberia), Bhadreswar, Baidyabati, Uttarpara, Tarakeswar, Khanakul, Kristanagar etc."[25] The word *tol* is, in fact, a word of non-Sanskrit origin, and is in use only in Bengal where *tols* are also called *Chaupadi* or, *Chaubadi* from Sanskrit *Chatuspathi*, a place for teaching the four *Vedas*.

Incidentally, the Sanskrit College at Calcutta had received generous contribution from him for the promotion of learning in Sanskrit. Madhabchandra Giri's munificence also transcended the regional barrier with his endeavour to set up a Sanskrit School in Benaras to impart education to the residential students there, along traditional line. Besides, his generous contribution to the fund for repairing the old structure of Tarakeswar High School speaks highly of his interest in imparting education on modern line.[26]

Meanwhile, the growing fame of this place of pilgrimage in Eastern India led to the steady increase in the inflow of pilgrims which correspondingly resulted in the increase in the number of residence-cum-rest houses for pilgrims in and around the sacred complex. Taking the cue from Samudranath Giri, the eighteenth *Mohanta*, this incumbent *Mohanta* masterminded the digging up of two big tanks-*Kumkumi* and *Sankardighi* - within the distance of a stone's throw of the *Tarakeswar Math*. Besides, a few temples had been built up in and around Tarakeswar with direct financial help from this *Mohanta* of which the *Kali* temple of Bhanjipur, an adjacent village, deserves special mention in this context.[27]

As a matter of fact, a few wealthy pilgrims had taken part in the maintenance and development of the temple as well as other establishments associated with the sacred complex during the tenure of Madhabchandra Giri. Notable among them were Chintamani De of Howrah and Gangadhar Sen who took part in the rejuvenation of the sacred complex at the behest of this *Mohanta* of the *Tarakeswar Math*. The former took the initiative for the remodelling of the *Natyamandira* or the marble hall and financed the laying of the floor of the temple with costly tiles in 1891. He also spent money generously for the repair of several roads. He is said to have done it "in gratitude for having been miraculously cured of disease in answer to prayer offered at the shrine."[28] The latter was involved in the reconstruction of the staircases of *Dudhpukur* or *Siddhapukur* in 1893.[29] The Magistrate and Collector of Hooghly, George Toynbee, had referred to the existence of "a very celebrated medical temple" on the road from Haripal to Tarakeswar, in his study of the administration of the Hooghly District.[30] He seems to have referred to the temple of Lord *Taraknath* which, by then, had become famous for miraculous cures.

The tenure of Madhabchandra Giri also witnessed the arrival of Sarada Debi, the consort of Sri Ramakrishna, at this place of pilgrimage along with her mother and brother to offer prayers to Lord *Taraknath*, in March 1881 (1287 B.S.).[31] Tarakeswar was revisited by her in the month of August, 1886 with the intention of performing the *dharna* ritual for the cure of Sri Ramakrishna. A memorial has been erected on the Tarakeswar railway station platform only recently in honour of this memorable visit.

It is noteworthy that a few fairs and festivals like *Sivaratri* and *Gajan* began to take place on a massive scale in the month of *Phalgun* (Feb-March) and *Chaitra* (March-Apr.) under the supervision of this *Mohanta* which ultimately led to an all-round development of this pilgrim town.[32] Although these fairs and festival had begun immediately after the revelation of the cult of *Siva*, under the guidance of *Rao* Bharamalla along with the participation of Mukunda Ghosh and his associates, these indeed got a fillip during the tenure of this twenty-fourth *Giri Mohanta*.[33] The participants in these festivals were mostly rural folk, who belonged to the villages of the districts of Midnapur, Howrah, 24 Parganas, Hooghly as well as of Jessore and Khulna in Bangladesh.[34] This coincided with the creation of a railway link between

Tarakeswar and the surrounding region following an extension of railway network during this period.

IV

One of the memorable events during the tenure of Madhabchandra Giri was the extension of the railway line, from Sheoraphuli to Tarakeswar, which in its turn helped Tarakeswar grow rapidly in popularity. In fact, "the East India Railway line from Howrah to Hooghly was opened for passenger traffic on the 15th August, 1845.... Among the subsequent additions to the line, the following may be mentioned :- the opening of a branch line to Tarakeswar, a noted place of pilgrimage. The line was constructed by private enterprise and handed over to the East India Railway to work on the 1st January, 1885".[35] This extension of the railway line from Sheoraphuli to Tarakeswar had its natural impact not only on the flow of pilgrims to Tarakeswar, but also on the creation of an economic bond between the pilgrim town and the surrounding region linked to it by the railway network.[36] Moreover, the initiative for opening up the Bengal Provincial Railway was also undertaken during this period although the programme came into effect during the tenure of the last *Giri Mohanta* of the *Tarakeswar Math*.[37]

The project for the construction of this railway was first mooted in 1885 by Annadaprasad Sinha, a resident of Sitiplassey in the district of Hooghly, who was incidentally an important officer in charge of Indian Midland Railway project at Bhopal. He was helped in his endeavour to form the Bengal Provincial Railway Company Limited by Amritalal Roy, the editor of the Hope- a weekly in English. The Head Office of this company was opened at Tarakeswar.

The proposer of the scheme for the opening of this railway line was Annada Prasad Roy, a young engineer from Roorkee Thomson Civil Engineering College and the agent was Amritalal Roy. They urged the respectable and wealthy Bengalis to buy the shares of this light feeder railway line and to apply for the same to A.L. Roy - the editor of the Hope at 65, Akhil Mistri Lane, Calcutta. A few reputed personalities of the then Bengal led by *Raja* Peary Mohan Mukherjee, the *zamindar* of Uttarpara in the district of Hooghly, came forward to purchase shares in order to facilitate the creation of this company. *Raja* Peary Mohan alone bought six hundred shares to help the completion of this project.[38]

This scheme for opening up the Provincial Railway line was applauded in the issue of the Indian Daily News on 28 May, 1889. It supported "the project for forming a native company to construct light feeder lines of Railway in Bengal, connecting prosperous districts with the main arterial lines" ..... Ultimately, "the Bengal Provincial Railway Line, on the 2 feet 6 inches gauge, was built by a company formed through the exertions of Mr. A.L. Roy. The first section from Tarakeswar to Basua (12.5 miles) was opened to traffic on 7 November, 1894, the second section from Basua to Magra (18.12 miles)on 8 March, 1895, and the third section from Magra to Tribeni (2.15 miles) in 1904."[39] The news of the opening ceremony of the Bengal Provincial Railway Line from Tarakeswar to Magra on 2nd April, 1895 was published in the Indian Messenger on 7 April, 1895. The opening ceremony was presided over by Sir Charles Elliot, the Lieutenant Governor of Bengal. It reported that "before a large and respectable gathering, the Lieutenant Governor formally declared open the Tarakeswar-Magra line of the Bengal Provincial Railway Company, the first railway in

India which has been entirely financed and constructed by the sole agency of the natives of this country...."

"The Railway was constructed by *Babu* Ananda Prasad Roy, a 'passed' student of Roorkee Thomson Civil Engineering College, and a young engineer of exceptionally high abilities who with Mr. Amritalal Roy of 'Hope' projected and planned the line". Although it was the first undertaking of its kind solely conducted under native management, it failed to pay the expected dividend.[40] Despite the earnest endeavours of this enterprising Joint Stock Company to connect Tarakeswar with the arterial railway system of India, it failed to keep itself alive after 1956. Even the urgent efforts of Hirendranath Roy, who was for long the General Manager of the Bengal Provincial Railway went in vain.[41]

The direct result of this extension of the railway network connecting Tarakeswar with the surrounding region was the gradual increase in the inflow of pilgrims as well as the steady development of this pilgrim town. Madhabchandra Giri, the *Mohanta* of the *Tarakeswar Math* during this period was, indeed, the eyewitness to this process of the rapid transformation of a hamlet into a vibrant pilgrim centre.

The result of this rapid transformation was visible particularly in the growth of vibrant business centres in and around the sacred complex during this period. In fact, business centres like *Chaulpatti* dealing mostly in rice, jute and vegetables, *monoharipatti* dealing in pictures, items necessary for daily rituals in the households and toys of various types for children, as well as *kaparpatti* dealing in woven fabrics came into being during this phase of evolution of this pilgrim town.[42]

Hence, an all-round transformation of this pilgrim centre in the second half of the 19th century owed definitely to this extension of the railway line, the process of which had begun in 1884.

V

Despite the all-round development of this place of pilgrimage, the diminishing power of the *Giri Mohantas* eventually became conspicuous during the regime of Madhabchandra Giri. In fact, the rot had already set in the institution over the years owing to the lack of enlightenment among a few *Dashnami Sannyasis* who had purposely facilitated the demoralisation of the whole system.[43] A few *Mohantas* of the *Giri* order at the *Tarakeswar Math* became callous and perverted particularly during the later phase, because of their excessive indulgence in mundane affairs. Naturally, grievances began to arise with reference to the immoral character of the *Mohantas,* as manifested in their alleged role in the violation of the chastity of women and their autocratic behaviour in relation to their tenants around the sacred complex.

Madhabchandra Giri was never up to the mark in so far as moral character was concerned and, therefore, he was put in the dock to answer for his alleged immorality. He had to face severe criticism in and around this pilgrim town for his direct involvement in the infamous Elokeshi affair. The Elokeshi Case of 1873 had caused a great sensation throughout Bengal and led to a perceptible scepticism in the psyche of the Bengalis in general about the holiness associated with the *Mohanta*.[44] He was accused of violating the chastity of Elokeshi, a housewife of the village Kumrul under Dhaniakhali Police Station in the district of Hooghly. This tiny village, not far from

Tarakeswar, became very prominent during this period simply because of this case.[45]

The Tarakeswar Adultery Case, in which the *Mohanta* of the *Tarakeswar Math* stood charged, marked an important epoch in the annals of Hooghly. It would have been very strange, indeed, if it had not created the sensation which it did. The *Mohanta* of the *Tarakeswar Math* usually commanded much respect as much for his immense wealth, as for his supposed superior sanctity. The reverence he received from the Hindu community at large, was almost without parallel. When it was reported that such a venerable monk had grossly misbehaved with a housewife of sixteen without caring for rigid rules of his holy order, it was only natural that there followed a terrible commotion in Hindu society. The facts regarding his deviation from the strict vow of celibacy soon became public.

The young housewife of the village Kumrul was the daughter of one Nilkamal Chakrabarty of the same village in the vicinity of the sacred complex. Elokeshi was the daughter of his first wife, and she was married to a high caste *Brahmin*, named Nabinchandra Bandyopadhyaya. Nabinchandra was an employee in the Government Printing Office at Calcutta and generally resided there. As was usual, he paid only occasional visits to his wife in his father-in-law's residence. Meanwhile, Nilkamal married again after the death of his first wife and his second wife was incidentally in touch with Madhabchandra Giri, the *Mohanta* of the *Tarakeswar Math*. The *Mohanta* lost control over himself when he saw Elokeshi in her stepmother's company. He attempted to seduce Elokeshi, using all possible means, with the help of her stepmother. As people are generally fond of discussing their neighbour's shame, Nabinchandra, before long, heard slanderous reports of his wife's misconduct. Under these circumstances, he came to Kumrul on a visit to his wife after having obtained leave from his office. Suspicion soon ripened into certainty.[46] On the fatal night of 27 May, 1873, the much afflicted and enraged husband suddenly asked his wife point-blank about the real state of affairs. He was already in utter tension, and became highly exasperated by her repudiating the imputation. Nabinchandra found no other way to save his wife from the lust of the *Mohanta*, so he killed her.

The news of this brutal murder spread like wild fire everywhere in Bengal and caused an instant reaction against the *Mohanta* of the *Tarakeswar Math*. Nabinchandra surrendered himself to the police of his own accord. He was brought before Joint Magistrate of Sreerampur, who ordered him to *hajat*. While confined to *hajat*, Nabinchandra preferred a charge of adultery against the *Mohanta* under Section 497 of the Indian Penal Code.[47]

Accordingly, a preliminary enquiry was held by Mr. William Fitzpatrick Meres, the Joint Magistrate of Hooghly. The *Mohanta*, who had disappeared after the murder of Elokeshi, did not appear in the court until 1 August. Meanwhile, a warrant for his arrest had been issued on 16 June, 1873. The role of Joykrishna Mukherjee, the *zamindar* of Uttarpara had been commendable in this context. He, indeed, earnestly endeavoured to bring Madhabchandra Giri, the lecherous *Mohanta* of the *Tarakeswar Math* to justice in 1873. The *Mohanta* escaped to the French territory of Chandernagore. Joykrishna, as the most influential *zamindar* of the district, helped the Government in proceeding against the fugitive *Mohanta* and getting him arrested.[48] Mr. Meres, however, thought that a prima facie case had been made out already against the *Mohanta* and he, therefore, committed him to the sessions.

This commitment was quashed by the Sessions Judge of Hooghly Mr. H.T. Princep, on the technical ground of non-jurisdiction. He was of opinion that the preliminary enquiry should have been held by the Joint Magistrate of Sreerampur, within whose jurisdiction the offence was said to have been committed. But Nabinchandra was a very determined opponent. He, indeed, renewed his complaint upon which a second enquiry was held by the Magistrate empowered in this context. The ultimate result was a second commitment.

This time the trial came before Mr. Charles Dickinson Field who was then officiating for Mr. Princep. The Judge was assisted in the trial by Shibchandra Mallick and Shambhuchandra Gargory, the two native Assessors of repute and residents of Chinsura in the district of Hooghly. The trial commenced amidst considerable public interest. The crowd that used to assemble during the period was immense. There was a sea of human heads in and around the court room and the place looked, indeed, like a great *mela*.[49] Ishanchandra Mitra, the able Government pleader, conducted the prosecution, while Mr. Jackson and Mr. G.H. Evans, the two well-known counsels of the Calcutta Bar, defended the prisoner. The main points for determination were, first, whether the accused *Mohanta* had had intercourse with Elokeshi or not, and secondly, whether at the time of such intercourse, he knew or had reason to believe her to be the wife of another man. However, it had already been established beyond doubt that Elokeshi was the wedded wife of Nabinchandra Bandyopadhyaya.

Gopinath Sinharoy was the material witness in this case. He was the *durwan* (gatekeeper) of the *Mohanta* when the adultery was said to have been committed. His evidence disclosed certain circumstances which raised a strong presumption that the *Mohanta* had consciously committed the crime. The prisoner's counsel fought tooth and nail to demolish the testimony of Gopinath, but truth triumphed in the end. The Judge believed the witness. There were some other material witnesses but they had disappeared from the scene before the second enquiry began. Only Gopinath remained. Some attempts seem to have been made to buy him over, but he stood firm and unmoved. His evidence, in fact, turned the balance in favour of the prosecution. The Judge, after a very patient and careful consideration of the evidence and the attendant circumstances, found the prisoner guilty on both counts. While Shibchandra Mallick concurred with the viewpoint of the Judge, the other Assessor Shambhuchandra Gargary differed on the ground that there was no direct evidence as to sexual intercourse between the two. He forgot that such evidence was hardly expected to be forthcoming in such a case.

The Judge, disregarding the opinion of dissenting Assessor, convicted the accused under Section 497 of the Indian Penal Code and sentenced him to undergo three years' rigorous imprisonment and to pay a fine of Rs. 2,000/-. The maximum punishment, as provided in the Penal Code was five years' imprisonment with or without fine. This order which was generally satisfactory to the country, was passed on 20 November, 1873.[50]

There was, of course, an appeal to the High Court but the *Mohanta* was refused bail in this case. He was made to put off his holy saffron dress and put on the ignoble dress of a convict. The jail is always a great leveller as it makes no distinction between a pariah and a priest.

The appeal of the *Mohanta* was heard by a Divison Bench consisting of Mr. Justice Markby and Mr. Justice Birch on 15 December, 1873. His counsel, Messrs. Jackson and Evans fought hard to get him off, but their Lordships held that the conviction was good and valid. As regards the sentence, they observed in no uncertain terms that despite the severity inherent in the sentence, it ought not to be mitigated in view of the public position of the accused.

The observation of Mr. Justice Birch on this point was very proper and pertinent. His Lordship said that the offence of the accused was considerably aggravated by his position as head of a venerated shrine, by virtue of which he was regarded by his co-religionists as an impersonation of the deity whose shrine was in his charge. A man in his position had immense power and influence in this country. If he "is faithless to his trust, and if under the cloak of religion, and regardless of the decided prohibition of such conduct in the writings which he holds sacred, he employs his opportunities to debauch married women, he merits condign punishment."[51]

Based on the Tarakeswar Adultery Case, there was staged a play titled, *Ish! Mohanter Eki Kaj* (Oh! what a mischievous deed of the *Mohanta* is this) at the Bengal Theatre on 6 September 1873.[52] It achieved immense popularity. The overwhelming success of this drama had in its turn encouraged also the Great National Theatre to stage another play, *Ami to Unmadini* (I have gone mad) with almost the same theme on 3 January, 1874. Rasaraj Amritalal Basu enthralled the audience by virtue of his role as the hapless father of Elokeshi. This was the most sensational play of the time, which drew crowds to the theatre.[53]

Even ballads were composed at that time on the *Mohanta*-Elokeshi episode. These sometimes displayed vulgar taste of their anonymous composers. Besides, satirical compilations also began to be published which referred to the immoral *Mohanta* Madhabchandra Giri. Of these, *Mohanter Eki Dasha*

(What a distressed being the *Mohanta* is) and *Aha! Mohanter Ei Kaaj* (Oh! What a mischievous deed of the *Mohanta* is this), both published in 1873 by Jogendranath Ghosh, seem noteworthy. Moreover, *Mohanter Eki Kaj* - Vol. I and II published consecutively in 1873 and '74 from Howrah were written by Laksmi Narayan Das. Again, *Mohanter Chakra Bhraman* (Circular trip of the *Mohanta*, 1874) by Bholanath Mukherjee as well as *Mohanta Pakshe Bhuto Nandi* (Bhuto Nandi on behalf of the *Mohanta*, 1874) by Harimohan Chatterjee characterise the *Mohanta* as a misfit.

Apart from these, over a dozen satires had been compiled as a reaction to this unhealthy development.[54] These were, however, the reflections of perceptible changes in the psyche of the Bengalis, caused by the misdeeds of the *Mohanta*. The ripples created because of these developments gradually died down after the *Mohanta* breathed his last in 1893.

Poor Nabinchandra was not spared. He was tried for the murder of his wife. He was convicted also for the crime he had committed on the spur of the moment and was sentenced to transportation by order of the High Court. Efforts were made afterwards by the well-wishers of Nabinchandra to expedite his release. An appeal was made to the Lieutenant Governor of Bengal praying for his intervention in this regard.[55] In view of the peculiar character of his offence, he was released in 1877, on the occasion of the assumption by Queen Victoria of the title of Empress.

Meanwhile, Shyamchandra Giri, the senior disciple of the convicted *Mohanta* took charge of the administration of the twin institutions at Tarakeswar as the pro tem *Mohanta*. The term of imprisonment, however, at last expired and Madhabchandra Giri was released in the latter part of November, 1876. He returned and instantly demanded the restoration of the administration of the *Math* to himself. Shyamchandra Giri was not at all desirous of obliging his preceptor and refused to vacate the *Guddee* in his favour. He was supported at this crucial stage even by the Mukherjee-*zamindars* of Uttarpara in the district of Hooghly.[56] Despite these developments, Madhabchandra Giri forcibly re-entered the temple premises and resumed possession of them and of the landed property.

Shyamchandra Giri brought a Summary Suit for the recovery of possession under Section 15 of Act XIV of 1859 in the District Court of Hooghly. Mr. Justice G.P. Grant, the Judge, decreed the suit on 28 August, 1877. On 3 September, the defendant Madhabchandra Giri, moved the High Court under Section 15 of the Charter Act. As a result a rule was granted, calling upon the other party to show cause as to why the order of the District Judge should not be set aside. This rule was heard by a Division Bench consisting of Mr. Justice R.C. Mitra and Mr. Justice W. Markby on 24 November, 1877. Their Lordships while finding fault with the Judge as to the way in which he had tried the suit, held that they could not interfere with his decision under their general powers of superintendence, and they, accordingly dismissed the application. Thus defeated, Madhabchandra Giri brought a Civil Suit for declaration of the title and recovery of possession, and in this he was signally successful.[57] He was restored to the *Guddee* which he occupied up to the time of his death which took place in Calcutta in *Phalgun* (Feb.-March) 1299 B.S. (1893 A.D.)

In fact, the evolution of the *Tarakeswar Math* during the nineteenth century was dominated by at least three *Giri Mohantas* of whom Madhabchandra Giri was the best-known. The expansion, as well as consolidation of the estate-*zamindari* along with the all-round development of this sacred complex that happened during this period was commendable. Yet, this twenty-fourth *Mohanta* himself was very responsible for the ignominy that attached itself to the *Tarakeswar Math*, leading to its erosion in the long run.

Note

1. Title Suit No. 28/1922. Suit Under Sec. 92. C. P. C. Para. 17A.

2. The list of properties submitted by the defendant in the Court of the District Judge. Hooghly.
   Title Suit No. 28/1922. D. Sinharoy and others Vs. Satishchandra Giri.

3. Prafulla Chakrabarty - Social Profile of Tarakeswar. P.-18.

4. Title Suit No. 28/1922. Suit Under Sec. 92. C. P. C. Para.-18.

5. Verdict of Mr. Justice K. C. Nag, the District Judge, in relation to the Suit Under Sec. 92. C. P. C. Serial No. of Order or Proceeding - 798. Date of order - 17.07.28.

6. Satishchandra Giri - Tarakeswar Sivatattva. P.-127.

7. A. K. Banerjee (ed.) West Bengal District Gazetteers. Hooghly. P.-43.

8. Satishchandra Giri - Tarakeswar Sivatattva. P.-127.

9. A. K. Banerjee (ed.) - West Bengal District Gazetteers. Hooghly. P.-725.

10. L. S. S. O'Malley and M. M. Chakrabarty - Bengal District Gazetteers. Hooghly. PP.-320-321.

11. Prafulla Chakrabarty - Social Profile of Tarakeswar. P.-19.

12. Title Suit No. 28/1922. Suit Under Sec. 92. C. P. C. Para. 6.

13. Title Suit No. 28/1922. Suit Under Sec. 92. C. P. C. Para. 23 & 32.

14. Ibid. - Para.- 32.

15. Ramakanta Chakrabarty - Bange Vaisnava Dharma. Cal.1996. PP.-139-140.

16. Title Suit No. 28/1922. Suit Under Sec. 92. C. P. C. Para. 22 & 32

17. Ibid.- Para-33.

18. The list of properties submitted by Satishchandra Giri in the Court of the District Judge, Hooghly. Title Suit No. 28/1922.

19. Prafulla Chakrabarty - Social Profile of Tarakeswar. P.-20-21.

20. Kamal Chattopadhyaya - Swadhinata Sangrame Hooghly Jela. 'Paschimbanga' Hooghly Jela Sankhya. 1403 B.S. Department of Information and Culture. West Bengal Government. P.-58.

21. Narendranath Bandyopadhyaya - Tarakeswar Satyagraha Sangram. PP. -52-56.

22. Amrita Bazar Patrika - 6.5.24, 6(3).

23. Buddhadeb Bhattacharya - Satyagrahas in Bengal. P.-89.

24. Prafulla Chakrabarty - Social Profile of Tarakeswar. P.-19.

25. L. S. S. O'Malley and M. M. Chakrabarty - Bengal District Gazetteers. Hooghly. PP.-239-240.
Also,
Dr. Rameschandra Mitra - 'Education' in Narendrakrishna Sinha ed. The History of Bengal (1757-1905). Calcutta University. 1967. PP.-431-432.

26. Prafulla Chakraborty - Social Profile of Tarakeswar. P.-19

27. Ibid. - PP. - 19-20.

28. L. S. S. O'Malley and M. M. Chakrabarty - Bengal District Gazetteers. Hooghly. PP.-322-323.

29. S. K. Mitra - Hooghly Jelar Itihas O Bangasamaj. Vol.-II. P.-1115.

30. George Toynbee - A Sketch of the Administration of the Hooghly District. From 1795 to 1845, Cal. 1888. P.-107.

31. Tarit Kumar Bandyopadhyaya - Sri Sri Ma O Dakatbaba. PP.- 35, 241 and 245.

32. Prafulla Chakrabarty - Social Profile of Tarakeswar. P.-20.

33. Satishchandra Giri - Tarakeswar Sivatattva. P.-81-85

34. Ashok Mitra (ed.) - Paschim Banger Puja Parban O mela. Vol.-II, P.-605.

35. L. S. S. O'Malley and M. M. Chakrabarty - Bengal District Gazetteers. Hooghly. P.-203.

36. The Statesman - April, 29; 1884 (editorial).

37. Benoy Ghosh - Samayik Patre Banglar Samajchitra. (in Bengal). 1962. PP.-129-130.

38. S. K. Mitra - Hooghly jelar Itihas O Bangasamaj. Vol. II. P.-1132.

39. L. S. S. O'Malley and M. M. Chakrabarty - Bengal District Gazetteers. Hooghly. P.-204.

40. C. E. Buckland - Bengal Under the Lieutenant Governors. P.-937.

41. S. K. Mitra - Hooghly Jelar Itihas O Bangasamaj. Preface and Vol. I, P.-324.

42. Prafulla Chakrabarty - Social Profile of Tarakeswar. P.-20.

43. Swami Satchidananda Saraswati - Jnanapradip. Vol.-II. P.-102.

44. Sri Pantha - Mohanta-Elokeshi Sambad. Ananda Bazar Patrika. Autumn Special. Calcutta. 1976. PP.-27-37.
Also,
Narendranath Bandyopadhyaya - Tarakeswar Satyagraha Sangram. PP.-32-33.
Also,
Pramathanath Sanyal - Tarakeswar. P.-32.

45. S. K. Mitra - Hooghly Jelar Itihas O Bangasamaj. Vol.-II. PP.-817-818.

46. Durgacharan Roy - Debganer Martye Agaman. PP.-431-432.

47. S. C. Dey - Hooghly Past and Present. PP.-309-318.

48. Friend of India - July 17, 1873.
Also,
Hindu Patriot - July 21, 1873.

49. Bharat Sanskarak - 12.9.1873.

50. S. C. Dey - Hooghly Past and present. PP.-309-318.

51. 12 W.R. PP.-13-21.

52. S. K. Mitra - Tarakeswarer Itikatha. P.-17.

53. Hemendranath Dasgupta - The Indian Stage. 2nd edition. Vol.-II. PP.-235-236.

54. Jayanta Goswami - Samaj Chitre Unabingsha Satabdir Bangla Prahasan. Cal. Sahityasree. 1381 B.S. 1381 B.S. (1974) PP.-254-300.

55. Bharat Sanskarak - 12.9.1873.

56. S. K. Mitra - Hooghly Jelar Itihas O Bangasamaj. Vol.-II. PP.-1118.

57. S. C. Dey - Hooghly Past and present. PP.-309-318.

Chapter - V

Satishchandra Giri : the last
Giri Mohanta

I

On 2 *Chaitra*, 1299 B.S. (i.e., March 1893 A.D.), Satishchandra Giri became the *Mohanta* of the *Tarakeswar Math* following the *Guru Sisya Parampara* after the death of Madhabchandra Giri.[1] Satishchandra Giri began his tenure in the transitional period and was a witness to the process of complete elimination of the *Giri* regime at the *Tarakeswar Math*. The tenure of this last *Giri Mohanta* was eventful in all respects.

However, his succession to the office of the *Mohanta* was in no way peaceful as he had to face strong opposition from the co-disciples of his preceptor who challenged his allegedly illegal assumption of office. Since Madhabchandra Giri's death, there had begun a scramble for the *Guddee* (seat of administration), which resulted in the taking over of the properties of the *Math* by Satishchandra Giri, the incumbent *Mohanta*, by virtue of an alleged will of his predecessor. Therefore, his position was anything but secure. The fight was raging when Shyamchandra Giri, one of the most potential challengers, died leaving Satishchandra Giri almost without a rival.[2]

The last *Giri Mohanta* was alleged to have been the *durwan* (gatekeeper) of his preceptor prior to his nomination as the favourite disciple and consequent initiation into the office of the *Mohanta* at the *Tarakeswar Math*. Contrary to the allegation, he claimed to have possessed the necessary qualities, as required by religious instructions. His subsequent conduct and sense of responsibility were said to have convinced his preceptor, who bequeathed all the *debutter* (in the name of the deity) as well as *nij* (self) properties to his successor by virtue of a will.[3] It has already been noted that the *Giri Mohantas* were traditionally accustomed to bequeathing their properties to their favourite disciples, who were in fact marked out for succession. The differences regarding the categorisation of properties took shape only incidentally during the tenure of Satishchandra Giri.

Besides Shyamchandra Giri, the incumbent *Mohanta* had found another potential rival in the person of Srischandra Giri. His spiritual brother Srischandra Giri instituted Suit No. 686 of 1898 in the High Court for a declaration that the deceased Madhabchandra Giri had only been a trustee and had no right to either dispose of the *debutter* property or to appoint his successor through a will. This case had been raised before Mr. Justice Sale. Bhupendranath Bose was the attorney for the *Mohanta* while Debi Prasad Sarbadhikari appeared on behalf of Srischandra Giri.[4] The case, however, moved upto the Privy Council and continued for six years after which the appellant came to a term with Satishchandra Giri following the receipt of a substantial sum of money from him.[5] The incumbent *Mohanta* was not at all against the compromise as the continuation of litigation would have caused immense loss to the *debutter* property. He admitted to have paid 25000/- to Srischandra Giri along with a small annuity of Rs. 100/- per month as the price for compromise which, in its turn, had left the former without another potential contender in the immediate future.[6]

As a matter of fact, a considerable part of his tenure had been spent in contesting litigation in the courts of law and in fighting acrimonious issues out with his rivals. They always wanted him to step down from his *Guddee* at the *Tarakeswar Math*. The allegations they made in the courts of law generally included moral turpitude, defalcation of funds and damage to religious property.

Satishchandra Giri spent most of his time as a magnificent *zamindar* with the same luxurious lifestyle considered to be characteristic of the late nineteenth century *zamindars*. He had to withstand not only the attack from his contestants who, working from within, tried always to throw him out of the office of the *Mohanta*, but also the jealousy and wrath of contemporary *zamindars*. Of these, the *zamindars* of Uttarpara, Chakdighi, Narajole and Mymensingh were very jealous and therefore, instrumental in attempting to curb his power as far as possible. Although Prafulla Chakrabarty reasoned that Satishchandra Giri had been granted the title of *Raja* by the British *Raj* in recognition of his influence on the colonial administration, the version of Sri *Sri Tarakeswar Lila* published at the behest of *Sri Sri Taraknath Jiu Seba Samiti* seems completely different in this context. This booklet asserts in clear terms that the last *Giri Mohanta* sought the title of *Raja* from the British *Raj* but ultimately had to remain satisfied with the traditional title of *Mohanta Maharaj* as the British *Raj* turned a deaf ear to his request.[7]

The last *Giri Mohanta* was very frank in his admission that he was on terms of enmity, particularly with the

Sinharoys of Haripal (Dharanidhar Sinharoy, Ranjanlal Sinharoy and Birendralal Sinharoy) and also the *zamindars* of Uttarpara. He had referred to the envy of his enemies as the sole reason for the enmity. While he did clarify no reason for the envy on the part of the *zamindars* of Uttarpara, he was more assertive about the Sinharoys of Haripal whose endeavours, in fact, brought about the overthrow of the *Giri* regime in the long run. The Sinharoys were in charge of the management of estate of the *Math* ever since the tenure of Madhabchandra Giri. Gurudayal Sinharoy was appointed with the aforesaid charge at the behest of the preceptor of the last *Giri Mohanta*. As the estate suffered immense loss during his tenure and also under the management of his descendants, Kshetrapal Sinharoy and Jnanendra Sinharoy, Satishchandra Giri took over the management. This was said to have been the cause for the anger of the Sinharoys.[8] However, the verdict given by the District Judge on 6.11.29 in the context of the Title Suit they filed, sounded the death knell of the *Giri* regime that had dominated the pilgrim town for over two centuries.

Several Title Suits had been filed by the rivals of the incumbent *Mohanta* prior to the filing of aforementioned Title Suit 28/1922. Of these, the Title Suits No. 33 of 1902 and No. 38 of 1910 were very important. These covered allegations of waste, breach of trust, devastation and misconduct. The former was withdrawn after one year while the latter was dismissed. Besides these, another Title Suit No. 9 of 1903 under Sec. 539 of the Code of Civil Procedure 1882 was instituted with similar allegations and met the same fate. These consecutive Title Suits annoyed and harassed the *Mohanta* to a considerable extent.

II

The Title Suit No. 28 of 1922 in the District Court that ultimately brought down the *Giri* regime was initiated under allegations on several counts against the last *Giri Mohanta*. As before, it was alleged by the complainants that the twin institutions were exclusively public, religious and charitable endowments meant for the entertainment of pilgrims, guests and ascetics and also for the maintenance of *Sadabrata* (hospitality). Therefore, the property and the income therefrom as well as the property acquired out of such income constituted the *debutter* (in the name of the deity) property of the *Math* and not *nij* (self) property of the *Mohanta*. Although the *Mohanta* was required to be bound by the practice of *Brahmacharya* (lifelong celibacy) and the exercise of no occupation except that of *Mohanta*, Satishchandra Giri fell far short of these requirements.

Despite the lack of clarity in the will of reference to the nature of the properties by virtue of which he claimed to have become the *Mohanta*, Satishchandra Giri was believed to have been overzealous in having claimed almost all the *debutter taluks* and *zamindari* along with *debutter* lands as his *nij* holdings. Even the property declared by the District Court in Suit No. 2 of 1878 as *debutter* was claimed by him as *nij* property of his predecessor. He was also accused of having acquired *taluks* and other landed property out of the income of the *debutter* property appertaining to the *Tarakeswar Math* in the *benami* (in the name of the other) of his brother-in-law. He was incidentally made responsible for the grant of a *mokarari* settlement of a very valuable piece of land near the temple to the detriment and injury of the *Tarakeswar Math*. Moreover, the properties dedicated over the years in the name of idols associated with the presiding deity were said to have not been devoted to the maintenance of those deities.[9]

The charges of misappropriation of large sums of money as well as his indulgence in usury were also brought against him. This usury was carried on in the name of his relatives as well as in his own name and on his own account. He was also made guilty of having spent money thus accumulated, on acts calculated to serve his personal interests. This he did while ignoring the *Sadabrata* (hospitality) on one hand and maintaining his relatives within the *Math* premises out of the income of the estate on the other.

The last *Giri Mohanta* was put in the dock also for his being instrumental in not allowing the pilgrims to worship Lord *Taraknath* without his permission. They were said to have been forcibly administered oaths, and subjected to forcible collection at the behest of the *Mohanta*. These accusations against the *Mohanta* facilitated, in fact, the Tarakeswar *Satyagraha* of 1924 which led ultimately to the erosion of the base of the *Giri* regime at the *Tarakeswar Math*.

In short, the *Mohanta* was made "guilty of breach of trust, neglect of duty and fraudulent acts". Therefore, the primary concern of those who put the last *Giri Mohanta* in the dock, was the removal of the incumbent along with a declaration by the court categorising the whole property as *debutter*.[10]

III

In fact, Satishchandra Giri did never accede to the proposition that the *Tarakeswar Math* was a charitable as well as public endowment. He claimed to be the *Malik Sebayet* (worshipper-cum-owner) of Lord *Taraknath* managing the *debutter* (in the name of the deity) property in accordance with long established customs and usages. At the same time, he was against the notion that no *Mohanta* of the *Tarakeswar Math* could acquire the *nij* (self) property. He denied that he had ever endeavoured to transform the movable and immovable property of Lord *Taraknath* into his *nij* (self) property which had been bequeathed to him by his late preceptor. Instead, the property acquired and dealt with by his predecessor as the *nij* property was claimed to have been the only *nij* property of the incumbent *Mohanta*.[11]

While clarifying his so-called *nij* property, the incumbent *Mohanta* emphatically stated that the *mouzas* Mirzapur, Khasbag, Nachipur, Talpur and Bagbari in the district of Hooghly were acquired out of income of the *nij* property belonging absolutely to him and possessed by him under the conditions of the will of his late preceptor. As the source of accumulation of such property, he referred to *pranamis* (money given with due reverence) given by his disciples as well as by those obliged with the divine remedies for diseases. Besides, *pranamis* rendered to him for the performances of *santi-sastayans* (propitiatory rites) with reference to Lord *Taraknath* also resulted in such accumulation.[12]

The *Mohanta* also refuted the accusation that he had purchased landed property from the income of the *debutter* property of the *Math* in the *benami* (in the name of the other) of his brother-in-law Mahabir Prasad Missir. This accusation had been directed to him in relation particularly to the purchase of landed property in Balia and Arrah districts of Bihar. He, however, disputed the contention of the complainants with the statement that the landed property in question had been purchased by his predecessor with the purpose of building a house there and he was bound by the urge to the realisation of the dream of his late preceptor.[13]

He, indeed, stood firmly against the proposition that the grant of *mokarari* settlement of a very valuable piece of land near the temple had been made under his purview to the detriment and injury of the Tarakeswar estate. He submitted that he had for the benefit of the *Math* granted this lease of a small piece of waste land measuring over 19 *cottahs* outside *Tarakeswar Bazar* (market) as it yielded no income at all. However, this lease for building a *dharmasala* was granted on the receipt of Rs. 5250/- as premium and at a fixed annual rent of Rs. 305/-, thus benefitting the *debutter* estate of the *Math* to a considerable extent.[14]

Incidentally, he emphasised that the idols associated with the presiding deity of this place of pilgrimage had been placed at the *Math* by his predecessors at different times. The arrangements for the worship of these idols were stated to have been made from the income of the *debutter* estate as well as from that of the *nij* property.[15]

He was, however, evasive about the existence of rent-free and *jamai* lands as also about the *nazurat* property which he claimed to have been his *nij* property.[16]

Although he claimed that he had in no way altered or fabricated the accounts maintained from the time of his predecessor, he was at the same time against rendering the accounts of the *debutter* (in the name of the deity) as well as the *nij* (self) properties to an outsider for auditing. This obstinacy on the part of the *Mohanta* seems curious despite his claim that he had never spent any sum calculated to serve his own interest.[17]

He also contradicted the proposition that he was a man of loose and immoral character and not an ascetic *Mohanta*. Here he seems to have been suffering from self-contradictions because he asserted at the same time, that the

Mohanta of the *Tarakeswar Math* was not always bound by the observation of the rites and ceremonies of the *Sannyasis* belonging to *Brahmacharyasram* and, therefore, could hold any other occupation except that of the *Mohanta*.[18] These self-contradictory assertions were necessitated possibly because of his urge to refute the allegation that Kashinath Missir was his illegitimate son and not the legitimate son of Mahabir Prasad Missir, already referred to. Besides, his objection to the complaint that he had been living in the *Math* with his relatives and his denial of the existence of *Sakar* and *niskar* properties in the name of *Maiji* at Tarakeswar, were parts of his attempts to project himself as a *Mohanta* committed to the observation of all the practices and customs of the *Math* as well as "the rules and religion of the *Dashnama Sannyasi Mandali*."[19]

To keep himself fully in accordance with the customs of the *Math*, he claimed to have been looking after the comforts and conveniences of the *Sannyasis* and pilgrims coming to the *Math* though not duty-bound to do so. He contended that the pilgrims thronging this place of pilgrimage to worship Lord *Taraknath* were allowed to do so obviously with the prior permission of the *Mohanta*. But he emphatically argued that it had never been the practice among the pilgrims to worship the deity directly, nor had they any right to do so without the permission of the *Mohanta* which was, however, not refused without just and reasonable cause. In fact, the pilgrims, in accordance with the prevailing practice, had to pay "one pice each at the door of the temple and one pice each within the temple as a mark of respect to the deity and none were allowed to enter the temple without payment of the same." He instantly denied the allegation that the pilgrims were forced to take oaths and were compelled at the behest of the *Mohanta* to part with whatever money they had with them.[20]

The *Mohanta* claimed confidently that he was already accustomed to the making of proper arrangements for the worship of the presiding deity as well as for the carrying on of the *Sadabrata* (hospitality) as usual, along with the distribution of alms to the poor and proper medical arrangements for the pilgrims through a charitable dispensary.[21]

The endeavour of the last *Giri Mohanta* was however, commendable for the opening of a hospital run by qualified medical personnel at this place in 1894, with a general ward and one cholera ward. The hospital, now in ruins, was built near the Bengal Provincial Railway gate at Tarakeswar. He had also taken all possible steps to improve the sanitary condition of the town. To maintain general cleanliness in and around the sacred complex, he contributed liberally from the estate funds and ordered the building of community latrines for the use of pilgrims and local inhabitants. Besides, rest houses were constructed during this period to accommodate the inflow of an increasing number of pilgrims.[22] Besides, a few tanks were dug up for supplying water to the pilgrims and to the residents. The construction of roads in the vicinity of the twin institutions was also taken up. Moreover, he took interest in the establishment of a *chatuspathi* or *tol* for the traditional education of the boys of the locality and those from distant places.[23] In fact, the programme usually undertaken for general welfare by the municipal administration in these days was put into practice by the incumbent *Mohanta*.

Given this background, the *Mohanta* presented himself as a person who had performed his duties to the satisfaction of the Hindu public for nearly thirty years.

IV

Immediately after the initiation of the Title Suit No. 28 of 1922, a compromise had been reached between the incumbent *Mohanta* and the plaintiffs barring particularly the original plaintiff, Dharanidhar Sinharoy. Satishchandra Giri was, in fact, instrumental in installing Prabhatchandra Giri as his successor at the *Tarakeswar Math* by dint of this compromise. Certain property was admitted to have been given over as the *nij* property to this favourite disciple by the last *Giri Mohanta*. However the case might have been, the rights of the deity and the interest of the endowment had seriously been compromised by this deed of compromise between the *Mohanta* and the others. The then District Judge termed this comprise as unlawful simply because the admissions as well as concessions were made without reference to the customs and rules of the religious institution.[24]

Meanwhile, Mr. Justice P.C. De, the District Judge, appointed Amulya Chandra Bhaduri on 7 July, 1925 under order XI, C. P. C., as the Receiver for the administration and custody of the properties in the suit. Earlier, Shyamacharan Ukil Banerjee had been appointed the Receiver of a portion of the properties by order of this court. As he had already applied for leave to resign and his resignation had been accepted, the appointment of a new Receiver followed normally. However, the new Receiver was an M.A., and an orthodox *Brahmin* by caste. Coming from a family of landholders, he possessed extensive practical experience of *zamindari* management. The salary of the incumbent Receiver was fixed at Rs. 600/- per month and was ordered for the execution of a security bond for Rs. 20,000/- to the satisfaction of the court.[25]

The *Mohanta* instantly appealed to the High Court, expecting an order to restrain the Receiver from taking possession of the properties of the *Tarakeswar Math*. To the delight of the *Mohanta*, the High Court ordered on 8.1.26, the setting aside of the appointment of the Receiver for the property which was said to have been the *nij* property of the incumbent. Therefore, the Receiver was left with the responsibility only of the *debutter* property.

Hence an appeal was made to the Privy Council against the judgement of the High Court. But here again the decision went in favour of the defendant *Mohanta* who was, however, allowed to remain in possession of his so-called *nij* property so long as the original suit continued.[26]

The Receiver, indeed, was allowed to remain in charge of the palace (*Math*), the *bazar* (market) and the *debseba* (service to the presiding deity) by virtue of the aforesaid order of the High Court.[27] Besides, the Receiver was empowered by the District Court to allow the *Mohanta* to inspect and also to take copies of all necessary documents, particularly those relating to collection of rents and administration of the *nij* property through his officers. These were given on condition that the same would be returned within the given time as decided by the Receiver. But the *Mohanta*'s incidental claim to all the plots comprising the Sahapur garden-house, to which reference has already been made elsewhere, as the *nij* property was turned down due to some of the plots admittedly being *debutter*. However, the new management of the estate began immediately agricultural experiments there in association with the Department of Agriculture of the Government of Bengal.[28] As a matter of fact, the Receiver was required to submit the accounts of alleged personal estates in the interest of safeguarding the endowment.[29]

The incumbent Receiver also attempted to prepare forthwith a list of the *debutter* holdings in each of the villages as ordered by the District Court. As regards the *chaukidari chakran* holdings in the village, it was held that those which had been settled in favour of the *Mohanta* after the Governmental takeover, should be treated as appertaining to the parent villages and that the *Mohanta* should get possession of the same along with the villages. But the properties relating to *Maiji*'s (Mohanta's mother) properties referred to earlier, remained in the possession of the Receiver along with the charitable institutions in and around the sacred complex. Pending the decision of the court, the properties in the districts of Arrah and Balia were also ordered to the possession of the Receiver.[30] He was also entrusted with the responsibility of preparing the accounts of the *jama, baki* and *washil* of all the *Mahals* of the estate and also a statement of the rents payable to superior landlords of the estates.[31] The administration of the Receiver was initially carried on under the assumption that there were separate sources of income - *nij* and *debutter* and separate expenses - *nij* and *debutter*. But ultimately entire income from separate sources was adjudged *debutter* income, just as all the expenses were considered *debutter* expenses.[32]

Despite the incumbent *Mohanta*'s exclusive claim to his alleged *nij* property, the District Judge Mr. Justice K. C. Nag unequivocally ordered that the *Mohanta* could in no way alienate, sell or mortgage the property and, therefore, must submit regular accounts to the District Court of the *nij* property. He decided against the standpoint of the *Mohanta* who had referred to contribute not even one *paisa* towards the various charitable and religious objects of the endowment. This, in his opinion, was tantamount to stultifying the *Mohanta*'s esteemed position at the *Tarakeswar Math*.[33]

Apart from the debate surrounding the nature of the properties during the tenure of this last *Giri Mohanta*, no prima facie proof of the alleged possession of promissory notes, debentures etc. was found in so far as the incumbent was concerned.[34]

The whole perspective had, in fact, gone a sea change with the verdict of Mr. Justice K. C. Nag on 6.11.29. Initially, the issue was whether the *Mohanta* was liable to be removed for having violated his duties as the religious head of the establishment and also for having violated his duties as the manager or trustee of the endowed properties. The latter issue was part of a scheme aimed at the removal of the last *Giri Mohanta* of the Tarakeswar estate.[35] However, the developments that took place during the years to come, revolved round these aforesaid issues as well as the verdict delivered on 6.11.29.

The last *Giri Mohanta*'s obsession with his *nij* property was instantly turned down by means of this verdict. It put in clear terms that the properties had been held by the court "on unimpeachable evidence to be *debutter* or trust properties appertaining to the endowment by my judgement delivered yesterday."

The District Judge unequivocally stated that "the defendant *Mohunt* is guilty of misappropriation and gross breach of trust and that he cannot be entrusted with the possession of the trust estate even for a single minute for it has been proved that he utilises every single minute in committing breaches of trust and misappropriation of the trust property." He also commented that Satishchandra Giri "misappropriated *lakhs* and *lakhs* of *debutter* money for indulging in a most luxuriant and vicious mode of living and for making a most lavish provision for his illegitimate sons, Kashinath and Ramananda, for whom he has bought *zamindaries* at Arrah and Balia with *debutter* money yielding an annual income of Rs. 40,000/- (Forty Thousand) in the *benam* of his brother-in-law, Mahabir Prasad. The defendant *Mohunt* himself has admitted in his evidence that he has been indifferent to the affairs of the endowment for the last 10 or 12 years and that it is no business of his to look after the interest of the *Math*. This application of his for allowing him to continue in possession even after the admission of his, comes with a very bad grace from him and cannot possibly be allowed by any Court of Justice. To allow him to do so would be to defeat the ends of justice and give him further opportunities for misappropriation. He does not say how he will be prejudiced if the court assumes possession through the Receiver for the ends of justice pending the framing of a scheme for the management of the trust estate."[36] Therefore, the verdict of the District Judge on 6.11.29 as well as the turning down of the proposition of the last *Giri Mohanta* with the appeal for the staying of the Receivership sounded the death knell of the hegemony of the *Giri Mohantas* at the *Tarakeswar Math* that had lasted for over two centuries.

V

Satishchandra Giri did not tamely accept the verdict delivered on 6.11.29. He appealed for a stay-order to the High Court, against the decree of the lower one. Instead of granting this with regard to the *debutter* (in the name of the deity) property in possession of the Receiver, it allowed the *Mohanta* his possession of the *nij* (self) property, except that in Balia and Arrah. The *Mohanta* was asked in this context to file a list of alleged personal property showing the amounts of Government revenue as also payments in the form of rents along with original receipts. Proper accounts of all receipts, disbursements and expenses were also required for the period commencing from the date of the decree.[37]

The *Mohanta* responded accordingly. A critical analysis of the list thus submitted puts him and his predecessors in the category of *talukdars* in relation to the *zamindars* of Burdwan, Chakdighi, Champdani, Sreerampur and also to the collectorates in the districts of Hooghly and Midnapur. Even Satishchandra Giri claimed that he himself was a *talukdar* in relation to innumerable Union Presidents' Office at different places including Baligari, Kulbatpur and elsewhere. Besides, his commitment for sending an annual subscription of Rs. 3500/- to the Benaras Hindu University referred to his status as *talukdar*.[38]

As a matter of fact, the *Mohanta* had by then become instrumental in creating hindrances to smooth administration of the properties by the Receiver. He tried his best to coerce the Receiver to make over to himself all the papers with reference to the *debutter* as well as the alleged *nij* properties of the *Mohanta*. Moreover, he endeavoured to misappropriate almost all the *chittas, khatians, thak* maps and field-books as well as other survey maps of the estate which were in the possession of the Receiver. Even certain papers which were mistakenly made over to the *Mohanta*, were not returned for the same reason. The *Mohanta* kept up his vituperative campaign against the Receiver despite his consent to the delivery of papers concerning *kistibandis* and *kabuliyats* along with the sale-deeds relating to the alleged personal propety.[39]

Meanwhile, the District Judge, by virtue of an order dated 9th June, 1930, directed the Receiver of the *Tarakeswar*

Math to frame a scheme for the management and control of the estate in the eventuality of the removal of Satishchandra Giri. Accordingly, the Receiver called upon various bodies to elect their representatives to the committee entrusted with the management and to nominate a person to be appointed as the *Mohanta* of the *Tarakeswar Math*. Thereupon, the various bodies elected their members to the committee.

The meeting of the members of the family of *Raja* Bharamalla, the original founder of the Tarakeswar endowment, elected unanimously Dr. Dharanidhar Sinharoy M.B. as the representative of the family to the committee.[40] The District Board of Hooghly held its meeting in response to the order of the District Judge and resolved that Taraknath Mukherjee, the Vice Chairman and member of the District Board as well as *zamindar* of Uttarpara had been elected as the Hindu representative of the Board to the committee.[41] Besides, the *Bangiya Brahman Sabha* passed a resolution to the effect that the President of the *Sabha*, Panchanan *Tarkaratna*, and Chirasruhit Lahiri, the manager of the estate of *Raja* Kishorilal Goswami of Sreerampur had been elected to the aforesaid committee.[42] It had also been decided that two members of the proposed committee would be elected from the Hindu tenants of the Tarakeswar estate. In fact, those who used to pay not less than two rupees as *chaukidari* tax and not less than one rupee as road tax would be eligible as voters as well as candidates for election to the committee.[43] Ashutosh Pakhira and Girindrakumar Shome were elected eventually as representatives to the committee.[44]

In order to select two representatives from among the *Maths* under the purview of the *Tarakesvar Mandali* for the committee of management, the letters of invitation had been sent from the Receiver to :

1. Kshitish Chandra Puri, *Mohanta* of *Santoshpur Dashbhuja Math* in the District of Hooghly.

2. Khagendrananda Ashram, *Mohanta* of *Guptipara Math* in the District of Hooghly.

3. Niranjan Parbat, *Mohanta* of *Nayangarh Math* in the District of Hooghly.

4. Prabhat Chandra Bharati, *Mohanta* of *Chaipat Math* in the District of Midnapur.

5. Prasanna Kumar Bharati, *Mohanta* of *Gumgarh and Reyapara Math* in the District of Midnapur.

6. Surendranath Bharati, *Mohanta* of *Santoshpur Bishalaksi Math* in the District of Hooghly.

7. Trilok Chandra Giri, *Mohanta* of *Bhotbagan Math* in the District of Howrah.

None but Prasanna Kumar Bharati, *Mohanta* of *Gumgarh* and *Reyapara Math* turned up to attend the intended meeting of the *Mandali* for the selection of two representatives of the proposed Managing Committee for the Tarakeswar estate. Naturally, the endeavour in this direction proved fruitless.[45]

In the meantime, heads of the following religious institutions were requested to forward the names of such persons as were considered eligible for appointment as the *Mohanta* of the Tarakeswar endowment. Accordingly appeals were made to :-

1. Sri Raj Rajeswar Ashram, Sri Shankaracharya, *Saradamath*, Bombay.

2. Sri Shankaracharya, *Gobardhan Math*, Puri, Orissa.

3. Sri Shankaracharya, *Shringeri Math*, Mysore.

4. Sri Shankaracharya, *Kanchi Kamkuti Math*, Conjeeveram.

5. Sri Shankaracharya, *Kumbhakonam Math*, Madras.

6. Sri Shankaracharya, *Shankheswar*, Madras.

7. Sri Jagannath Ashram, *Kanko Math*, Katrasgarh, Manbhum.

8. Sri Krishnadayal Giri, *Mohanta*, Buddhagaya.

9. Sri Mahadebananda Giri, *Bholananda Giri Ashram*, Hardwar.[46]

Besides, an advertisement signed by Mr. Justice K. C. Nag on 20.9.30 had been published in various newspapers in different parts of the country calling upon fit and proper candidates for appointment as the *Mohanta* of the *Tarakeswar Math* in place of Satishchandra Giri. It was clearly stated in the advertisement that the applications should reach the District Judge on or before 25 October, 1930.

The Receiver was ordered in this connection to get the advertisement published in the following newspapers:-

1) *Amrita Bazar Patrika*, Bagbazar, Calcutta; 2) *Biswamitra* (Hindi), Harrison Road, Calcutta; 3) *Basumati* (Bengali Daily), Bowbazar Street, Calcutta; 4) *Brahman Mahasammelan* (Hindi), Bamghat, Benaras City; 5) *Hindi Bangabasi*, 6, Bhabani Dutta Lane, Calcutta; 6) *Hindu Sansar* (Hindi), Delhi.[47]

Accordingly, numerous applications for the post of the *Mohanta* at the *Tarakeswar Math* reached the District Judge of Hooghly and he provisionally fixed 10 November, 1930 as the date on which the final selection of the *Mohanta* would be made.

The last *Giri Mohanta* apprehended that if a new *Mohanta* and a new committee of management were appointed by virtue of the order of the District Judge, complications would certainly arise and the incumbent would certainly be prejudiced. Therefore, he appealed for the staying of the decree dated 9 June, 1930 in the High Court along with further proceedings in F.A. File No. 234 27 of 1930.

The last *Giri Mohanta* was fortunate enough, at least for the time being, in having the wind-blown in his favour by virtue of the stay-order issued by the High Court that kept in abeyance the endeavours of the District Judge.[48]

VI

The complacency of Satishchandra Giri resulting from his temporary success with the stay-order of the High Court was very short-lived. This was evidenced by the endeavour of the same to frame a scheme outlining a new form of management of the temple and the trust estate as compared to the scheme framed at the behest of the District Court in the event of the removal of the incumbent *Mohanta*.

Accordingly, it propounded the composition of the body for management of the twin institutions with following persons : (a) the *Mohanta* of *Tarakeswar Math*, (b) a Hindu representative to be selected by the District Board of Hooghly, (c) a member of the family of *Raja* Bharamalla to be elected by such members of the family, residing in the village Bahirgarh and usually paying *chaukidari tax*, (d) one representative of the Hindu tenants of the Tarakeswar estate with qualification to vote at the election of the Bengal Legislative Council, (e) two representatives of the *Bangiya Brahman Sabha* of Calcutta, (f) a representative of the Sanskrit Association of Calcutta, (g) a representative *Mohanta* of the *Tarakesvar Mandali*, to be elected by the *Mandali*, (h) two Hindus, one of whom would be an official nominated by the Magistrate of the District of Hooghly and (i) one representative of the *Marwari* Chamber of Commerce, Calcutta.

A critical study of the schemes for the management of the twin institutions prepared initially by the District Court and then by its higher counterpart reveals certain common features barring a few dissimilarities. However, it called upon the opinion of the *Tarakesvar Mandali* for filling up the vacancy caused by the removal of Satishchandra Giri in accordance with the custom of the *Math*. But the District Judge was not made susceptible to the recommendation of the *Mandali*, if the person recommended was not considered to be fit for the office.

Although the High Court took cognizance of the remark of the District Judge with reference to Prabhatchandra Giri, the pet *Chela* of the incumbent *Mohanta*, as "the most unsuitable person for the office of the *Mohanta*", it was at the same time against putting constraint to prevent Prabhatchandra from coming in as an ordinary candidate for the office at the *Tarakeswar Math*.[49]

VII

Despite his earnest efforts to stick to his position as the *Mohanta* of the *Tarakeswar Math*, Satishchandra Giri failed in the long run, as was proved by the aforementioned judgement of the High Court delivered on 24.8.34. Accordingly, the then District Judge of Hooghly, Mr. Justice K. C. Basak directed the Receiver to take possession of the property held as *debutter* along with all collection papers, decrees, title deeds, account books and other papers relating to the property by 5 P.M. on 12 September, 1934. Besides, the keys of the Sahapur garden - house, the rooms in the palace and of all *Mofussil Kutcheries* in possession of the last *Giri Mohanta* were also ordered to be made over to the Receiver within the stipulated period.

The District Magistrate was requested to render police help to the Receiver while he was taking possession of the property and prevent thereby any breach of peace by Satishchandra Giri and his henchmen.[50] The Receiver was ordered to continue as possessor until further orders or until the new *Mohanta* was appointed. Although Satishchandra Giri raised no objection to this process of taking possession of the property mentioned in the decree, controversy cropped up in respect of certain other property that was not included in the decree. The way out had, however, been found in the body of the judgement where that had been declared as either *debutter* or property purchased with *debutter* funds. Incidentally, the allegation against the *Mohanta* of possessing promissory notes was not proved on review.

Given the background of the outstanding developments that had taken place during the past few years, and which had culminated in the judgement of the High Court on 24.8.34, the last *Giri Mohanta* came ultimately to realise that the days of the *Giri* regime at the *Tarakeswar Math* were numbered.

VIII

In the light of the incidents already related, an endeavour was made to choose the successor of Satishchandra Giri with the help of at least seven *Mohantas* of different *Maths* under the purview of the *Tarakesvar Mandali*. Of them, Khagendrananda Ashram, Kshitish Chandra Puri, Niranjan Parbat, Sibchandra Giri, Prabhat Chandra Bharati and Prasanna Kumar Bharati recommended Prabhatchandra

Giri as the successor of the incumbent while only Trilok Chandra Giri, an aspirant to the *Guddee* of the *Mohanta* at the *Tarakeswar Math* dissented.[51]

Despite being supported by the majority of the *Tarakesvar Mandali,* Prabhatchandra Giri's case was lost by virtue of the order of the then District Judge on 29 June, 1937 which, however, was challenged by him in the High Court. As a matter of fact, he was held responsible for persistently setting up a title hostile to the deity in so far as the *Putni Mahal* Jagannathpur was concerned as well as for his claim to the premises Nos. 51 and 53, Ramesh Mitra Road, Calcutta, as his personal property. Besides, he was accused of operating a bank account formed of *debutter* funds in his name, from which the withdrawals were made over to his preceptor Satishchandra Giri.

Despite his frank admissions that he had been forced to perform misdeeds as a mere puppet of his preceptor due to his bond to obey him in all respects, the High Court upheld that Prabhatchandra Giri's appointment as the *Mohanta* would certainly prejudice the interest of the twin institutions. This was because he was still bound to obey his spiritual father. Therefore, he was considered unfit for the twin institutions at an important evolutionary moment.[52] The rejection of the claim of Prabhatchandra Giri to the *Guddee* at the *Tarakeswar Math* belied, indeed, the last hope of Satishchandra Giri to control the office of the *Mohanta* through his disciple for as long as would be possible. Over the above, this judgement resulted also in ending the *Giri* ascendancy which had administered the sacred complex at Tarakeswar for over two centuries.

The long-drawn tenure of the *Giri* regime had practically come to an end with the appointment of *Dandiswami*

Jagannath Ashram. He had, meanwhile, been appointed the *Mohanta* of the *Tarakeswar Math* by order of Mr. Justice Satchidananda Mukherjee in the month of *Agrahayan*, 1344 B.S. (1937 A.D.). This appointment of a Bengali *Mohanta* from a different division of the *Dashnami Sannyasis* in place of the traditional non-Bengali *Giri* division of monks marked the beginning of a new era in the history of Tarakeswar.[53]

Note

1. Title Suit No. 28/1922. In the Court of the District Judge of Hooghly. Suit Under Sec. 92. C. P. C. Plaintiffs Vs. S. C. Giri, Para.-7.

2. S. C. Dey - Hooghly Past and Present - PP.-309-318.

3. Title Suit No. 28/1922. D. Sinharoy and others Vs. S. C. Giri. Suit Under Sec. 92. C. P. C. Paras.- 25 and 27.

4. The Statesman - 07.09.1897.

5. Pramathanath Sanyal - Tarakeswar (in Bengali). Dacca. 1936.

6. Title Suit No. 28/1922. D. Sinharoy and others Vs. Satishchandra Giri. Suit Under Sec. 92. C. P. C. Para.- 26.

7. Prafulla Chakrabarty - Social Profile of Tarakeswar. P.-21-22.
   Also,
   Sri Sri Taraknath Jiu Seba Samiti (ed.) - Sri Sri Tarakeswar Lila. P.-13.

8. Title Suit No. 28/1922. D. Sinharoy and others Vs. S. C. Giri, Suit Under Sec. 92. C. P. C. Paras.- 5 and 13.

9. Title Suit No. 28/1922. In the Court of the District Judge of Hooghly. (Suit Under Sec. 92. C. P. C.) Paras.-2,4,9,12 and 13.

10. Ibid. - Paras 11, 14-19.

11. Title Suit No. 28/1922. D. Sinharoy and others Vs. S. C. Giri, Suit Under Sec. 92. C. P. C. Paras.- 20 and 28.

12. Ibid. - Para. - 35.

13. Ibid. - Paras. - 35 and 37.

14. Ibid. - Para. - 39.

15. Ibid. - Para. - 21.

16. Ibid. - Paras.- 32 and 35.

17. Ibid. - Paras. - 42 and 43.

18. Ibid. - Paras. - 15 and 44.

19. Ibid. - Paras. - 35 and 44.

20. Ibid. - Paras. - 15, 19 and 40.

21. Ibid. - Para. - 41.

22. Prafulla Chakrabarty - Social Profile of Tarakeswar. P.-22.

23. Title Suit No. 28/1922. D. Sinharoy and others Vs. S. C. Giri. Suit Under Sec. 92. C. P. C. Para.- 41.

24. Serial No. of Order of Proceeding - 121. Date of Order - 28.3.25.

25. Ibid. - 133.

26. Ibid. - 650. Date of Order - 18.1.28.

27. Ibid. - 720. Date of Order - 21.3.28.

28. Ibid. - 831. Date of Order - 20.8.28.

29. Ibid. - 720. Date of Order - 21.3.28.

30. Ibid. - 720. Date of Order - 21.3.28.

31. Ibid. - 440. Date of Order - 9.12.26.

32. Ibid. - 652. Date of Order - 18.1.28.

33. Ibid. - 798. Date of Order - 17.7.28.

34. Ibid. - 143. Date of Order - 2.3.26.

35. Ibid. - 290. Date of Order - 28.6.26.

36. Ibid. - 981. Date of Order - 7.11.29.

37. In the High Court of Judicature at Fort William in Bengal. Civil Appellate Jurisdiction. Appeal from original decree of 1929 (filed in the court on 25th Nov. 1929). In Title Suit No. 28 of 1922 of the Court of the District Judge of Hooghly (Chinsurah). Decree dated 6.11.29 and of stay of further proceedings. D. Sinharoy and others Vs. Satishchandra Giri.

38. In the Court of the District Judge, Hooghly. T. S. 28 of 1922. D. Sinharoy and others Vs. Satishchandra Giri.

39. Letter from A. C. Bhaduri. Receiver, Tarakeswar estate to the Hon'ble District Judge. Date. 29.3.30.

40. Resolution passed at the meeting held at Bahirgarh on 17 August, 1930.

41. Resolution passed at the meeting held on 30 July, 1930 at the behest of Rai Satishchandra Mukherjee Bahadur B. L.; M. L. C.; Chairman of the District Board, Hooghly.

42. Resolution passed at the meeting of Bangiya Brahman Sabha held on 25 Bhadra, 1337 B.S. at the behest of Ramranjan Roy, Assistant Secretary, Bangiya Brahman Sabha.

43. Notice put up with signature of A. C. Bhaduri M. A., Receiver, Tarakeswar estate, at Receiver's office on 11 Bhadra, 1337 B.S.

44. Letter from A. C. Bhaduri Esq. M. A. Receiver, Tarakeswar estate to Mr. Justice K. C. Nag, District Judge, Hooghly. Date-11 Sept., 1930.

45. Ibid.

46. Petition submitted by the plaintiffs in relation to the Title Suit No. 28 of 1922 in the Court of the District Judge of Hooghly. Date-18.9.30.

47. Advertisement made in the newspapers signed by the District Judge on 20.9.30 at the behest of the Receiver, Tarakeswar estate.

48. High Court of Judicature at Fort William in Bengal. Present - Hon'ble Manmathanath Mukherjee. Hon'ble Surendranath Guha. Date of order - 11.11.30.

49. In the High Court of Judicature at Fort William in Bengal. Civil Appellate Jurisdiction. Appeal from original decree No. 255 of 1930. Appeal against the decree of Mr. Justice K. C. Nag, District Judge of Hooghly. Satishchandra Giri Vs. D. Sinharoy and others Date - 29.3.34. Also,
In the High Court of Judicature at Fort William in Bengal. Civil Appellate Jurisdiction. Appeal against the decree of Mr. Justice K. C. Nag, District Judge of Hooghly. Satishchandra Giri Vs. D. Sinharoy and others Date - 24.8.34.

50. Serial Number of Order or Proceeding - 1000. Date of order - 10.9.34.

51. Ibid. - 39. Date of order - 3.8.35. Also, Ibid. - 40. Date of order - 10.8.38.

52. In the High Court of Judicature at Fort William in Bengal. Civil Appellate Jurisdiction. 13th January, 1938. Present : The Hon'ble Sir Robert Earnest Jack and David Clarke Patterson. Appeal against the order of S. Mukherjee, District Judge of zillah Hugly in the Title Suit No. 28 of 1922, dated 29th of June, 1937; Prabhatchandra Giri Vs. D. Sinharoy.

53 S. K. Mitra - Hooghly Jelar Itihas O Bangasamj. Vol.II. PP.-1120-1121. Also, Jnananjan - Acharya Sri Sri Jagannath Ashrampad. 1978. P.-196.

Chapter - VI

Tarakeswar Satyagraha : 1924

I

Satyagraha had, in fact, been considered to be an effective weapon by Mahatma Gandhi to fight against the British *Raj* through non-violent means in the then Indian political perspective. The authoritarian rule of the British *Raj* had certainly been shaken to its roots owing to the *Satyagraha* movement organised under the illustrious leadership of Gandhiji in course of the Indian struggle for freedom. Taking cue from the phenomenon of *Satyagraha* with its inherent thrust for obliterating the malaise from public life in all respects, there had developed *Satyagraha* movements in different parts of India with regional orientation.

Gandhiji had unequivocally propounded that when "there is an occasion, everyone has a right to practise non-cooperation or *Satyagraha*" against every sort of injustice.[1] Therefore, the *Satyagraha* was resorted to at Tarakeswar in 1924 with the intention to remove the glaring abuses of all sorts that had crept into the management of the age-old religious institution. In fact, the monastery at Tarakeswar was alleged to have been a den for corrupt and immoral activities under the regime of the *Giri Mohantas*. The last phase of the *Giri* regime in particular witnessed a few *Mohantas* at the helm of affairs who were supposed to have given up their commitment to the injunctions of *Brahmacharya*. Mention must be made of Madhabchandra Giri and Satishchandra Giri who were alleged to have been the embodiments not only of irresponsible power and authority, but also of sensuality. Hence, the *Satyagraha* movement in this pilgrim town had been organised as a genuine reaction against the aberrations of the later *Mohantas* who had taken over the reins of administration one after another in accordance with the *Guru-Sisya Parampara* or preceptor-disciple lineage.[2]

The bubble of the authoritarian halo of the *Giri* regime had burst during the administration of Satishchandra Giri, the last *Mohanta* of the *Giri* order at the monastery at Tarakeswar. In spite of his commendable activities in different spheres of administration of the temple as well as the estate, he could in no way escape the usual allegations put forward by his opponents. The inhabitants of this pilgrim town as well as the pilgrims in general, were very much antagonised by the authoritarianism of Satischandra Giri in almost all spheres. This, in fact, led to a rise in opposition at this famous place of pilgrimage in Eastern India during the first half of 1924. Even eminent persons of contemporary Bengal extended support to the organisation of a full-fledged movement in order to thwart the last vestiges of the *Giri* regime.

There is no denying the fact that Satishchandra Giri had earnestly endeavoured to facilitate the smooth inflow of pilgrims round the year. But grievances against him in so far as the pilgrims were concerned began to take shape also during his tenure. The pilgrims who thronged this place of pilgrimage were alleged to have been under constant pressure to accede to forcible exactions of different kinds inside as well as outside the temple by the agents of the *Mohanta*. The *Birbhadra Dal* was organised under the personal supervision of the *Mohanta* to perpetrate his authoritarianism in this place of pilgrimage. The pilgrims in general were aggrieved over the utter callousness of the authority towards ensuring convenience of the women pilgrims in respect of bathing as well as sanitary arrangements. Moreover, accusing fingers were raised against the *Mohanta* for his voluptuous character which, indeed, added fuel to the fire in the mobilisation of the movement. But it must been taken note of that he was in no way the trend-setter in the given context.[3] Besides, the *Mohanta* during this phase behaved like an authoritarian *zamindar* to his subjects living in and around the sacred complex. The grievances of the tenants fortified also the base for *Satyagraha* at Tarakeswar.

In order to redress these grievances, a proposal had been put forward for the formation of a popular committee. It was suggested that the committee should be entitled to exercise supervisory authority over the management of the trust and performance of rituals in accordance with the *Shastras*. The *Mohanta* would simply carry out the directives of the proposed committee with his role only as an important member of the committee. The proposal was also put forward for the instant abolition of all sorts of forcible exactions perpetrated for so long in this pilgrim town at the behest of the *Mohanta*.[4] Therefore, the *Satyagraha* movement at Tarakeswar had primarily begun with the purpose of abolishing all sorts of forcible exactions from the tenants as well as pilgrims. The *Satyagrahis* were above all committed to ensure the honour of the female pilgrims. The need of the hour also necessitated the earnest endeavour to determine not only the real proprietor of the estate but also to define the actual role of the *Mohanta* as a functionary of the trust.[5]

However, one *Swami* Viswananda had taken earnest initiative to build up an organisation of the *Sannyasis* known as *Mahabir Dal* and came forward to stand against the ensuing oppression in this place of pilgrimage. He had mercilessly been beaten up for his courage in standing up against the *Mohanta*. This, indeed, in no way dampened his spirit.[6] He had chalked out a programme for taking recourse to *Satyagraha* at Tarakeswar in collusion with his trusted lieutenants on the eve of the *Sivaratri* festival in the month of *Phalgun* (Feb-March, 1924).[7] He got support not only from the oppressed tenants and irritated pilgrims but also gained overwhelming support from the *Pundits*. This, in fact, strengthened his ethical standpoint in the struggle against the *Mohanta*. Mention should be made of *Pundit* Dharanath Bhattacharya and *Pundit* Sarat Chandra *Sankhya Vedantatirtha* who had played an important part in the movement.[8] *Pundit* Dharanath Bhattacharya joined hands with *Swami* Viswananda in the initial phase of the movement.

The office bearers of the *Mahabir Dal* were named at the behest of *Swami* Viswananda. *Swami* Viswananda, the chief protagonist, was declared the founder of the *Dal* while *Swami* Satchidananda, Makhan Lal Roy, Durga Singh and Swabhab *Brahmachari* (alias Kali Krishna Ghosh) were named Commander, Secretary and Assistant Secretaries respectively.[9]

Prior to the start of the movement *Swami* Satchidananda made a fervent appeal to all concerned to help the *Satyagrahis* in terms of money as well as through enrolment as volunteers. In his appeal, he put forward certain proposals for consideration to the people. He had primarily proposed the overthrow of the *Mohanta*, followed up by the creation of a trust for all the properties of the monastery at Tarakeswar. He had also put forward the idea of the organisation of a committee, composed of learned persons of commendable morality, for supervising the sacred performances within the temple. He also made it a point that three-fourth (3/4) of the total income accruing from the property of the temple would be spent for the maintenance and improvement of the temple. Moreover, arrangements for public amenities and improvement of the condition of tenants were also suggested. The remaining one-fourth (1/4) of the total income was to be left as a fund in reserve. Provision was also made for the rejuvenation of the temple as and when it would be necessary and for the livelihood of the *Mohanta* till his death. It was incidentally proposed that the money for expenditure owing to the arrangements of daily worship and for other charitable activities would come from the income accruing from the temple. He had, indeed, pleaded also for the deposition of jewels worth *lakhs* of rupees, which were lying in the custody of the then *Mohanta*, in the banks. The income accruing from it was proposed to be spent in accordance with the direction of the temple committee. Finally, he opined in favour of the appointment of anyone in future as *Mohanta* who would be a high-profile person conversant with the scriptures.[10]

II

To make the whole project a complete success, *Swami* Satchidananda prayed for permission from the President of the Bengal Provincial Congress Committee (B. P. C. C.) to start the *Satyagraha* movement at Tarakeswar on the eve of the *Sivaratri* festival. In his letter to the President of the B. P. C. C, he assured in unequivocal terms that the *Satyagrahis* would always remain non-violent in body and spirit although there was very little possibility of the *Mohanta's* as well as the Government's remaining non-violent.[11]

Meanwhile, *Swami* Viswananda tried his best to organise the volunteers of the *Mahabir Dal* for the impending *Satyagraha* movement. He opened an office for this purpose at 179, Harrison Road, Calcutta, and another at Tarakeswar.[12] He appealed to the residents of this pilgrim town to prepare themselves for participating in the intended movement for non-payment of rents to the *Mohanta* through the Manager of the monastery. Besides, the members of the monastery willing to take part in the movement were asked to get themselves ready to render service for the movement, for their help would be required in need.[13] The *Satyagrahis* were directed to remain ever alert to save the pilgrims from the agents of the *Mohanta*. But at the same time, they were advised to remain non-violent alongside their determination to undo all wrongs.[14]

In fact, the organisers of the *Satyagraha* movement were very much aware of the fact that the success of the movement depended to a large extent on organisational skill. Therefore, emphasis was given to the steady recruitment of volunteers from the initial phase of the movement in order to make it a success. Immediately after the B. P. C. C. took the decision to sanction the *Satyagraha* movement in this place of pilgrimage, the volunteers from outside were urged to proceed through District Congress Committees. Besides, an alternative channel for recruitment of volunteers was also arranged through *Hindu Sabha* with its office at 10/1/1 Syed Gally Lane, Calcutta. The temple of *Baldeoji* at 25, Grey Street was also made a centre for recruitment of volunteers for the movement at Tarakeswar.[15] Besides, innumerable centres for recruitment of volunteers had been opened in Calcutta to gear up the course of movement. Of these, the following were important centres.[16] :

NAME	ADDRESS
Bengal Provincial Congress Committee	38/1, Sukia Street
Bagbazar Darjipara Rastra Samiti	62, Shyampukur Street
Central Calcutta Rastra Samiti	1, Lalbehari Thakur lane
Jorabagan Rastra Samiti	2, Laksmi Narayan Mukherjee Lane
North Calcutta Rastra Samiti	42, Banamali Sarkar Street
Simla Garpar Rastra Samiti	69, Simla Street
South Calcutta Rastra Samiti	Bhabanipore

Moreover, the volunteers were also requested to register their names at 9, Russa Road, Calcutta.[17] Thus the *Satyagraha* movement, that had primarily been initiated with the assistance of the local people, transcends its local context with the involvement of the B. P. C. C.

No arrangement for their travelling allowance was made in this context. But these volunteers were assured of meals at the *langarkhana* (feeding centre) set up by the *Akalis* at *Tarakeswar*.[18] A large number of *Satyagrahis* were fed from this *langarkhana* on daily basis as long as the *Satyagraha* was in full swing. The interest of the *Akalis* in this movement can be explained with reference to the nature of the *Akali* movement that had been started also during the freedom movement with similar effort to remove the glaring abuses in the management of religious institutions. The *Akalis*, incidentally, received their inspiration from the *Satyagraha* movement launched by Gandhi.[19]

However, an office was also opened at Tarakeswar station. There had been constituted nine departments to carry on several types of activities in relation to the course of movement.[20] Of these departments, the medical and sanitary department in charge of Dr. Ashutosh Das achieved great popularity in this pilgrim town by virtue of its commendable service, free of cost, to those in distress. This department took utmost care to ameliorate the sanitary condition in order to prevent the outbreak of epidemic diseases.[21] The *Satyagrahis* were ever alert with regard to the propaganda and publicity campaigns. They were in touch with reporters of Calcutta Press and Associated Press in order to publicise the cause of the movement. They were, indeed, successful in rousing public sympathy for the movement at Tarakeswar.[22]

The leaders of the *Mahabir Dal* were, in fact, conscious of the end as well as means of the *Satyagraha* movement. They wanted the removal of the *Mohanta* along with the transference of the *debutter* property to the representatives of the Hindu Committee for management. They were ready to give the upper hand to the Congress in the matter of selection of members of the committee immediately after it came forward to take up the reins of the movement. To achieve the end, they emphasised the necessity of resorting to peaceful means. The *Satyagrahis* were, however, urged to elect their leader from among themselves in course of the movement. The leader was expected to have a commitment to the proposed end, which would always remain beyond question. In fact, the *Satyagrahis* were always keen to take help from the Congress for mobilisation, once the movement had started.[23] The *Satyagraha* committee had the sagacity to carry on earnest endeavour for keeping itself always informed of the reaction of all concerned about the arrangements made by the organisers. Sometimes, inquiries were made by this committee to ascertain this objective as far as possible.[24]

However, the B. P. C. C responded promptly to the letter written by the Commander of the *Mohabir Dal* on behalf of the *Satyagrahis*. Accordingly, Deshbandhu Chittaranjan

Das, President of the B. P. C. C; Subhas Chandra Bose and Srish Chandra Chatterjee visited Tarakeswar on 8 Apr. 1924 to inquire into the matter and chalk out a line of reforms following a spot-study of the developments as had taken place at Tarakeswar in the meantime.[25]

A preliminary survey convinced the leaders of the reign of terror let loose in this place of pilgrimage. The people could hardly venture to speak out in public against the *Mohanta* as they were in stark fear of danger to their lives and property. The leaders were prompt to assure the inhabitants of the pilgrim town as well as the pilgrims in general of protection against the agents of the *Mohanta*. They had declared in no uncertain terms, their commitment for rendering adequate service to them. An Enquiry Committee was, therefore, set up to enquire into the whole matter in association with members like Deshbandhu Chittaranjan Das, Netaji Subhas Chandra Bose, Srish Chandra Chatterjee, Maulana Akram, Dr. J. M. Dasgupta, *Pundit* Dharanath Bhattacharya and Sri Anil Baran Roy.[26] In his statement Subhas Chandra urged the progressive section of the *Hindu Sabha* (Bengal branch) to take up the matter. He had also made it completely clear that the B. P. C. C would be compelled to take action if the *Hindu Sabha* failed in its duty at this stage.[27]

However, the findings of another Enquiry Committee instituted by the *Hindu Sabha*, Burrabazar, also referred to the illegal exactions by the agents of the *Mohanta* from the pilgrims, shopkeepers as well as residents of the pilgrim town. Besides, it also referred to the cases of the violation of women visiting this place of pilgrimage. This amounted naturally to violation of all the principles of decency and morality.[28] *Swami* Viswananda, the founder of the *Mahabir Dal* had primarily thought of taking recourse to direct action to achieve the goal. But his wisdom guided him to convey prior information to the Divisional Commissioner of Burdwan and District Magistrate of Hooghly before undertaking such a momentous step. Urging the Government to take immediate step to settle the dispute amicably, he requested the authorities concerned at the same time to come forward with necessary measures in keeping with the popular demand for the recognition of the people's right to the possession of the temple to which they were entitled.[29]

III

On 7 Apr. 1924, a confrontation occurred in this place of pilgrimage when a few volunteers of the *Mahabir Dal* reached Tarakeswar for the proposed movement and were assaulted on the spot by the agents of the *Mohanta*. Allegations and counter allegations ensued. In fact, a few agents of the *Mohanta* took on the volunteers of the *Mahabir Dal* while they were busy in distributing leaflets in the market place at the behest of *Swami* Satchidananda. The untoward turn of the event was indeed checked with the timely arrival of the Subdivisional Officer (S. D. O.), Sreerampur and the Assistant Superintendent of Police, Hooghly.[30]

The *Mohanta* was capable of sensing the implication of the brewing storm and he promptly endeavoured to move against those who were supposed to have been making capital on public grievances. To foil their campaign against him, he planned the attack on the *Mahabir Dal*, accusing it of its earnest endeavour to dislodge him from the office of the *Mohanta*. Meanwhile, he began to conduct meetings and conferences at Tarakeswar with a view to ensuring proper state of affairs in this place of pilgrimage and to reassert the *Mohanta*'s rights enjoyed over the years.[31]

In order to instil fear into the mind of his opponents he arranged to bring hired miscreants from different places and began to oppress the tenants as well as to coerce the students of the locality.[32] As his oppressive measures yielded little or no result, he made an appeal to the Government for help. In a letter dated Apr. 21, he complained against *Swami* Viswananda and *Swami* Satchidananda, accusing them of fomenting trouble at Tarakeswar. In order to overcome the impasse, he proposed a conference and, agreed on arbitration with leading members of the public. But he was always over conscious to emphasise the fact in this connection that the temple was in no way a public endowment and therefore, the public had no right to interfere in any way with the management of the trust.[33] The *Mohanta*, meanwhile, met Sir Ashutosh Mukherjee to seek his advice in the context of this development, but in vain.[34]

The *Mohanta* incidentally prayed for an injunction against the *Mahabir Dal* which he suspected to have contemplated not only interference with the management of the temple and the properties of the deity, but also to take possession of the palace of the *Mohanta*.[35] It had also been reported that the *Mohanta* was making efforts to create communal disturbances to complicate matters.[36]

But none had faith in him. Naturally, he failed to create any impact on the public. The *Mahabir Dal* got overwhelming support from the people which, however, resulted in an increase in the number of volunteers.

The ensuing *Gajan* festival brought a chance for the volunteers of the *Mahabir Dal* to rise to the occasion for making arrangements to relieve the sufferings of the people caused by the extortions of the *Mohanta*. All sorts of collections were stopped except the *pranami* offered in obeisance to the deity. No extra charge was taken for even *mundan* (tonsure) except the charge of the barber.[37] Moreover, the other religious rites within the sacred complex were performed by the pilgrims with the help of the volunteers, free of cost.

The movement was put off for the time being immediately after the *Gajan* festival was over. In the meantime, the volunteers devoted themselves earnestly to initiating intensive propaganda in order to mobilise the public opinion in favour of the movement. The pressure of work on the volunteers became considerably less as the flow of pilgrims ceased to a large extent after the *Chaitra Samkranti* i.e., end of the month *Chaitra* (March-April) in the Bengali calendar. The volunteers of the *Mahabir Dal*, meanwhile, had taken over the right of performing the sacred rituals within the shrine.[38] At this stage, the rumour of an impending compromise between the contending groups was in the air. Sensing the mood of the people of the pilgrim town *Swami* Viswananda warned against any such rumour and declared that the *Dal* would work as usual in relation to the sacred performances within the sacred complex.[39] Even the rumour of a compromise initiated by Deshbandhu C. R. Das in exchange for two *lakhs* of rupees embarrassed the leaders of the movement, who refuted the charge immediately.[40]

The *Mohanta* got exasperated by these developments and appealed to the Government for help. The Government was very prompt to respond to the appeal of the *Mohanta*. It set up a committee to inquire into the matter.[41] Henceforth, the movement began to take a political overtone in spite of its religious character. The volunteers of the *Mahabir Dal* under the guidance of their leaders were determined to launch the *Satyagraha* movement with a view to occupying the palace (*Math*) of the *Mohanta* on May 20, 1924.[42]

A few days prior to the formal launching of the *Satyagraha*, a rumour was again heard about an alleged endeavour on the part of Deshbandhu to initiate a selfish compromise. In order to scotch the rumour Deshbandhu in a frank statement said- "I assure everybody that I shall be no party to any settlement which will not protect the people of Tarakeswar or those who stood by a true religious spirit against the *Mohunt*. The temple and the *debutter* property (property devoted to god) must also be protected."[43] This statement reassured those concerned with the course of movement in the pilgrim town.

The B. P. C. C intervened at this juncture and in a meeting on 14 May, 1924; the B. P. C. C was directed by its Executive Council to strengthen the movement. The decision was also taken for sending a contingent of volunteers immediately to the pilgrim town for the relief of the residents as well as pilgrims.[44]

Just four days prior to the commencement of the movement an incident occurred at Tarakeswar which, however, increased the tension in an already grave situation. A few vendors had brought vegetables and fruits for sale from adjacent places. As they were getting ready to leave the market after transactions were over, the *ijaradar* of the market appeared to claim toll by order of the *Mohanta*. They naturally refused to oblige as they were well aware of the developments of the last two weeks during which the volunteers of the *Mahabir Dal* had achieved commendable success in thwarting forcible exactions by the agents of the *Mohanta*. As a result, the vendors were severely beaten up by the hired goons of the *Mohanta* in the scuffle that ensued.[45] As soon as the news of the scuffle spread, *Swami* Satchidananda arrived at the spot with volunteers. His arrival added fuel to the fire. He was mercilessly beaten up by the Gurkha goons engaged by the *Mohanta* and was ultimately carried to an unknown place. The rumour of his murder aggravated the whole atmosphere of the pilgrim town. Even *Swami* Viswananda sent a telegram to Calcutta on the basis of this rumour that *Swami* Satchidananda had been killed.[46] However, the police was successful, following rigorous enquiries, to find out the severely injured *Swamiji* in a room on the ground floor of a nearby *dharmasala*. A few miscreants were apprehended and arrested by the police. The *Swamiji* in his statement referred to an attempt on the part of the *Mohanta* to kill him on the spot.[47]

This infuriated the people who organised a sit in demonstration on the nearby railway line to protest against the event. The B. P. C. C responded promptly in this context and sent Shyamsundar Chakrabarty to inquire into the matter. His talk with *Swami* Satchidananda and the volunteers of *Mahabir Dal* convinced him that the irate mob would in no way allow any train to run until and unless the *Mohanta* and his agents were stopped from carrying on atrocities on this scale. They even demanded the arrest of the *Mohanta* along with his trusted lieutenants as soon as possible. However, the information regarding the arrest of culprits from no less an officer than the S. D. O partly pacified the demonstrators. He was at the same time candid in his admission that the *Mohanta* could not be apprehended owing to the lack of evidence against him. This, indeed, pacified the volunteers and they at once decided to lift the barricade.[48]

In a meeting organised the following day, the leaders of the movement urged the people to carry on the *Satyagraha* movement to a fruitful end. Moreover, *hartal* (general strike) was observed in the pilgrim town, the day after the incident took place.[49]

Meanwhile, one Subodh Krishna Basu, who identified himself as the Secretary of Hindu Temple Reform League, despatched a telegram to the Governor, the Viceroy and Mahatma Gandhi respectively. He clearly stated in that telegram that "after the publication of Deshbandhu Das's message to adopt *Satyagraha*, riot and violence have started this morning in Tarakeswar temple... . Public apprehends repetition of Chauri Chaura. Pray immediate intervention and investigation through reliable agency."[50] An enquiry into the authenticity of the person and his telegram proved without doubt that the person was a trusted agent of the *Mohanta*. The telegraphic message was instantly contradicted by Makhanlal Sen of *Ananda Bazar Patrika* who assured Gandhiji of the falsehood of the message.[51]

IV

The Government intervened at this stage with the earnest endeavour to achieve a settlement. In the meantime, the District Court of Hooghly ordered the appointment of a Receiver for the temple of Lord *Taraknath* as well as for the vegetable market in pursuance of an appeal made by the plaintiffs.[52] The Government expected that the bone of contention between the *Mohanta* and his opponents would become non-existent immediately after the appointment of the Receiver as he would henceforward be entitled to look after the management of the temple. Moreover, the complaints against the *Mohanta* would naturally cease to exist once he was kept away from the management of the temple by virtue of the verdict of the court. However, the course of events took a different turn with the bold assertion of *Swami* Viswananda that the people alone should have the right to appoint the Receiver.

But the Government made it unequivocally clear that the standpoint of the *Swamiji* necessitated the vindication in the court that the property assumed the character of public *debutter* property. Moreover, relevant laws enacted by the legislature were also thought to be necessary to vindicate the right of the people in this context. *Swami* Viswananda was in favour of legislation based on public opinion. He did not hesitate to make it distinctly clear that the *Satyagraha* would be started in no time to vindicate the right of the people. Naturally, an arena of confrontation developed, following the eagerness of the public to assert its right and the strong determination of the Government to maintain law and order.[53]

Armed with the decree of the District Court and the accompanying police officers, Shyamacharan Ukil Banerjee appeared as Receiver to take charge of the shrine and the local market. The organisers of the *Satyagraha* were, in fact, completely against the appointment of a Receiver. They were very much in favour of the formation of a committee by the public for the management of the *debutter* property. Realising his helplessness, given the hostile mood of the people, the Receiver thought it wise to leave the place at the earliest.[54] He, however, sent a report to the District Judge in which he admitted that he had been able only to prepare an 'Inventory' of the properties belonging to the temple. But the list of properties remained incomplete owing to unavoidable reasons. As the *Mohanta* was away and his whereabouts were not known, he suggested that 'the ornaments of the deity' might be left in the custody of Prabhatchandra Giri, the favourite disciple of the incumbent *Mohanta*.[55] Hence, the upshot of the action of the *Satyagrahis* was that the Receiver could not take charge of the temple.

V

Ultimately the fateful date 20 May, 1924 scheduled for the start of *Satyagraha* came.[56] The District Magistrate invited Sri Anil Baran Roy, Secretary of the B. P. C. C on behalf of the Government to reach an amicable settlement. The District Magistrate proposed the full access of the Receiver to the possessions of the temple. He also solicited support from all concerned to make his endeavour for the creation of an Arbitration Board to settle disputes, a success. Moreover, he argued in terms of deciding the issues related to the temple by a committee acceptable to both the contenders. The Secretary of the B. P. C. C had his own terms for a compromise in the given context. He had pressed for the acceptance by the *Mohanta* of the Arbitration Board to be appointed by Deshbandhu as the President of the B. P. C. C. Pending the creation of this Board, the *Satyagrahis* were to have been in possession of the temple. He had also argued in favour of releasing all the prisoners arrested on previous occasions. But the difference between the two parties was insoluble.[57]

When the talks for compromise failed, the *Satyagraha* began on May 20, 1924 and continued for about four months under the illustrious leadership of Deshbandhu Chittaranjan Das.[58] Accordingly, four volunteers offered *Satyagraha* in front of the monastery at 12 noon on May 20, defying the prohibitory order.[59] The actions of the *Satyagrahis* were vividly reported in the contemporary newspapers. The volunteers tried to enter the palace (monastery) of the *Mohanta* claiming it as public property. The *Satyagrahis* had to break through the cordon set up by the police at the gate and were consequently arrested.[60] The day after the start of the movement, *Swami* Viswananda was arrested on the ground that he was trying to foment trouble in the pilgrim town.[61]

However, the entire situation had taken a turn for the worse on May 22 following an order of the Government for the cancellation of trains from Howrah to Tarakeswar. The Government was anxious to stop the further inflow of the *Satyagrahis* to Tarakeswar. It was already very much worried about the information regarding the arrival of about two hundred workers from the Liluah Workshop to the pilgrim town to join the *Satyagraha*. Even the District Traffic Superintendent of Liluah was asked to take appropriate steps to prevent willing sympathisers of the movement from boarding the train. In spite of the best efforts of the station authority as well as the Railway Police, they entrained themselves as soon as the train for Tarakeswar reached Liluah. The cancellation of the train was responded to with the setting up of a barricade on the line and with no result.[62]

Meanwhile, the Government was becoming very anxious about the tense situation in the pilgrim town. Initially, a special Magistrate was posted at the temple as breach of peace was apprehended. An armed police force was stationed at Tarakeswar in addition to the local police to withstand any sort of disturbance.[63] That the Government was instrumental in suppressing the movement is evident from its order for reinforcement by police contingents from Sreerampur and elsewhere.[64] The District Magistrate warned against any endeavour to violate law and order.[65] A keen perusal of the course of events will clearly show that the Government showed no hesitation to side with the *Mohanta* and to apply its power to suppress the *Satyagrahis*. The *Satyagrahis* were arrested at random and were sent to jails in different districts of Bengal. The way the *Satyagrahis* were maltreated in jails speaks much of the high-handedness of the Government. It was reported that fourteen *Satyagrahis* of minor age were mercilessly beaten up in Bankura jail.[66] The *Satyagrahis* were compelled to take recourse to a hunger strike as a result of the merciless oppression of the jail authorities.[67] The imprisoned *Satyagrahis* in different jails were deprived of basic amenities. The *Satyagrahis* in Sreerampur jail were huddled together in unhygienic conditions and were deprived of even beds at night. Moreover, the prisoners in Berhampore jail were the victims of indecent assaults every now and then. To make the matter worse, the jail authorities denied necessary medical aid to the ailing *Satyagrahis*.[68] The reaction of the Government in this connection no doubt smacked of its revengeful attitude towards the *Satyagrahis* at Tarakeswar.

VI

The *Satyagraha* movement at Tarakeswar achieved considerable impetus with the visit of Deshbandhu to Tarakeswar on 30 May, 1924. He was not permitted by the police to enter the temple. He, however, conferred with *Swami* Satchidananda, the Commander of *Mahabir Dal*, about recent developments. This meeting resulted in the decision that he would assume the responsibility to head the movement in right earnest after his return from the Serajgunj Conference. In the meantime, some differences cropped up between, *Swami* Satchidananda and the volunteers of *Mahabir Dal* over the question of conducting the *Satyagraha* movement at Tarakeswar. Things went so far that he decided to resign from the leadership of the *Mahabir Dal* and even thought of offering himself for arrest in disgust. He was dissuaded by Deshbandhu from taking such an extreme step as it would jeopardise the common cause. He also requested the volunteers of the *Dal* to maintain cordial relation among themselves and work in unison. The intervention of C. R. Das at this juncture, indeed, amicably settled the matter.[69]

After his visit to Tarakeswar, Deshbandhu said :

"From what I have seen, I am confirmed in my view that it is the duty of every Hindu in Bengal to support this *Satyagraha* movement. In my opinion, unless the *Mohunt* accepts a reasonable settlement, the Provincial Conference at Serajgunj should take it up and invite the whole of Bengal to this struggle for the purification of one of the most important shrines in the province."[70]

He was deeply perturbed at the "unwarrantable position" taken up by the Government in relation to the developments in the pilgrim town. He was unequivocal in contradicting the claim of the *Mohanta* that the Tarakeswar estate was his private property.

However, an appeal, bearing the signatures of over two thousand residents of this pilgrim town, was sent to the B. P. C. C and also to the Provincial Conference at Serajgunj. The B. P. C. C was earnestly urged in this appeal to take charge of the *Satyagraha* movement at Tarakeswar. Accordingly, the conference rose to the occasion and resolved to extend full-fledged support to the movement. It asked the B. P. C. C to take charge of it.[71]

In accordance with the resolution taken up at the Serajgunj Conference, the B. P. C. C came forward to shoulder the responsibility for continuing the movement at Tarakeswar. Accordingly, C. R. Das reached Tarakeswar along with his wife Basanti Devi and Dr. Pratap Chandra Guharoy on 6 June, 1924. After his meeting with *Swami* Satchidadananda, the Commander of *Mahabir Dal*, he gave the responsibility of conducting the *Satyagraha* movement to Dr. Guharoy.[72]

The B. P. C. C organised a committee to direct the course of the movement. Deshbandhu was declared President while Lal Mohan Ghosh was appointed the Secretary of the committee. The other members were Sasadhar Roy (President, *Hindu Sabha*), Pijush Kanti Ghosh (Secretary, *Hindu Sabha*), Panchanan *Tarkaratna* (President, *Brahman Sabha*), *Mahamahopadhyaya* Laksman *Sastri* (Secretary, *Brahman Sabha*), Binoy Bhusan Mukhopadhyaya (Secretary, *Brahman Sabha*), Surendra Mohan Ghosh, Basanta Kumar Majumdar, Amarendranath Bose, Srish Chandra Chatterjee, Satish Chandra Sarkar, Dr. J. M. Dasgupta, Dharanath Bhattacharya, Shyam Sundar Chakrabarty, *Swami* Viswananda, *Swami* Satchidananda, Gaur Hari Som, Tulsi Charam Goswami (Treasurer), Madan Mohan Barman, Satkari Pati Roy and Anil Baran Roy.[73]

Henceforward, the volunteers of the movement began to court arrest under the direction of the B. P. C. C. Initially, the volunteers of the *Mahabir Dal* and of the Congress joined hands and stood shoulder to shoulder in managing the affairs of the temple. The door of the temple was opened to all, and all sorts of exactions were stopped forthwith. All other suspected malpractices were also done away with. Chiraranjan Das, the son of Deshbandhu, was also among the large contingent of *Satyagrahis* at Tarakeswar who courted arrest during the movement which continued for about four months.[74]

Meanwhile, public meetings were arranged not only at Tarakeswar but also in Calcutta to give vent to the gravity of the situation caused by the misdeeds of the *Mohanta* and his followers. One such meeting was held at Harish Park, Calcutta on May 16, where the speakers resolved to support the Congress which had started the *Satyagraha* to oppose the *Mohanta*, in order 'to keep the fair name of the fair sex' intact.[75] Although the volunteers from outside thronged this pilgrim town everyday, the local people did not lag behind.[76]

The *Tarakeswar Satyagraha* was, in fact, a religious movement organised sedulously to weed out corruption from the religious complex. But it is important to note that Muslims also sympathised with the *Satyagraha* movement at Tarakeswar. The Calcutta *Khilafat* Committee extended its support for the movement and expressed its willingness to render practical help if called upon to do so by the Hindu community.[77] It was reported that a large number of Muslim youths had already reached Tarakeswar from Dacca and Tripura to join the *Satyagraha*.[78] They were given the responsibility of mobilising mass support and of collecting money for the movement.[79] Thus the *Satyagraha* movement achieved a wide base with the participation of the people irrespective of creed and caste.

VII

The most interesting development in course of the *Satyagraha* movement was, in fact, the overwhelming participation of female volunteers, who dared to stand against the all-pervasive corruption which prevailed in this pilgrim town at the behest of the *Mohanta*. A large number of women volunteers were arrested on June 11 but were set free by order of the Magistrate. They eventually refused to leave the spot until and unless *Swami* Satchidananda was released.

He was, meanwhile, ordered to be remanded in police custody since the Police Inspector took exception of the endeavour of the *Swamiji* to exhort those around him to join the *Satyagraha* movement in large numbers. At this stage, the Inspector of Police issued order for escorting the

Swamiji to the police station. The endeavour of the police to implement forcibly the order of the Inspector resulted in a scuffle following which the *Swamiji* fell down unconscious. However, he regained his senses in hospital.[80]

The participation of women volunteers, indeed, raised the eyebrows of those sceptics who questioned their personal characters. This became clear from the application of the plaintiffs in the District Court for the examination of a few women with reference to their being *pardanashin*. Some of them were land-ladies of lodging houses, some were prostitutes and some of them joined the *Satyagraha* movement and publicly mixed with male volunteers. They were arrested by the police and sent up before the court. It was also stated that the names of the fathers or husbands of those women were not given which led to the assumption that they were not respectable women. Incidentally, proofs were given in support of this assumption in the court of the District Judge of Hooghly.

The defendant *Mohanta* alleged that Kali Dasi, a woman *Satyagrahi* was a fish-seller by profession. Therefore, the application for her being examined was rejected by the District Judge. The same happened to Rashmoni Dasi, a *Keora* woman by caste and a sweeper by profession. Krishna Bhabini Debi, a prostitute, was also disqualified for the known reason along with Aghorebala Dasi, a mid-wife by profession and a *Keora* woman by caste.

The remaining four women -- Hari Dasi Debi, Kali Dasi Debi, Jnanadabala Debi and Laksmimani Debi were all *Brahmin* women by caste. Hari Dasi Debi joined the *Satyagraha* movement publicly as well as actively and was sent up to Sreerampur Court on being arrested by the police. Joining the *Satyagraha* movement was exceptional, as many women who otherwise used to observe *parda*, discarded it during the *Satyagraha*. Hence the Judge allowed her for being examined.

Kali Dasi Debi, as had been alleged by the defendant *Mohanta*, was a sister of one Guiram Chatterjee and had incidentally been turned out of her home for immorality. She appeared in public as an assistant of Jnanada Debi who had joined the *Satyagraha* movement publicly. The District Judge allowed also the prayer for her examination despite allegation against her.

Jnanada Debi was the most active participant in the *Satyagraha* movement. The defendant's allegation against her was that she always used to appear in public. She was arrested and sent up by the police for having joined the *Satyagraha* movement. The District Judge was of opinion that a landlady of a lodge of her type, common to Tarakeswar, might not be termed a *pardanashin* woman. "But if she comes from a respectable *Brahmin* family and claims the privilege of the *parda*, I do not see any reason for not respecting her wishes. So I order that she also may be examined on commission."

Laksmimani Debi was stated to have been the owner of a shop and hotel at Tarakeswar and went about in public. She had also joined the *Satyagraha* movement actively and publicly. Again, the District Judge found no reason for rejecting the application for her being examined on commission.[81]

The discussion about women participants in the *Satyagraha* movement must not lead us towards generalisations. It seems that the repeated emphasis on the examination of a few women, with reference to their being *pardanashin*, was a pointer to the endeavour to generalise social status of the women volunteers in the *Satyagraha* movement from the standpoint of the sceptics.

VIII

However, the *Satyagrahis* had already chalked out a plan for approaching the palace of the *Mohanta* through the eastern as well as the southern gate. The course of events meanwhile took a serious turn on *Janmastami* (Aug. 22). Tradition demanded that the deity of *Laksmi-Narayan* should be taken out of the temple, which was within the monastery, to the temple of Lord *Taraknath* for worship on auspicious date. The *Satyagrahis* were desirous of asserting their right of entering the temple of *Laksmi-Narayan*, despite the fact that negotiations with the Magistrate were under way. But the endeavour of *Swami* Satchidananda, along with a large number of his associates to rush through the eastern gate disregarding even the warning of the Magistrate made the situation worse. The Magistrate was left with no other alternative but to order the police to fire on the irate *Satyagrahis*. The *Swamiji* along with a few of his associates suffered injuries as a result of this. However, the police report referred to a premeditated attack on the Magistrate as well as the constables on duty in the context of sporadic violence that continued for sometime.[82]

But the version of Satishchandra Chakrabarty, Superintendent of the *Satyagraha* Committee at Tarakeswar contradicted the police report. He boldly asserted that "missiles and brickbats were thrown at the innocent people and gunshots were also made".[83] The Statesman in its editorial column observed that "the disturbance which took place at Tarakeswar on Friday evening was clearly no part of Congress agitation, and deserves to be considered in its proper light. It was caused by genuine pilgrims who had arrived in large numbers at the shrine for worship and who had the right to expect that the images of *Laksmi-Narayan* should be exposed on the *Janmastami* day. The *Mohunt's Chela* refused to allow the images to leave the place, because he feared that they would not be brought back after the ceremony and the loss would be fatal to his master's prestige. Whether the images would have been restored or not it is impossible to say, though it is easy to understand the *Chela's* fears."[84] *The Ananda Bazar Patrika* also reported the arrest of sixteen *Satyagrahis* as a result of the fracas that ensued because of the attempt to forcibly enter the precinct of the temple of *Laksmi-Narayan Jiu*. Moreover, the demise, owing to pneumonia, of one Paritosh Kundu, a *Satyagrahi*, in the prison at Krishnanagar, was also reported in the same edition of the *Patrika*.[85]

IX

There opened a rift between the leaders of the movement, while it was in full swing. In fact, the campaign of vilification at this stage had told heavily on the course of this movement. Even Deshbandhu was not spared from this campaign of vilification. Certain glaring allegations were put forward against him by his opponents. He was alleged to have the motive to create friction between landlords and tenants. He had already been branded as an earnest propounder of the Permanent Settlement. Moreover, his identity as a *Brahmo* had given scope to his detractors to complain that he wanted always to do away with Hindu shrines. Over and above, he was also accused of trying to take control of the shrine with an eye to the financial gain of his *Swarajya* Party. The allegation against him of taking fullest political advantage of this movement was not difficult as he was by then at the helm of affairs of the B. P. C. C, in which the *Swarajya* Party was dominant. To make his endeavour a success, he was thought to have been instrumental in installing a *Mohanta* of his choice following the consequent removal of the incumbent. Deshbandhu was prompt to refute the allegations labelled against him. In his statement he argued : "I do not desire any friction between landlords and tenants. I have opposed the idea of such class war from public platforms. The question of the repeal of Permanent Settlement is an undesirable question to raise and in my opinion whatever steps are taken must be taken after the attainment of self-Government and even then only as a matter of agreement between landlords and tenants."

"I am not a *Brahmo*. I am a Hindu and I claim to be sincere. It is absolutely untrue that I want to take up Hindu shrines to finance my party. My point of view is the Hindu point of view. I want the shrines to be purified and reformed. I do not want to remove *Mohuntship* but to have a devout *Mohunt* appointed, so that the service in the temple may be properly supervised and income applied to the good of the pilgrims and the locality by establishing such educational and charitable institutions as may be required for the good of the people. In my opinion this is not politics. But if it is so regarded I am not ashamed of it."

"Nor is it true that I want the *Mohuntship* to go to some Bengali instead of Hindi-speaking gentleman. I do not wish to interfere in the slightest degree with the traditions of the particular sect to which the *Mohunt* belongs."[86]

The whole situation had become somewhat tense with the rumour gaining momentum that a settlement had been arrived at, between C. R. Das and the incumbent *Mohanta*. The *Mohanta* on his part was by then quite willing to initiate the process of settlement only if he was left with his absolute right over his own fortunes. He thought it wise to be a party to a settlement immediately, as he had no other choice in the given state of affairs. He was, however, not averse to the idea of the formation of a committee for management of the temple with its property worth a *lakh* of rupees.[87] Deshbandhu initially contradicted the report to this effect, published in the *Amrita Bazar Patrika*, but did not hesitate to rise to the occasion. He eventually published certain terms for a settlement. Accordingly, he pleaded for the abdication of Satishchandra Giri, the incumbent *Mohanta*, in favour of his *Chela* Prabhatchandra Giri. The new *Mohanta* Prabhatchandra Giri would remain under the control of the committee vested with the power to, if necessary, remove him from the seat of the *Mohanta*. The properties with a net annual income of over Rs. 30,000/- and the ever increasing income accruing from the temple offerings would be left in charge of the committee for the purpose of necessary charities. The other properties with a net annual income between Rs. 25,000/- and Rs. 32,000/- would be managed by the *Mohanta* Prabhatchandra Giri. The income would be utilised for the maintenance of whoever the *Mohanta* might be in future. The *Mohanta* would henceforward not claim any other sum for his maintenance. The *Mohantas* from Prabhatchandra Giri onwards were proposed to be subservient to the scheme of management to be devised by the committee. It was also made clear in his terms for settlement that the committee should have the absolute right to take immediate possession and manage directly the properties vested with the *Mohanta* if he was found to be an oppressor to his tenants. The temple as well as the estate along with other properties would be considered as public properties, managed by the committee. Finally, C. R. Das's terms for settlement demanded that the worship of *Laksmi-Narayan Jiu* would have to be opened to the public at the earliest.[88]

However, *Swami* Satchidananda, the Commander of the movement, did not accept these terms for settlement. Not only he was completely against the appointment of Prabhatchandra Giri as the *Mohanta* but also was against the constitution of various committees on the ground that the *Swarajyists* would form a majority in them.[89] The denial of the *Swami* to accept the terms for settlement stands for the fact that the local participants in the *Satyagraha* movement were becoming sceptical about the role of Deshbandhu C. R. Das.

X

At last the day of reckoning dawned on Satishchandra Giri. He was ultimately compelled to announce his decision to abdicate in favour of his *Chela* (disciple) Prabhatchandra Giri on 22 September, 1924. The police personnel were withdrawn from the gate of the *Mohanta*'s palace (monastery) and none of the *Satyagrahis* were arrested thenceforward, after the monastery was declared as public property. The *Satyagraha* was, however, withdrawn on September 23, 1924 to make the terms of settlement effective.[90] A meeting was arranged later on, at which Satishchandra Giri, in the presence of Deshbandhu and *Swami* Viswananda, apologised to all for the harm he might have knowingly or unknowingly caused to them.[91]

The announcement of his abdication of the *Mohantaship* in favour of his *Chela* Prabhatchandra Giri, however, facilitated the process of a compromise for the withdrawal of the Civil Suit pending in the District Court, Hooghly. It is to be mentioned here that one Dharanidhar Sinharoy along with six others had already filed a suit against the incumbent *Mohanta*. Nobody dared present himself as a witness against the *Mohanta*. But Sripati Hazra and Tirthabasi Sinharoy were the only two persons who had the courage to stand against the *Mohanta* of the *Tarakeswar Math* at least in the initial phase.[92] Despite this development, a prayer had been made for the withdrawal of the Civil Suit immediately after the termination of the *Satyagraha* movement.

It has been alleged in the 'Satyagrahas in Bengal' (Chapter-IV) with reference to the *Tarakeswar Satyagraha* that Dharanidhar Sinharoy and six others agreed to withdraw the Civil Suit by reason of a deed of compromise.[93] In fact, D. Sinharoy was never a party to this deed of compromise which was agreed to between the *Mohanta* and the other six plaintiffs. Meanwhile, three persons claiming to be interested in the trust applied for being considered as plaintiffs to the suit. The court added them as plaintiffs after notices were duly given to the defendant *Mohanta* and the original seven plaintiffs on 23.8.24.[94] These additional plaintiffs were from the *Brahman Sabha* which objected instantly to the compromise on several grounds.

Primarily, the *Brahman Sabha* was against the compromise as it was an endeavour to stifle judicial enquiry into the merits of several important questions. Moreover, they emphasised that the question already raised in the original suit could not be disposed of by virtue of a private adjustment, as it affected the orthodox Hindus in general. This compromise was also in no way satisfactory to them as it failed not only in the matter of ensuring the rights of the deity but was also not at par with existing laws and customs. The plaintiffs were also of opinion that the terms of compromise were contradictory in character and, thereby, failed to create confidence in the devotees, in the matter of management of properties and other affairs of the temple. They even characterised as illusory, the nature of constitution of the proposed committee.[95]

It will not be out of context to refer to the fact that the expenditure incurred by the *Brahman Sabha* in relation to the suit, was made up by one Brojendra Kishore Roychowdhury of Gauripur, Mymensingh. He had incidentally contributed one *lakh* of rupees with the desire to make the whole process a success.[96]

The *Brahman Sabha*, composed of mostly orthodox *Brahmins*, had pitted itself against the *Satyagraha* movement. Initially, a few members of the *Sabha* were included in the committee formed by the B. P. C. C. But it resolved later on not to join and support the committee as it was in favour of dislodging the *Mohanta* by legal means.[97] It was always in favour of an appointment of a successor to Satishchandra Giri in accordance with the orthodox Hindu scriptures and traditions.[98] The *Sabha* was completely against the implementation of the terms of settlement put forward by Deshbandhu Chittaranjan Das and formulated its own terms instead.

Accordingly, the *Sabha* argued in terms of ensuring the right of the public to have a *darshan* of *Laksmi-Narayan* whose *Seba* and *puja* should be in accordance with the *Shastras*. It was against allowing either Satishchandra Giri or his *Chela* Prabhatchandra Giri to reside in the monastery at Tarakeswar after its legal categorisation as *debutter*.

It was not against the creation of a permanent Arbitration Committee. But it emphasised the point that the members of this committee should in no way be the members of the Managing Committee. It had incidentally put forward an exclusive list of eleven members who were to form the first Managing Committee. Besides, it had also made propositions regarding the composition of the *Deb-seba Samiti*. All the seven members of this committee were proposed to be orthodox *Brahmins*, prominent in Hindu society. Finally, it argued in favour of installing, in accordance with the rules of the temple, a young *Brahmachari* of commendable character in the office of the *Mohanta*. Hence, the deed of settlement was required to record clearly the rules relating to the appointment of the *Mohanta*.[99]

The *Brahman Sabha* exposed itself as a congregation of fanatics by virtue of its terms of settlement in this regard. Therefore, it was only natural that the *Brahman Sabha* would create difficulty for the terms of settlement already arrived at the behest of Deshbandhu C. R. Das from being effective.

However, the new plaintiffs of the *Brahman Sabha* prayed before the District Court not only for the cancellation of the terms of settlement but also for the appointment of a Receiver. *Swami* Satchidananda also appealed, in the meantime, to the Government for the appointment of a Receiver to overcome the impasse.[100] The court, in its judgement, ordered the appointment of a Receiver. Amulya Chandra Bhaduri was appointed as the Receiver and took charge of the temple as well as the monastery on 7 July 1925 by virtue of the order of the court.[101] The aggrieved *Mohanta* was prompt in appealing to the High Court for an instant stay-order against the verdict of the District Court with reference to the appointment of the Receiver.[102] Ultimately, the High Court in its judgement sanctioned the appointment of a Receiver exclusively for the *debutter* property.[103]

XI

In spite of commendable organisational skill and activity, the *Satyagraha* movement in this place of pilgrimage lost much of its thrust simply because of the lack of human and material resources.[104] Deshbandhu C. R. Das had become excessively eager to initiate at least an honourable settlement as he was getting very tired of the allegations made by his opponents. But his cherished objective was fulfilled in the long run with the exit of the corrupt regime of the *Giri Mohantas.* In fact, the appointment of the Receiver changed the whole scenario and the *Satyagraha* movement ultimately lost much of its edge as a result of this appointment. This development, however, marked the beginning of a new era in the history of this place of pilgrimage in Eastern India.

There is no denying the fact that the *Satyagraha* movement launched under the leadership of Deshbandhu Chittaranjan Das, Netaji Subhas Chandra Bose and *Swami* Viswananda to eradicate the evils associated with the *Tarakeswar Math* achieved the desired goal in the long run. The Title suit No. 28 of 1922 filed in the Court of the District Judge, Hooghly challenging the rights of the *Mohanta* resulted in the verdict that the *Math* was a public endowment. The *Mohanta* was allowed to remain as the executive head, functioning under the directions of the Managing Committee with its power to remove the *Mohanta* as and when needed.

Note

1. Amrita Bazar Patrika - Editorial. 20.05.24.

2.   Sudhir Kumar Mitra - Hooghly Jelar Itihas O Bangasamaj. Vol.-II, P.-1119.

3.   Narendranath Bandyopadhyaya - Tarakeswar Satyagraha Sangram. PP.-32-33.
Also,
Pramathanath Sanyal - Tarakeswar. P.-32.

4.   Forward - 25.4.24, 4(2).

5.   Narendranath Bandyopadhyaya -Tarakeswar Satyagraha Sangram. PP.-52-56.

6.   Sudhir Kumar Mitra - Tarakeswarer Itikatha. P.-13.

7.   Ananda Bazar Patrika - 20.2.24.

8.   Sudhir Kumar Mitra - Hooghly Jelar Itihas O Bangasamaj. Vol.-II. P.-1120 and P.-1128.

9.   Swarna Kumar Ghoshal - Tarakeswar Satyagraher Itihas. P.-14.

10. Ananda Bazar Patrika - 27.2.24, 3(6).

11. Amrita Bazar Patrika - 28.2.24, 6(3).

12. The Bengalee - 9.4.24, 4(4).

13. Amrita Bazar Patrika - 2.3.24, 7(4).

14. Ananda Bazar Patrika - 3.4.24.

15. Amrita Bazar Patrika - 4.5.24, 5(6).

16. Ananda Bazar Patrika - 25.5.24.

17. Ibid. - 13.6.24, 3(3-4).

18. Amrita Bazar Patrika - 4.5.24, 5(6).

19. R. C. Majumdar - History of the Freedom Movement in India. Vol-III. P-200.

20. Swarna Kumar Ghosal - Tarakeswar Satyagraher Itihas. P-30.

21. Amrita Bazar Patrika - 17.8.24. 6(6).

22. The Bengalee - 22.6.24, 5(6).

23. Ananda Bazar Patrika - 22.5.24, 3(2).

24. Amrita Bazar Patrika - 18.7.24, 3(4).

25. Forward - 8.4.24, 3(5).

26. S. K. Mitra - Hooghly Jelar Itihas O Bangasamaj. Vol II. P-1120.

27. Forward - 10.4.24, 3(5).

28. Amrita Bazar Patrika - 6.5.24, 6(3).

29. Ibid - 20.4.24, 3(4).

30. The Bengalee - 9.4.24, 4(4).

31. Ananda Bazar Patrika - 6.3.24, 2(3-4) & 20.3.2024, 4(2).

32. Ibid. - 20.2.24 & 13.4.24, 2(5-6).

33. Amrita Bazar Patrika - 25.4.24, 8(1).

34. Ananda Bazar Patrika - 27.4.24, 2(4).

35. The Bangalee - 9.5.24, 6(3) & 14.5.24, 3(7).

36. Ananda Bazar Patrika - 11.5.24, 2(7).

37. Amrita Bazar Patrika - 16.4.24, 6(5).

38. Ananda Bazar Patrika - 20.4.24, 2(4-5).

39. Ibid. - 19.4.24, 2(6).

40. Ibid - 24.4.24, 2(6).

41. Ibid - 2.5.24, 2(2).

42. Buddhadeb Bhattacharya - Satyagrahas in Bengal. P-88.

43. The Bengalee - 9.5.24, 4(7).

44. Amrita Bazar Patrika - 16.5.24, 6(2).

45. Buddhadeb Bhattacharya - Satyagrahas in Bengal. P-89.

46. Ananda Bazar Patrika - 17.5.24, 2(1).

47. Ibid - 18.5.24, 2(7).

48. Ibid - 17.5.24, 2(1).

49. Ibid - 18.5.24, 2(5-6).

50. Amrita Bazar Patrika - 17.5.24, 5(2).

51. Ananda Bazar Patrika - 18.5.24, 2(7).

52. Ibid - 17.5.24. 2(4).

53. Amrita Bazar Patrika - 18.5.24, 5(1-5).

54. Ibid. - 20.5.24, 5(1-2).

55. Narendranath Bandopadhyaya - Tarakeswar Satyagraha Sangram.
     PP.-94-95.

56. Swarna Kumar Ghoshal - Tarakeswar Satyagraher Itihas. Chaps. III and IV.

57. Amrita Bazar Patrika - 21.5.24, 5(4).

58. Sudhir Kumar Mitra - Hooghly Jelar Itihas O Bangasamaj. Vol.II. P-1120.

59. The Bengalee - 21.5.24, 4(4).

60. Ananda Bazar Patrika - 30.7.24.

61. Ibid - 22.5.24. 3(1).

62. Ibid. - 23.5.24, 3(1-2).

63. Amrita Bazar Patrika - 15.5.24, 6(3) & 18.5.24, 5(1-5).

64. Ibid. - 20.5.24, 5(1-2).

65. The Bengalee - 21.5.24, 4(4).

66. Ibid. - 26.6.24, 5(7).

67. Amrita Bazar Patrika - 6.7.24, 5(3).

68. Ibid. - 8.7.24, 6(5) & 9.7.24, 5(6).

69. The Bengalee - 31.5.24, 4(7).

70. Amrita Bazar Patrika - 31.5.24, 5(4).

71. Ananda Bazar Patrika - 5.6.24, 2(7).

72. Ibid. - 7.6.24, 2(5).

73. Amrita Bazar Patrika - 10.6.24, 8(2).

74. Sudhir Kumar Mitra - Hooghly Jelar Itihas O Bangasamaj. Vol II. P.-1120.

75. Amrita Bazar Patrika - 17.5.24. 5(2).

76. Ibid - 20.5.24, 5(1-2).

77. Ibid - 16.5.24, 6(2).

78. Ibid - 5.7.24, 6(1).

79. Ananda Bazar Patrika - 22.5.24, 3(1).

80. Amrita Bazar Patrika - 12.6.24 & 13.6.24.

81. Serial Number of Order or Proceeding - 212. Date of order - 28.4.26.

82. The Bengalee - 24.8.24, 5(1).

83. Ibid - 26.8.24, 3(4).

84. The Statesman - 26.8.24, 6(3).

85. Ananda Bazar Patrika - 30.7.24.

86. The Bengalee - 20.7.24, 6(4).

87. Amrita Bazar Patrika - 31.8.24, 6(1).

88. The Bengalee - 20.9.24, 4(6-7) & 6(4).

89. Ibid. - 29.9.24, 4(6).

90. S. K. Ghoshal - Tarakeswar Satyagraher Itihas. P.-59.
Also,
Narendranath Bandopadhyaya - Tarakeswar Satyagraha Sangram.
PP.-52-56.

91. The Bengalee - 25.9.24, 5(7).

92. S. K. Mitra - Hooghly Jelar Itihas O Bangasamaj, Vol. II, P.-1120.

93. Buddhadeb Bhattacharya - Satyagrahas in Bengal. P-101.

94. Serial Number of Order or Proceeding - 121. Date of order - 28.3.25.

95. Amrita Bazar Patrika - 12.3.25, 3(3).

96. S. K. Mitra - Hooghly Jelar Itihas O Bangasamaj. Vol. II, P.-1128.

97. Ananda Bazar Patrika - 13.6.24, 3(3-4).

98. The Bengalee - 20.7.24, 2(3).

99. Amrita Bazar Patrika - 25.9.24, 6(3-4).

100. Ibid. - 18.2.25, 7(2).

101. Ibid. - 10.7.25, 3(4). Also, A.K. Banerjee - West Bengal District
Gazetteers. Hooghly. P.-155.

102. Serial Number of Order or Proceeding - 134. Date of order - 9.7.25.

103. Ibid. - 142. Date of order - 22.2.26.

104. Bengal Administrative Report - 1924-25. (XII - XIII).

Chapter - VII

The Aftermath

I

The interregnum between the passing of the *Giri* regime into oblivion and the advent of the *Ashram* order of the *Dashnami Sannyasis* in the administration of the twin institutions witnessed the tenures of two Receivers. Of them, Amulya Chandra Bhaduri was the first. He was appointed on 7 July, 1925 and worked until mid-May, 1937. His efficient role in the development of the sacred complex necessitates special treatment in the ensuing discussion.

Apart from his efficiency as the administrator of the *Math* and its property, he was equally commendable for the keen interest he showed in the all-round development of Tarakeswar. Primarily, he actively endeavoured in 1927 to renovate the only High School in the pilgrim town. As a mark of gratitude, a marble plaque bearing his name was put up in the High school. Besides, he sanctioned substantial grants for the Girls' Primary School as well as for the repair of the *chatuspathi* (an institution for learning the Sanskrit language). With a view to encouraging the physical education of the students of the locality, he also sanctioned a playground for the High School, from the Tarakeswar *estate*.[1] He was said to have spent upto Rs. 1200/- at a time for the development of the school during his tenure.[2]

He was much concerned about public health at Tarakeswar, in view of its fame as a pilgrim town. He undertook special measures to keep away epidemics through proper sanitation, as well as through the inoculation of the residents and pilgrims, particularly during the pilgrimage season. Besides, an *Ayurvedic* centre was also set up at the Tarakeswar estate at his instance.

The *Chandina Sattva* which was followed during the tenure of the last *Giri Mohanta* was abolished during his term as the Receiver. Besides, he took special care of the *dharnayatris* and endeavoured to lessen their plight. The tradition of the distribution of the *prasad* (consecrated food) of Lord *Taraknath* to the ascetics and pilgrims was also established by him. This expensive ritual, known as *bhandara* (distribution of consecrated food) is still practised within the sacred complex.

His encouragement to agricultural experiments at the Sahapur garden-house coincided with his interest in improved breeds of cattle. Moreover, one Hiralal Shaw, a wealthy merchant of Calcutta, arranged for the marble flooring and decorative tiling of the temple walls during Bhaduri's Receivership.[3]

Notwithstanding the commendable services he rendered to this pilgrim town, he could not avoid the charges brought against him and, ultimately, he had to resign. Initially, he was accused of preferring the candidature for appointment of those from his native North Bengal. Besides, his handling of the finances of the *Tarakeswar Math* rendered him open to accusation. However, he failed ultimately to withstand the charges, ranging from nepotism to deliberate self-projection at the cost of temple funds, brought against him.[4]

His resignation from the post of the Receiver was followed by an advertisement seeking eligible candidates for the post. Of the applicants for the post, Mr. Justice S. Mukherjee favourably considered a retired District Judge Rashbehari Mukherjee, an orthodox *Brahmin* and an ex-President of the Bengal Provincial Service, Judicial Branch.

The salary of the new Receiver was fixed at Rs. 500/ per month and he was required to furnish security, or a fixed deposit of Rs. 10,000/- and the balance of Rs. 10,000/- in personal security from any reliable company within 7 days of his appointment.[5] He was, in fact, the Receiver for the estate for a short while as, within a few months, the District Judge decided on the appointment of *Dandiswami* Jagannath Ashram as the next *Mohanta* of the *Tarakeswar Math.*

II

The appointment of *Dandiswami* Jagannath Ashram to the office of the *Mohanta* at the *Tarakeswar Math* coincided with the setting up of a new administrative hierarchy in accordance with the order passed on 29.8.34 by the Calcutta High Court.

The new *Mohanta* as the *Tirtha-Guru* (preceptor of the religious complex) was directed accordingly to adhere to the advice of the newly constituted Managing Committee which had also been put together following the same order.

This Bengali *Mohanta* was born in the district of Pabna, now in Bangladesh, in the month of *Kartik* in 1301 B.S. He was a reputed and learned person, with a keen interest in the promotion of the learning of the Sanskrit language.[6] Initially, *Dandiswami* Jagannath Ashram had been the head of the *Kanko Math* at Katrasgarh, Manbhum, for a long time prior to his appointment as the *Mohanta* of the *Tarakeswar Math*. Of all the heads of the religious institutions, he alone displayed sufficient initiative in taking over the administration of the twin institutions, when invited to do so in the changed perspective.

His interest in the promotion of the Sanskrit language materialised in the establishment of a Sanskrit College within the premises of the *Tarakeswar Math* in 1345 B.S. The marble plaque engraved on the southern gate of the monastery still bears witness to his achievement in this regard. The boarders of the *Brahmachari Ashram* were mainly the students of this residential Sanskrit College. Scholars in Sanskrit literature who generally came from East Bengal (Bangladesh) and Bihar were appointed to teach the Bengali as well as non-Bengali students of this college. The non-Bengali students were mostly from Bihar, Uttar Pradesh and Assam and this trend continues even today. It is interesting to note that these non-Bengali students often get regular allowances from their respective states even in these days.[7] The new *Mohanta* did not sever his relationship with the *Kanko Math* in Bihar even after taking over the office of the *Mohanta* of the *Tarakeswar Math*. He endeavoured to establish a Sanskrit College there. He also enthusiastically arranged *Yajnas* (ritual sacrifices) on auspicious occasions at that *Math*.[8]

He took keen interest in initiating remarkable changes with regard to the rituals performed over the years within the temple, immediately after his appointment as the *Mohanta* of the *Tarakeswar Math*. He was, indeed, instrumental in doing away with the animal sacrifice within the precinct of the temple particularly during the worship of the Goddesses *Durga* as well as *Kali*. The alternative to animal sacrifice that he insisted on is still being followed.

Despite his limited power and resources, Jagannath Ashram tried to improve the condition of this place of pilgrimage. Permanent structures were put up around the sacred complex during his tenure. He fought boldly against the corruption which had flourished over the years, thus polluting the sanctity of the twin institutions. Besides codifying the norms to be put into effect by the priests of the temple, he also brought the errant employees of the estate to book since they were well-known for corruption. This naturally led to a growing dissatisfaction among those employees who created trouble for the new *Mohanta*.[9]

He was also bent on recovering the *benami* (in the name of the other) property, in Arrah and Balia districts of Bihar, of the erstwhile *Giri Mohanta* in order to strengthen the finances of the Tarakeswar estate.[10] At the same time, he enthusiastically continued the philanthropic work that had been started during the *Giri* regime. He helped the people in and around the sacred complex through donations from the surplus funds of the estate when they were in distress. A few refugee *Brahmins* from East Bengal (Bangladesh) were granted lands for residence and, also provided with employment at the Tarakeswar estate.[11] This perhaps spoke much of his inclination to help those who came from his place of birth.

Despite his earnest desire to change the overall atmosphere of the pilgrim town, he had to face the antagonism of a large number of local residents which, in the long run, caused him much distress. His disenchantment with the litigation in which he got himself entangled, against his will, strengthened his determination to resign in favour of his trusted disciple *Dandiswami* Hrishikesh Ashram.

The causes of the litigation were simple. Immediately after his assumption of the office of the *Mohanta*, he began to think of himself as the sole possessor of the Tarakeswar endowment and its assets. Moreover, he believed that all the traditional powers allowed to the *Mohantas* of the sacred institution, concerning the management of the shrine, were also given to him. This he believed, in spite of his awareness that he had no control over those which were taken away by order of the court, under Sec. 92. C. P. C.

Although he did not object to the power of the committee with reference to the appointment and dismissal of the Manager, Treasurer and the Accountant, he wanted them to work under him as laid down in the authorised scheme. Besides, he denied the power of the committee in relation to the appointment of the Superintendent of the estate which, according to him, had been vested exclusively in the *Mohanta*.

He also stuck to his standpoint that the annual budget of the estate (from 1st of *Sravan* to 30th of *Ashar* of a Benali year), prepared at his initiative, would be submitted to the committee for sanction, and once sanctioned would be the basis of the endowment for the year concerned.[12]

This viewpoint of the *Mohanta* had faced opposition from his opponents, who contested the claim that the assets of the endowment had been vested in the *Mohanta* as its owner. Therefore, the *Mohanta* had neither authority over the Manager, Treasurer and Accountant, regarding their appointment or dismissal, nor in matters relating to the sanction of leave and the enforcement of discipline. Besides, the ultimate authority to provide funds or to sanction budgets was always within the jurisdiction of the committee alone. Hence, following the terms of the authorized scheme would not be derogatory to the prestige of the *Mohanta*.[13]

The District Judge, however, upheld that the committee should be treated with respect and utmost consideration as it had acted within its allotted powers in the appointment of the Manager and the fixation of his salary. The *Mohanta* was directed to be dependent on the committee for the supply of funds, and to take part in its deliberations as an important member of the committee, which was the only appointing authority with reference to everyday administration. The *Mohanta* was invested only with the authority to monitor the performance of the officers of the Tarakeswar estate including the Manager. Hence, the authority of the committee vis-a-vis the *Mohanta* had been upheld by virtue of the judgement given by the District Judge.[14]

The judgement made it amply clear that the *Mohanta* had got himself entangled in a quarrel with the committee on flimsy grounds. The fall out of this judgement led to a disenchantment with him, as it created an atmosphere within the *Tarakeswar Math* in which he himself felt uneasy to a considerable extent. Moreover, his inability to compromise with his personal problems compelled him to resign in 1952 (1358 B.S.), after nominating his disciple *Dandiswami* Hrishikesh Ashram as his successor.

Dandiswami Hrishikesh Ashram hails from the district of Bankura and is still in the office of the *Mohanta* at the *Tarakeswar Math* which he had taken over at the age of eighteen in the month of *Chaitra*, 1358 B.S. (1952 A.D.) by virtue of the order and approval of Mr. Justice Rebati Chattopadhyaya, the District Judge of Hooghly.[15] The initiation of *Dandiswami* Hrishikesh Ashram, in fact, disproves the statement in the West Bengal District

Gazetteers (Hooghly) that the age-old practice of *Guru-Sisya Parampara* had been abolished with the change in the order of *Dashnami Sannyasis* at the *Tarakeswar Math*.[16]

Note

1. P. Chakrabarty - Social Profile of Tarakeswar. P-23.

2. Serial Number of Order of Proceeding - 1328. Date of order - 24.5.37.

3. Prafulla Chakrabarty - Social Profile of Tarakeswar. P-24.

4. Serial Number of Order of Proceeding - 652. Date of order - 18.1.28.

5. Ibid. - 1320. Date of order - 18.5.37.

6. S. K. Mitra - Hooghly Jelar Itihas O Bangasamaj. Vol-II, P.-1121.

7. Yugantar - 23 March, 1995 (8 Chaitra, 1401 B.S.).

8. S. K. Mitra - Hooghly Jelar Itihas O Bangasamaj. Vol-II, P.-1121.

9. Jnananjan - Acharya Sri Sri Jagannath Ashrampad. P-197.

10. S. K. Mitra - Hooghly Jelar Itihas O Bangasamaj. Vol-II, P.-1121.

11. P. Chakrabarty - Social Profile of Tarakeswar. P-26.

12. Petition on behalf of Dandiswami Jagannath Ashram under Clause XVIII of the scheme framed under Sec. 92, filed on 11 March, 1946. Dandiswami Jagannath Ashram Vs. Sri Srijib Nayatirtha and others.

13. Petition of objection on behalf of Sri Srijib Nayatirtha and others filed on 9 July, 1946. Dandiswami Jagannath Ashram Vs. Sri Srijib Nayatirtha, Member and Secretary, Committee of Management, Tarakeswar estate, and others.

14. Judgement of the Court of the District Judge, Hooghly, Misc. Case No. 32 of 1946 dated 16th Apr. 1947. Present : B. M. Mitra. Esq. ICS.

15. S. K. Mitra - Hooghly Jelar Itihas O Bangasamaj. Vol-II, P.-1121.
    Also,
    P. Chakrabarty - Social Profile of Tarakeswar. P-26.

16. A. K. Banerjee - West Bengal District Gazetteers, Hooghly, P.-726.

Chapter - VIII

Tarakeswar Pilgrimage : Its bearing on fairs and festivals

I

Tirthayatras or, pilgrimages have the same cultural and religious importance in Hinduism as they have in other religions. *Tirthasthala* (place of pilgrimage) and *Ksetramahatmya* (fame of the place of pilgrimage) are important segments of the *Puranas* which deal with the importance of pilgrimages in detail as well as the ideal way of life the pilgrim is required to lead during the *tirthayatra*. The *Savdakalpadrumah* gives a list of two hundred and sixty-four *tirthas*, on the basis of information from the *Puranas* and the epics.[1] Incidentally, the epic Mahabharata contains a section in the *Vanaparba* (chapter 78-158), entitling *Tirthayatraparba*, which is exclusively devoted to pilgrimage.

The orthodox viewpoint laid down in the scriptures emphasises the purity of the motive arising from a devout feeling for undertaking a pilgrimage.[2] Hence the pilgrimage always facilitates co-ordination between the purity of life and perfect knowledge, springing from the manifestation of divinity already in man.

Therefore, a place of pilgrimage has a greater attraction for the traveller rather than a secular tourist spot. Pilgrims often tolerate great hardship to reach holy places and also care little for the discomfort they may face while temporarily living there. Therefore, a pilgrim town with its invariably congested lanes infested with pestering beggars and clusters of shops around the temple dealing in items for worship must have the ability to arouse great religious fervour in those who take the trouble to visit it. Usually, the religious character of a pilgrim town is manifested through the work of a few special groups of people who are responsible for religious services to the presiding deity of the temple.[3]

This is because of the all-pervasive influence of the presiding deity on those who throng the place of pilgrimage all through the year. This again helps creating a common bond between the inhabitants of the pilgrim centre and those from the surrounding regions. As the prosperity of a place of pilgrimage depends to a considerable extent on the pilgrims, secular and religious elements co-exist in its cultural heritage.

II

Tarakeswar, as a place of Hindu pilgrimage in Eastern India, has long been considered an ideal place of pilgrimage over the years. Despite being a *Saiva* centre, Tarakeswar seems to have accommodated in course of time people from diverse sects of Hinduism. But the fact remains that this pilgrim centre has achieved its present status due to the inflow of pilgrims following the revelation of the cult of Lord *Taraknath*. The gradual increase in the flow of pilgrims, however, began only during the latter half of the nineteenth century, following the improvement in communication, especially the extension of the railway line that connected

Tarakeswar with other places. Previously, only primitive modes of transport, such as the oxcart and the palanquin, were available to travellers in this region who preferred not to walk. Most of the people, however, had to travel on foot for financial difficulties.[4]

The pilgrims who wished access to Tarakeswar from Baidyabati near Sheoraphuli had to get there on foot owing to the lack of conveyance prior to the extension of the railway line from Sheoraphuli to Tarakeswar in 1885. Although a bungalow had been built at Baidyabati for the convenience of the pilgrims, nothing else was done to ensure their comfort and safety during this period. They were frequently attacked by the roving bands of dacoits and were robbed of their belongings on the way to Tarakeswar.[5] No sooner were the hindrances in the communication system overcome, the urge to visit this place of pilgrimage increased dramatically.

W. W. Hunter noticed and typified this development in his "A Statistical Account of Bengal". He referred to a large shrine dedicated to Lord *Siva* "where crowds of people assemble at all times of the year, but especially during the months of March and April." He also wrote about the pilgrims flocking at this place of great sanctity "principally for the fulfilment of vows on recovery from sickness. Two large religious gatherings for the worship of *Siva*, the deity of the temple, are held every year. The first of them is the *Sivaratri*, held in the month of February, on the fourteenth day after full-moon, in the month of *Phalgun*, a day specially sacred to *Siva*..... The second great religious festival held at the Tarakeswar temple is the *Chaitra Samkranti* on the last day of the Hindu month of *Chaitra* and of the Bengali year, falling within April. It is also the day of the swinging festival. The temple of Tarakeswar is visited by a large number of persons from the surrounding neighbourhood, within a circuit of forty or fifty miles during the whole of the month of *Chaitra*."[6]

From the month of *Baisakh* to that of *Chaitra* of the Bengali calendar year (corresponding to the period of one year from April to March) this "place of great sanctity" witnesses fairs and festivals of different types. Usually, casteism plays an important part in almost all the sacred performances before the presiding deity of this pilgrim centre. But it is only during the time of fairs and festivals that casteism assumes a secondary importance. In fact, these fairs and festivals, held at frequent intervals also represent the basic structural and functional features of the Hindu civilization. Moreover, these have traditionally been associated with the salient features of the puranic places of pilgrimage.

III

L. S. S. O'Malley referred to the pilgrims coming "to the shrine throughout the year and on all the days of the week, but Monday is the favourite day, as it is considered the day most auspicious to *Siva*".[7] Usually, most of the regular pilgrims take a holy bath in the *Dudhpukur*, the sacred tank adjacent to the temple of Lord *Taraknath*, prior to performing sacred rituals as directed by orthodox practice. Thereafter, they worship the presiding deity with flowers, garlands, sweets and a small pot, full of water of the Ganges mixed with unboiled milk bought generally from the shops dealing in goods for rituals. Most of the pilgrims take primary interest in the worship of Lord *Taraknath* and, only secondarily do they offer oblations to other deities within the sacred complex.

Of the many rituals performed by regular pilgrims, *mundan* (tonsure) and *dandi* (prostration) seem important.

These are performed "principally for the fulfilment of vows on recovery from sickness".[8] The "form of treatment - which can hardly be called a system of medicine and was designated the 'religious system' by Crawford - was to seek benedictions of the gods for effecting magical cure of ailments........."[9]

Although the males are primarily found to perform the *mundan* (tonsure) on almost regular basis, widows are also subjected to this ritual as is also common in Kashi, Prayag, Brindaban or in other places of pilgrimage in India.[10] Incidentally, this ritual has been initiated at the *kamansala* (tonsuring centre) under the supervision of the temple administration. The number of pilgrims performing this ritual increases or decreases in keeping with the flow of pilgrims.

The ritual is also performed within the sacred complex at major religious ceremonies like *annaprasan* (the first time a baby is fed rice) and *upanayan* (the wearing of the sacred thread) on auspicious dates given in the Hindu almanac. Irrespective of castes, both male and female babies, six or seven months old, are tonsured at the time of *annaprasan* and are, incidentally, fed the *paramanna-bhog* (rice boiled with milk) of Lord *Taraknath*. But the *upanayan* is exclusively meant for the sons of the *Brahmin* caste of a given age. These two ceremonies are generally held within the sacred complex during the lean pilgrim seasons.

The reference to *mundan* as a traditional religious rite can be bad in the *Skandapurana*.[11] Besides, the *Koran Shareef* has also prescribed this ritual for a devout Muslim in connection with the vow (*wajeb*) undertaken for a pilgrimage (*Hajj*) to *Kaba Shareef* in Mecca, and its consequent fulfilment.[12]

The ritual of *dandi* (prostration) is performed over the years by the regular as well as seasonal pilgrims at Tarakeswar.

It follows the fulfilment of desires, believed to have been possible by the grace of Lord *Siva*. The pilgrim performing this ritual is always found circumventing the temple, or, in some cases, covering a part of the way to the temple through consecutive prostrations, each prostration measuring out the distance equal to the length of the pilgrim's body. This ritual is also followed by those on pilgrimage to Deoghar, where also Lord *Siva* is the presiding deity.

In fact, this ritual is in no way peculiar in relation to the cult of Lord *Siva* as it is generally performed in honour of other gods and goddesses with local as well as regional importance all over India by the devotees. Reference can be made to the performance of the same particularly in honour of the sun-god, on the auspicious date of *Mitra Saptami* in the month of *Agrahayan* (Nov.-Dec.) of the Bengali calendar. However, the aforesaid rituals performed at Tarakeswar always adhere to orthodoxy as the pilgrims are traditionally required to complete the whole process while worshipping Lord *Siva*.

A few of the regular as well as seasonal pilgrims at Tarakeswar also perform the ritual of tying a fragment of a brick to either hair or with a string. Thereafter, the same is fastened together with other similar fragments on an upright column erected at the rear of the temple of Lord *Taraknath*. This ritual, indeed, stands for a prayer for a favour sought for long from the Lord, the fulfilment of which is believed beyond human endeavour. If the pilgrim feels that he or she has been obliged by virtue of divine grace, the necessity of honouring the unilateral contract assumes priority over others.

The Muslims also have a similar folkrite. This is evident not only from their visits to the *Mazar Shareef* of famous *Sufi* saints like Moinuddin Chisti in Ajmer or of Selim Chisti at Fatehpur Sikri but also from the visits to the sacred places associated with the *pirs* elsewhere in India. The hope for the fulfilment of worldly desires similarly acts as a driving force in this context too.

Apart from these, the ritual of inflicting wounds on the chest after the fulfilment of vows on the part of the devotee must also be mentioned. Despite being an abomination to rationalism, this folkrite has its antecedent in the *Sri Sri Chandi* where the king named Surath and his companion Baishya initiate the worship of the Goddess by inflicting wounds on their bodies for her propitiation.[13]

That this ritual is in no way peculiar to the pilgrims at Tarakeswar, is proved from the instance of similar ritual performed by the devotees of Abdul Sakur (*Fakir Baba*) at Tarava in Sonepur, Orissa for the fulfilment of wishes.[14]

Another noteworthy ritual performed by a few regular pilgrims is generally known as *Phul-karani*. With prior permission from the temple administration, the pilgrim is required to sit immediately before the presiding deity with rapt attention and in deep contemplation for sometime along with the priest concerned. The priest makes the ritual vow or *sankalpa* on behalf the pilgrim and ultimately places a few *bilwa*-leaves arranged in a special way on the *Lingam*.

Thereafter, a fully bloomed favourite flower of the Lord is placed over the *bilwa*-leaves. If the flower rolls down onto the stretched palms of the devotee on its own within specified time, it is taken for granted that his or her earnest desire will shortly be fulfilled owing to the divine grace of Lord *Taraknath*.

It seems that pilgrims, generally faced with and frustrated by insurmountable economic, physical as well as mental problems, adhere to this sort of ritual observance to ease their troubles. In fact, the flow of pilgrims over the years and the susceptibility of a few of them to seek miraculous solutions for their diverse socio-economic problems keep this ritual observance alive.

However, all the aforesaid ritual observances are performed almost daily by mid-day, with special emphasis on Monday, the favourite day of Lord *Siva* and also on auspicious dates during the lean seasons, in accordance with the Hindu almanac.

IV

In fact, oracles and miracles have swayed a large number of people around the world from time immemorial. There were a few temples in ancient Greece famous for their mysterious as well as oracular powers.[15] References to such oracular temples in the Iliad, lead us to the conclusion that the west does not lag behind the east in this matter.[16]

However, such a popular oracular temple in Eastern India is that of Lord *Taraknath*. The *dharna* ritual is performed in this place of pilgrimage by a section of pilgrims over the years with reference to this so-called oracular power of the *Lingam*. The *dharnayatris* (pilgrims desirous to performing this ritual) from all castes resort to *dharna* particularly for the curing of their diseases, and lie prostrate before the *Lingam*, vowing to die of starvation if no remedies are suggested to them.[17] A few of them are believed to have visualised the Lord while into a trance, and consequently recovered from incurable diseases by virtue of divine grace. No doubt that reason always takes the back seat in relation to belief in this context. However, the tradition of adhering to this rigorous ritual with an objective in mind, is in vogue till date.[18]

Initially, a *dharnayatri* is required to contact a priest who makes the necessary arrangements for him, resulting in his lying obstinately for days in the *Natyamandira* (court-hall) in front of the temple of Lord *Taraknath* till he receives the *pratyadesh* (direction to overcome crisis) of the Lord. The *dharna* ritual is in no way exclusively associated with Tarakeswar as it is also performed in other temples around India, including Deoghar in Bihar where Lord *Baidyanath*, a manifestation of Lord *Siva*, is the presiding deity.[19]

But, it must be conceded that no other temple has attained such distinction in this context in Eastern India as that of the temple of Lord *Taraknath*. However, the pilgrim desirous of performing this ritual takes shelter in the rest house or rest house-cum-residence of the priest. There the process begins with the cooking of sun-dried rice in an earthen vessel, along with specified vegetables after a holy dip in the *Dudhpukur* (sacred tank) at noon, and the partaking of the *habisyanna* (boiled sun-dried rice) mixed up with *ghee* (clarified butter).

The next morning, the concerned *dharnayatri* takes again a dip in the sacred tank and wears only a loin cloth. Such a pilgrim gets his or her name registered in the *Guddee* of the Tarakeswar estate within the sacred complex, and is then escorted to the temple where the priest directs the taking of the ritual vow or *sankalpa*, with incidental prayers for panacea through divine benediction. Thereafter, the *dharnayatri* sips *charanamrita* (water sanctified through the worship of Lord *Siva*) and is led towards the *Natyamandira* where he or she lies fasting on a new blanket stretched on the marble floor for a number of days with the hope of *prtyadesh* (divine direction) from the Lord. While bearing this ordeal, the *dharnayatri* is required to take a dip in the sacred tank every day whenever necessary without massaging oil on the body and to adhere to other restrictions. It is to be noted that the priest concerned always keeps an eye on his client while he or she is in such an ordeal, and prays regularly for his client through worship to the Lord. While fasting, a *dharnayatri* spends time observing daily rituals from dawn until the late hours of the night, remaining absorbed in the thought of the Lord and listening to the narration of mythological stories from the *Puranas* (*kathakata*) generally arranged in the afternoon within the *Natyamandira* at the behest of the *Tarakeswar Math*. Besides, arrangements for the *chandigan* (song sung in honour of the Goddess *Chandi*) have also been made in the afternoons on the dates and *tithis* of *Purnima* (full moon) and *Amabasya* (new moon) at the same premises. No doubt, these programmes help in the manifestation of divinity already present in the devotees.

Despite these, a few among the *dharnayatris* are believed to be endowed with divine grace within a few days, while in some cases the ritual bears no fruit. The priest, in fact, uses his discretion regarding the continuity of the ritual on the part of those from the second category. Irrespective of success and failure in the observance of this ritual, a *dharnayatri* usually completes his ordeal of *dharna* by offering worship to the presiding deity as directed by the priest. Thereafter, he or she breaks fast by taking the *charanamrita* of the Lord.

In fact, fasting to please a god or goddess has been emphasised from time immemorial for the followers of all religions. Fasting has been referred to as an important act in the *Anushasan Parba* of the *Mahabharata* (166/1) for the expiation of sin as well as the purification of the mind. The Lent festival of the Christians requires a devout Christian to observe a fast on the weekdays during a period of forty days before Easter as penitence.[20] Even a devout Muslim also takes recourse to *roja* or fasting during the entire month of *Ramazan* in order to attain the purification of body and mind.[21] Hence, fasting has always assumed an important role in the context of ritual observances for the followers of almost all the significant religions in this world.

However, the registers preserved in the temple office since the late forties show an increase in the number of *dharna* pilgrims from 3088 in 1945-46 to 3192 in 1950-51. But thereafter, a decrease is noticeable since there were only 2559 such pilgrims performing this ritual in 1960-61. This increased again in the late sixties. It seems striking that while *dharna* pilgrims coming mostly from the rural areas of the districts of Calcutta, Howrah, Hooghly, Burdwan, Midnapur, Nadia and 24 Parganas in West Bengal increased, the number of their Bangladeshi counterparts decreased. This was perhaps a secondary effect of the partition of India. Despite these perceptible developments, this ritual of *dharna* remains popular among a considerable number of people.

V

The ritual observances performed at Tarakeswar involve both folk as well as sanskritised elements. Though these ritual observances initially lead to the fulfilment of *artha* and *kama*, associated with earthly considerations, the ultimate goal remains *moksa* or the desire for overcoming the cycle of birth and death.[22] The citations from the *Gita* refer to this.[23]

Hence, the reason for the congregation of pilgrims at Tarakeswar round the year seems to be the belief that the cult of Lord *Siva* relieves the devotees not only from mundane sufferings but also generates the hope of salvation. Even those who endeavour to achieve material as well as psychological sustenance from the visit to the sacred complex follow the tenets of theology.

Despite the vivid description of these ritual observances with both folk and sanskritised elements, the last *Giri Mohanta* seems to have been silent about the folk rites, except those performed exclusively during the *Gajan* festival.[24] Moreover, the pilgrims on pilgrimage to Tarakeswar from the surrounding regions since the revelation of Lord *Taraknath* or even at the latter stages found no reference in this compilation. In spite of this omission, the fact remains that these ritual observances which are still performed, are similar to those in other *Sivaksetras* with puranic importance.

In fact, the rituals performed by the *Mohantas* as principal *Sebayets* as well as by the *Sebayet* priests for generations, within the temple of Lord *Taraknath* conform to the sanskritised prescription for such rituals. But the last *Giri Mohanta* was most probably against giving due importance to the role of the *Sebayet* priests with reference to ritual observances within the shrine. Neither the aforesaid compilation nor the Title Suit No. 28 of 1922 Under Sec. 92, C. P. C., in which the last *Giri Mohanta* defends himself as the *Malik Sebayet*, bear reference to the *Sebayet* priests as essential for rituals within the temple. However, it has been so despite their presence around the sacred complex for generations almost ever since the revelation of the cult of Lord *Siva*.

It is interesting to note that none of the successors of the *Sebayet* priests was able to show the letter of appointment as proof for strengthening the official standpoint in relation to the organisation of services within the temple since the beginning of the *Giri* regime. Hence, they were definitely at the mercy of the *Giri Mohantas*. This state of affairs ceased after the termination of the *Giri* ascendancy.[25]

The priestcraft that developed during the *Giri* regime was in contrast to its counterpart in the puranic places of pilgrimage all over India as it was devoid of professionalism. This is proved from the apathy to the tradition of maintaining systematic record of the families of clients of the *Sebayet* priests for future reference. This indifference still survives. In the absence of professionalism over the years, the acceptance of priestcraft as the last source of livelihood by the descendants of the *Sebayet* families has become the order of the day. Besides, the change in the outlook of society on the priestcraft over the years also gives rise to adverse reaction, as is obvious at present.

VI

The character of the pilgrim component, as well as its inclination to ritual observances as has been referred to earlier, go through perceptible transformation particularly during the period of fairs and festivals held at Tarakeswar.

The Bengali new year's day or *Poila Baisakh* dawns at this place of pilgrimage usually with the departure of the saffron brigade of Lord *Taraknath* whose congregation has kept up the vibrant tradition of the community festival i.e. *Gajan*. But at the same time it marks the beginning of the *Baisakhi mela* that continues for the entire month of *Baisakh* (April-May) as it "is looked upon as a favourable time for good deeds and for the performance of religious duties. While it lasts, a large number of people, mostly women, come from various parts of the province to pour water over the *Lingam* of *Siva*."[26] Unlike the regular pilgrims, the trek to Tarakeswar for the seasonal pilgrims begins from the *Nimaitirtha Ghat* at Baidyabati in the district of Hooghly. It is so named as Sri Chaitanya (Nimai) is said "to have stopped and bathed here in the Bhagirathi on his way to Orissa." According to prevalent custom, "devotees intending to pour holy waters of the Bhagirathi on the *Taraknath Linga* at Tarakeswar fill their pitchers after a ceremonial bath here and walk all the way to Tarakeswar, 37 k.m. (23 Miles) north-west of Baidyabati, carrying the vessels suspended from the ends of a bamboo pole...."[27] However, the inflow of seasonal as well as regular pilgrims increases specially on the holy *tithis* like *Aksay Tritiya*, *Baisakhi Purnima* and *Samkranti* or the last date of the month of *Baisakh*.

No doubt, the pilgrimage to Tarakeswar for regular pilgrims is naturally less strenuous and less time-consuming in comparison with their seasonal counterparts. The seasonal pilgrims, on this occasion, comprise mostly the younger people who are physically able to endure the strain of a pilgrimage to Tarakeswar on foot not just once in their lives, but also in some cases, a number of times in succession.

Despite this difference, both the regular and seasonal pilgrims are at one with their commitment to solicit help from the priests during this fair, for the offering of oblations to Lord *Siva*. To that extent, the pilgrims in general follow the directions enshrined in the scriptures.[28]

It is, indeed, interesting to note that neither W.W. Hunter's "A Statistical Account of Bengal' nor the *Tarakeswar Sivatattva* edited by Satishchandra Giri refer to this festival which takes place in the month of Baisakh. Only 'Bengal District Gazetteers' by L. S. S. O'Malley and M. M. Chakrabarty bears a casual reference to the *Baisakhi* pilgrims who congregate along with businessmen at this place of pilgrimage on the Bengali new year's day to offer oblations for the opening of new ledgers.

VII

There happens a steady decrease in the flow of pilgrims after *Baisakhi Samkranti*, which continues till the *Gurupurnima* (the tithi meant for the worship of the preceptor). In fact, the *Sravani mela* begins on the *Gurupurnima* which usually occurs in the month of *Ashar* of the Bengali calendar year, and continues thereafter till the *Rakhipurnima* (the festival of tying embellished thread on the wrist) that generally takes place in the month of *Sravan* of the same year. In fact, "the month of *Sravan* (mid-July to mid-August) is auspicious for *Siva* when *Sravani utsab* are held on each Monday.[29]

Although the *Sravani mela* has assumed an immense proportion at present by virtue of the improved communication and the influence of mass media, the reference to this can be had neither in Hunter's 'A Statistical Account of Bengal' nor in O' Malley's Gazetteers. Even the *Tarakeswar Sivatattva* is silent on the initiation of the *Sravani utsab*, which seems to have surpassed all other fairs and festivals in splendour and variety these days. Besides, the processing of the Title Suit No. 28 of 1922 that resulted in the end of the *Giri* regime in 1937 also bears no reference to pilgrims who visit the shrine on this particular occasion. Despite this, Prafulla Chakrabarty credits the last *Giri Mohanta* of the *Tarakeswar Math* with the introduction of the *Sravani mela* at Tarakeswar.[30]

In fact, the non-Bengalis mostly native to U.P. and Bihar, form the majority among the pilgrims during the *Sravani utsab* which is known also as *Marwari mela*. Besides them, non-Bengali Hindus from almost all over India throng here along with those from Calcutta and surrounding regions.[31]

Presumably, the erstwhile connection between this place of pilgrimage and U.P. as well as Bihar during the tenures of the last two *Giri Mohantas*, which has been referred to elsewhere, had something to do with the beginning of this festival. It is somewhat interesting to note that this festival takes place at the same time as that of Lord *Baidyanath* in Deoghar. Incidentally, the *Kaonrias* of Deoghar in Bihar and those attending this festival here, bear a certain resemblance in the given context.

Prior to their trek from *Nimaitirtha Ghat* in Hooghly or from Kalighat in Calcutta on barefeet, they wear new ochre-coloured loincloths and use bamboo shafts for carrying the sacred water of the Ganges in earthen or brass or bronze vessels. The beginning of the pilgrimage is similar to that of their *Baisakhi* counterparts. The journey begins generally in the afternoon or in the evening so that they can reach the destination early in the morning of the next day. The starting points of the *Sravani* pilgrims may be different but they are destined to reach and use the traditional main pilgrim-route, i.e. the Baidyabati - Tarakeswar road.

The seasonal pilgrims on pilgrimage to Tarakeswar throughout the year come from all walks of life and the *Sravani* pilgrims are no exception to that. But while on the road, as it happens elsewhere, the pilgrims adhere to equality and forget the differences among themselves, at least temporarily. Here lies, in fact, the basic strength of Hinduism, in the display of its traditional uniformity.

The seasonal pilgrims usually get no respite from sufferings even after coming close to the entrance of the temple as the same is used as the exit as well. Besides, the lack of adequate space within the temple only adds to their sufferings. The phenomenal increase in the flow of "pilgrims offering prayers to Lord *Siva*" on auspicious dates and *tithis* of the season makes it impossible for all of them to enter the temple and perform ritual observances.[32]

Noticeably, the female participants of the Bengali *Sravani* pilgrims are accustomed to performing ritual fast till the *bhogarati* (the ritual feeding ceremony of the Lord) is performed in the afternoon, on Mondays. Thereafter they have breakfast with fruits and cereals of specified kinds.

While going back from this place of pilgrimage, the *Sravani* pilgrims in general collect *prasad* (consecrated food) and *charanamrita* (water collected from the silver girdle of Lord *Siva*).

This *Sravani* festival held in association with the *Sravani* pilgrims gives rise to social cohesion and cultural unity. These are achieved through mutual co-operation between the pilgrims and those residing along the pilgrim-route, as well as the residents of this sacred complex.

VIII

The only noteworthy festival at this place of pilgrimage in the month of *Bhadra* (Aug.-Sept.) is the *Janmastami*, the anniversary of the birth of Lord *Krishna*. This festival, mostly a local affair, continues till midnight and the temple remains open until the worship is over. The whole process, however, requires the co-ordinated work of the *Sebayet* priests as well as the caste *Gopas* responsible for the organisation of services within the sacred complex. This traditional festival had been held even during the regime of the last *Giri Mohanta*, as is proved from the news items published with reference to it in The Bengalee as well as in The Statesman.[33]

Traditionally, the caste *Gopas* arrange for an embellished palanquin, to take the deity of *Laksmi-Narayan* from the temple within the monastery to that of Lord *Taraknath*, on the evening of this auspicious *tithi*. The *Sebayet* priests on duty take possession of the deity with due reverence as soon as the palanquin reaches the temple of Lord *Siva* in procession. After the celebration is over, the deity is carried back to the monastery with the same gaiety. As the festival continues till midnight, a few regular pilgrims as well as local people remain present until the conclusion of the festival.

The dawn of the next day becomes resonant with the cheerful voices of teenagers from the families of caste *Gopas* who participate in the frolic of *Nandotsab*, reminiscent of the boundless joy of king Nanda, King of the caste *Gopas*, after the birth of Lord *Krishna*. The *dharnayatris* are generally shifted elsewhere from the *Natyamandira* beforehand to facilitate the frolic that accompanies the *Nandotsab*. This, infact, exemplifies the eagerness of the *Giri Mohantas* to achieve a compromise with the *lokayata* (popular) culture.

IX

"The next month *Aswin* (Sept.-Oct.) is a highly auspicious month with the Hindus, as the *Durgapuja* takes place in it."[34] The *Durgapuja* is held accordingly within the temple of Lord *Taraknath* with great religious fervour. The painted image of the Goddess *Durga*, the variform of the consort of Lord *Siva*, is on the north-east inner wall of the temple and the special worship of the Goddess is traditionally arranged in accordance with the Hindu almanac.

Reference has already been made to the inclination of the *Giri Mohantas* to perform the *Saktipuja* simultaneously, alongside an unwavering commitment to the presiding deity. Despite the reluctance of the District Judge to admit the *Giri Mohantas* as *Tantrik Sannyasis* in his order dated 6 Nov., 1929 with reference to T.S. NO 28/1922, the fact remains that the last *Giri Mohanta* was somewhat correct in his assertion in this regard from an academic point of view.

In fact, perfect knowledge leads definitely to the revelation of the indivisible existence of *Siva* and *Sakti*, which precipitates the ultimate realisation of the power of *Sakti* as an imperative for emancipation from the cycle of birth and death.[35] This realisation perhaps led them to initiate the *Saktipuja*, with simultaneous emphasis on the *Tantrik* as well as *Vedic* rituals, as a means to achieve the will-power to renounce the world.[36] However, the overlapping of both types of ritual observances has incidentally been conceded in the *Srimadbhagabat*.[37] Hence, the proposition of the District Judge, drawing an exclusive dividing line between the *Tantrik* and *Vedic Sannyasis* with reference to the rituals observed, seems incorrect.

However, the worship of the Goddess follows tradition, with the exception of animal sacrifice to the Goddess. The alternative to animal sacrifice must have been introduced after the installation of the *Ashram* order in 1937 at the *Tarakswar Math*. The overt inclination of the *Giri Mohantas* to the *Tantrik* rites perhaps drew strength from the citation in the *Sri Sri Chandi*.[38]

The whole process of worship ends with the *Dhawjapuja* on the morning of *Bijoya Dashami* symbolising the impact of primitive community worship on that of the gods and goddesses mentioned in the Brahminical literature.[39] This ritual again remains a proof of compromise with the *lokayata* (popular) culture on the part of the upholders of Brahminical religion. However, the planting of the pole adorned with the *Dhawja* on the periphery of the sacred complex reminds one the lost splendour of the temple - *zamindari* which had evolved during the *Giri* regime.

Usually, the regular pilgrims are not allowed to enter the temple of Lord *Taraknath* until the worship of the Goddess is over on these auspicious *tithis* in association with those engaged in the organisation of services in the temple.

X

The fervour of the *puja* that begins in this place of pilgrimage with the *Durgapuja* continues till the night of *Diwali*, which is usually dedicated to the worship of the Goddess *Kali*. Reference has already been made to the initiation of the cult of the Goddess *Kali* by the second *Giri Mohanta* and the consequent endeavour of the twenty-second incumbent to erect a temple for the Goddess within the sacred complex. These, in fact, speak much for the inclination of the *Giri Sannyasis* at the *Tarakeswar Math* to *Saktipuja* through the *Tantrik* rites. Besides, the assertion of the last *Giri Mohanta* in this context, cited earlier, proves it.

Traditionally, a *Sebayet* priest is bestowed upon the responsibility of making arrangements for the regular as well as special worship on annual basis, in association with other priests within the temple of the Goddess. The special worship arranged on the night of *Diwali* in the month of *Kartik* (Oct.-Nov.) of the Bengali calendar year adheres to the *Tantrik* rites but with some modifications as are evident in the context of the *Durgapuja* at present.[40] In fact, *Saktipuja* in general and *Kalipuja* in particular seem inconceivable without the *Tantrik* rites.

This sort of development over the years has definitely created an ambience against which the sectarian affiliation of a considerable number of *Sebayet* priests to *Sakta* sect is revealed despite their dependence on Lord *Taraknath* for sustenance.

It is, however, interesting to note that neither the regular nor the seasonal pilgrims are allowed to enter the temple of the Goddess as they do in case of the presiding deity. They instead, are required to offer oblations only through *Sebayet* priests, in keeping with tradition.

XI

Reference has already been made to W.W. Hunter's observation with regard to two large religious gatherings at Tarakeswar, of which *Sivaratri*, held on the fourteenth *tithi* after full moon in the month of *Phalgun* (Feb.-Mar.), necessitates elucidation. Besides, O'Malley's Gazetteers also bears reference to a large *mela* (congregation) held at Tarakeswar in connection with *Sivaratri* festival.[41] But it seems curious that on no occasion the last *Giri Mohanta* referred to such an important festival held traditionally in this place of pilgrimage. This seems more obvious in the event of the publication of news regarding this festival in the *Ananda Bazar Patrika* and the *Amrita Bazar Patrika* on the eve of the *Satyagraha* movement, 1924 when he was in power at the *Tarakeswar Math*.[42]

In fact, "the ceremonies enjoined on this occasion are considered by the followers of *Siva* to be the most sacred of all their observances."[43] "It is primarily a woman's festival and most of the connected rituals are observed by devotees of the fair sex. Unmarried women fast and perform rites on this occasion to be blessed with tolerant husbands like *Siva*. Married women observe the same rituals with an identical prayer and for having children."[44] The three essential observances of the *Sivaratri* are fasting by day and night, holding a vigil at night and "worshipping *Siva* as the marvellous and interminable *Lingam*......".[45] This ritual observances result in "expiating all sins and securing the attainment of all desires during life, and union with *Siva*, or final emancipation, after death ... According to the *Ishana Samhita*, it was on this day that *Siva* first manifested himself as a marvellous and interminable *Linga*.... to typify the exaltation of *Siva* worship over that of *Vishnu* and *Brahma*, an event which no doubt at one time took place."[46]

The offerings during the whole ceremony generally include fruits and flowers of specified kinds, *bilwa*-leaves, incense-sticks and candles. While holding a vigil at night the devotee concerned is required to ritually bathe the Lord with milk in the first watch, in the second with curds, in the third with *ghee* and in the fourth with honey along with the customary prostration in the end of each watch in accordance with the directions of the *Sebayet* priest who leads in the rituals as well as prayers to Lord *Taraknath*.

The *Anadilingam* remains accessible to the pilgrims irrespective of castes throughout the night. As it happens round the year, casteism does not matter much for the regular as well as seasonal pilgrims on pilgrimage to Tarakeswar. That "the worship of Lord *Siva* at the time of *Sivaratri*, is permitted to all castes, even to *Chandals* and to women", had been acknowledged by H.H. Wilson in his 'Essays on the Religion of the Hindus'.

These ritual observances, in the belief of the devotees, elevate them to such an extent that they find themselves close to the Lord and enjoy the benefits of this as illustrated by the following legend given in the second part of the *Sivapurana*. Being benighted in the woods, once a fowler took shelter on the branches of a *bilwa*-tree (wood-apple) in a state of perpetual vigil owing to the dread of prowling and ferocious animals. He was completely unaware of the incidental importance of that auspicious night as it was *Sivaratri*. However, he was forced to remain awake through the night which was devoted to fasting and penitence. Incidentally, a few *bilwa*-leaves soaked in blood oozing from the wounds of his body were cast down on a deserted *Lingam* under the tree. Lord *Siva* was very pleased with the fowler and rewarded him for his involuntary observance of rites of the *Sivaratri*. The fowler was graced with the boon of securing the attainment of all his desires during his life, along with final emancipation after death. This legend, indeed, symbolises the accessibility of even the lower caste people to the worship of Lord *Siva*. The congregation of a large number of lower caste people, coming mostly from rural Bengal to this place of pilgrimage corroborates the aforesaid proposition. In fact, the three main conceptions of this divinity-*Siva*, the creator, *Siva*, the *Yogi* and *Rudra*, the destroyer-in the Brahminical *Puranas* are meaningful only in a very extended sense in the context of *Siva* worship in Bengal.[47]

"Although the religious ceremony in connection with the *Sivaratri* only lasts one night, a considerable *mela* or fair, which is held near the shrine on the occasion, continues for three days" and as many as "twenty-thousand people annually visit Tarakeswar shrine on the occasion of the *Sivaratri*."[48] Hunter's observation, made as early as 1876, with reference to the inflow of pilgrims during this festival differs considerably from the estimate given in the *Yugantar* after almost eighty-six years. It estimates the volume of the same from different parts of West Bengal at more than one *lakh*, thus pointing to the steady increase in the number over the years.[49]

Besides the regular pilgrims, a common sight on this occasion 'is the endless stream' of seasonal ones. They behave like their other seasonal counterparts and usually reach this pilgrim town on barefeet from Baidyabati with the water of the Ganges collected in small pitchers.[50] A considerable number of non-Bengali pilgrims are also found among the regular as well as seasonal pilgrims. But their number gradually decreases during the afternoon with the consequent increase in the number of Bengali pilgrims thronging at this place of pilgrimage.[51]

The flow of homeward-bound pilgrims begins generally at the end of the *Sivachaturdashi tithi*. While going back, they collect *prasad* (consecrated food) and *charanamrita* (water collected from the silver girdle) of Lord *Taraknath*.

XII

The *Dol* ceremony of *Laksmi-Narayan* which takes place in *Phalgun* (Feb-March) is also an important festival of Tarakeswar.[52] The *Dol utsab* (festival of colour) is a local celebration held on *Dol Purnima* (full moon), immediately after the *Sivaratri* and prior to the initiation of the *Gajan* festival on the first date of *Chaitra*, the last month in the Bengali calendar year. This spring-festival has been celebrated at this place of pilgrimage from time immemorial.[53]

As it happens on the occasion of *Janmastami*, this festival also centres on Lord *Laksmi-Narayan* who is placed during this festival on a *Dolmancha* (pedestal used for this festival) in the lawn adjacent to the monastery. The process begins with the *Chanchar utsab* (festival in relation to the burning of an effigy of a demon) held in the evening of the day before *Dol utsab*, within the Sahapur garden-house, in keeping with the tradition developed from the *Giri* regime. Initially, the caste *Gopas*, as they do during the *Janmastami* festival, carry the idol of Lord *Laksmi-Narayan* from the temple at the *Tarakeswar Math* to that of the presiding deity of the sacred complex. Hence, the ritual of exchanging *abir* (coloured powder) between *Hari* (Lord *Vishnu*) and *Hara* (Lord *Siva*) takes place in the presence of the *Sebayet* priests and others associated with the religious organisation of the temple complex.

After the completion of this ritual, the idol of Lord *Laksmi-Narayan* is taken back to the Sahapur garden-house where a special worship of the deity again takes place. Thereafter, the house temporarily set up for the *Chanchar utsab* is set on fire to the delight of a large number of onlookers, most of whom are locals.

At the dawn of the next day, the festival of colour begins immediately after the idol is customarily placed in the cradle erected on the *Dolmancha*. Irrespective of castes, the participants indulge in this festival and the whole of this pilgrim town gets a coat of bright colour on this holy occasion.[54]

Hence, the admixture of different trends in Hinduism has been the appreciable feature of this place of pilgrimage since the *Giri* regime. This was possible because of the cosmopolitan outlook of the *Giri Mohantas*, who patronised the *Janmastami* as well as the *Holi* festivals despite their inclination to the *Saktipuja* in this place of pilgrimage.

XIII

The last important festival held at the end of the Bengali calendar year in this place of pilgrimage is the *Gajan* festival. Presumably, the word *Gajan* derives from the din created by the village people in a congregation.[55] This festival is another vital proof of the assimilation of Brahminical rituals with popular religious rites or *lokacharas* that has been an important feature at Tarakeswar ever since the revelation of the cult of *Anadilingam*.

Interestingly enough, the worship of *Dharmathakur* and the worship of Lord *Siva* have found a common context in the *lokayata* (popular) form of *Saivism*. Hence, the *Gajan* festival, arranged in honour of *Dharmathakur*, was popular among the non-*Aryan* community. In fact, the worship of Lord *Siva* had become popular particularly in rural Bengal from time immemorial especially due to the interest shown by participants from the lower stratum of society.[56] However, the *lokadharma* or popular religion had gradually transformed the *Dharmathakur* into a village deity with the consequent evolution of the *Gajan* in the *Rarh* region. This *Gajan* festival gradually made way for the devotees of Lord *Siva* with the incidental transformation of the cult of Lord *Siva* into a village deity, adored mostly by the lower-caste people in the rural areas by virtue of the endeavours of the priestly community.[57] Often, the similarity of the rituals connected with the *Gajan* festival of *Dharma* and that of Lord *Siva* is emphasised to show the essential unity of the two godheads, as a result of which this festival is held to have become "one of the most popular of all religious ceremonies in West Bengal."[58]

It happens so, simply because of the change over from the *Vedic* concept of *Rudra* to the puranic concept of Lord

Siva as the creator or the *Yogi*.[59] Besides, the depiction of Lord *Siva* as a benign god in the medieval *Sivayanakavyas* "with power of endowing the earth with fertility" and "as a reluctant peasant" as well as "an inefficient head of a large household" in the *Mangalakavyas* facilitates this change.[60] Some say that the *Gajan* festival held in honour of Lord *Siva* has its antecedent in the religious ambience of Bengal prior to the Muslim conquest.[61]

However, the reference to the *Gajan* festival held traditionally at Tarakeswar can be had not only in W.W. Hunter's 'A Statistical Account of Bengal' but also in L. S. S. O. Malley's 'Bengal District Gazetteers'. Besides, the *Tarakeswar Sivatattva* edited by the last *Giri Mohanta* also bears reference to this festival with special emphasis on the rituals to be performed by the ascetics of Lord *Taraknath*.[62] Moreover, specific reference to this festival has also been made in the *Amrita Bazar Patrika* in connection with the *Satyagraha* movement against the last *Giri Mohanta* of the *Tarakeswar Math*.[63]

This place of pilgrimage is visited "during the whole of month of *Chaitra* (March-Apr.) by a large number of persons from the surrounding neighbourhood within a circuit of 40 or 50 miles" and the devotees "generally belong to the lower castes, who come to perform some penance, or to lead an ascetic life for a time, in fulfilment of a vow made to *Siva* in time of sickness or in danger, or in order to gain a reputation for piety"[64] "Throughout the month of *Chaitra* many devotees embrace *Sannyasa* to propitiate *Taraknath* by putting on saffron-coloured clothes, fasting during the day and taking their meals only after sunset."[65] Customarily, the priority for embracing *Sannyasa* during this festival rests with the family of Mukunda Ghosh.[66] Hence, the *Mul Sannayasi* or principal ascetic is chosen from among the successors to Mukunda

Ghosh in recognition of the importance of the caste *Gopas* in the revelation of Lord *Taraknath*.[67]

Usually, the initiation into *Sannyasa* materialises only when the priest concerned puts the *uttariya* (hand-woven cotton threads tied together with a tuft of *Kusha* grass) around the neck of the devotee, while chanting a *mantra* (incantation) : *atmagotram parityajya sivagotre pravisatu* (enter into the clan of Lord *Siva*, leaving the one of self). Austerity must be practised for the whole month. But in case of one's inability to go through the rigours of *Sannyasa* for the entire month of *Chaitra*, the devotee concerned is allowed to opt for *Sannyasa* only on days bearing odd numbers (3,5,7,9,15 and 17) in the auspicious month.[68] Once initiated into *Sannyasa*, a devotee is often found holding a stick made up of reeds.

L. S. S. O'Malley's assertion that "throughout the month of *Chaitra*, *Sudras* fast during the day-time, taking their meals only after sunset, as in the *Ramazan* fast of the *Muhammadans*" is not correct.[69] In fact, the *Brahmins*, the *Kshatriyas*, the *Baishyas* as well as the *Sudras* are allowed initiation into *Sannyasa* so long as they show due commitment to ritual observances.[70]

However, the enormity of the congregation on the occasion of the *Gajan* festival makes a broad regional division of the visitors a necessity. "The fair on the first four days of the eleven over which it is held is primarily earmarked for pilgrims from the south, coming mostly from Midnapur, Howrah, Southern parts of 24 parganas and Arambag subdivision and is called the *Dakne mela*. The *Purbe mela*, generally attended by pilgrims from eastern districts like Murshidabad, Nadia and North 24 paraganas, starts on the fifth day while visitors from Howrah, Hooghly, Calcutta and

Burdwan come after the ninth day. The eighth day is set apart for the pilgrims from Ramnagar, a nearby village."[71] Pilgrims from the districts of Jessore and Khulna in Bangladesh also visit Tarakeswar on this occasion.[72]

Generally, a *Gajan Sannyasi* partakes of *habisyanna* prepared of three handfuls of sun-dried rice boiled with milk and molasses in the evening, thus devoting the day to fasting and penitence.[73] This begins on the date of initiation into *Sannyasa* and continues until twenty-seventh day of *Chaitra*, marked as *Mahahabisya*-day (the concluding day for partaking of *habisyanna*).

The day after *Mahahabisya* is observed as the *Phal*-day (the day specified for offering fruits to the Lord). On this date, the *Gajan Sannyasis* along with the *Mul Sannyasi* achieve a state of frenzy, swinging swiftly the thorny twigs of the acacia tree and running all the way to Tarakeswar from Ramnagar.[74] Soon after they reach the sacred complex, there begins the rhythmic dance with the beating of drums by these *Sannyasis*, while they circulate the temple of the Lord. Then begins the ritual of *Kantajhanp* (jumping into the bed of thorns). On this date, they usually eat fruits in the evening, only when the rituals are over.

The *Gajan* festival tends to a climax on the next day, with that of the *Nil utsab* (the marriage anniversary of Lord *Siva*). The deity is dressed like a groom with a *topar* or conical *shola*-hat on the head. The *Sannyasis* assemble around the temple to light up earthen lamps and candles in the evening to celebrate the anniversary. The women in particular take part in this ritual, known as *Niler bati* with the incantation of *mantras* in the presence of the priests and breakfast therafter.[75] Traditionally, a spectacular procession reaches the temple, with the *Mohanta* in the palanquin to preside over the ceremony which is celebrated with a firework display in the evening.[76] A considerable number of *Gajan Sannyasis* leave Tarakeswar for home after this ceremony only to complete the remaining part of the ritual there.

The *Gajan* festival ends on the *Charak Samkranti* or the last day of the Bengali calendar year. The *Charakpuja* or the swinging festival "is celebrated with some pomp, more particularly at Tarakeswar" and "on this occasion men swing from high poles."[77] Usually, the *Gajan Sannyasis* undergo various forms of physical mortification sometimes by holding stalks in their mouth or "by walking upon live embers, throwing themselves down from a height, piercing their body and tongue with pincers, etc." with the desire for "obtaining favours from *Siva* and as an expiation for their sins." However, these practices along with the swinging festival, by means of hooks pierced through the fleshy muscles on both sides of the spine are now prohibited by order of the Government.[78] These rituals have not been replaced even by alternatives today.

In fact, the *Charakpuja*, which is associated with the rituals performed in honour of *Dharmathakur*, has intruded into the ritual observances associated with the cult of Lord *Siva*.[79]

This festival enters the concluding phase with the casting off of the *uttariya*, the ritual threads, by the *Gajan* pilgrims. Prior to this, they take a dip in the *Dudhpukur* (sacred tank), and appear before the priests concerned, who reinitiate them into their own clans by renouncing that of Lord *Siva*. This they do with the utterance of the incantation : '*sivagotram parityajya atmagotre pravisatu*' (enter into the clan of the self, leaving the one of Lord *Siva*).

Usually, these seasonal pilgrims perform *mundan, dandi* and all the other rituals as are performed by the regular pilgrims. They find no constraint of time at all in this context as most of them stay at Tarakeswar for a couple of days as compared to their counterparts.

As these pilgrims are mostly from rural areas of Bengal and elsewhere, their socio-economic background is embedded largely in agriculture. A large number of them are found coming to Tarakeswar in groups, owing to the nature of their commitment. Hunter has estimated the number of *Gajan* pilgrims at 'about fifteen thousand.'[80] This figure has risen very sharply with the inclusion of those not only from different parts of West Bengal and Bangladesh but also from Orissa, Bihar and Assam.[81] A large number of them are also found throughout this month fetching the water of the Ganges as happens in the case of other seasonal pilgrims. But with their comparatively unsophisticated socio-economic background, they are less prone to recreation while on pilgrimage.

Therefore, the sanskritised ritual observances mingled with popular rites provide this festival with a distinctive character, while reinforcing traditional values. Besides, this community festival also paves the way for the enjoyment of the fruits of group solidarity, achieved through an awareness of universal brotherhood. This was so strong that the *Giri Mohantas* through ages dared not to take on it despite their commitment to the sanskritised ritual observances. This tradition continues even today at the behest of the *Ashram Mohantas* of the *Tarakeswar Math*.

XIV

The pilgrimage to Tarakeswar and its bearing on fairs and festivals over the years make it amply clear that this pilgrim centre accommodates people from all the castes on the common platform of Hinduism. In fact, caste considerations and occupations do not stand on the way to interaction between the priestly community and devotees of Lord *Taraknath* or between the pilgrims and the local people. This kind of interaction which prevails at Tarakeswar seems peculiar, given the background of an otherwise caste-ridden and stratified society.

Despite this outstanding development, estimates of the specific number of pilgrims belonging to various castes over the years, are very difficult to obtain from the families of the traditional *Sebayet* priests. This is because, these families are not in the habit of maintaining the registers, bearing the names of their clients serially as are done today by their counterparts in other puranic places of pilgrimage.

A critical survey of the inflow of pilgrims over period of a few years, however, reveals that Tarakeswar as a place of pilgrimage has been visited and sometimes revisited by those belonging to certain specific castes. Of these, the *Brahmins*, the *Kayasthas*, the *Baidyas*, the *Mahisyas*, the *Sadgopas*, the *Tilis*, the *Gandhabaniks*, the *Gopas*, the *Modaks*, the *Kumbhakars*, the *Tantis*, the *Kansaris*, the *Napits*, the *Swarnabaniks*, the *Sunris*, the *Namasudras*, the *Baishyas*, the *Poundra-kshatriyas*, the *Dhopas* are noticeable. Incidentally, the pilgrims belonging to high as well as mid-level castes contribute to the maximum number of regular pilgrims while the *Baisakhi* and *Sravani* pilgrims come from all the castes. However, the low-caste pilgrims are found in greater number among those coming during the *Sivaratri* and *Gajan* festivals. These figures, which have been roughly consistent over the last few years, lead one to conclude that these trends have their source somewhere in the past.

The proximity to this place of pilgrimage and ritual commitment contribute possibly to the higher frequency of visits by those who are regular pilgrims from the aforesaid castes. Usually the majority of the pilgrims from high and middle castes are professionals or are involved in commercial activities, whereas those coming mostly during the *Sivaratri* and *Gajan* festivals are agriculturists.

It is interesting to note that all the pilgrims wish to achieve spiritual peace, irrespective of their socio-economic background. But those from the lower-caste groups desire panaceas from the presiding deity. Hence, they visit this place of pilgrimage more frequently than the others. However, the study of caste divisions so far as the *dharnayatris* are concerned does not show any significant change during the period under review. Therefore, Tarakeswar remains and will remain, if time permits, an important place of pilgrimage attracting pilgrims from all walks of life.

Note

1. Raja Radhakanta Deb - 'Savdakalpdrumah'. Part - II. PP. - 626-629. The Chowkhamba Sanskrit Series Office. Varanasi 1961.

2. Krishnachandra Smrititirtha (ed.) - Aryachar Paddhati or Purohit-Darpan. Vol. II. 'ParishistaKhanda'. Chap. - Tirthakrityaprakaran. PP. - 51-136.

3. Swami Saradananda - Sri Sri Ramakrishna Lila Prasanga. Vol. I. PP. - 139-171.

4. Swami Saradananda - Sri Sri Ramakrishna Lila Prasanga. Vol I. P.-346.

5. S. K. Mitra - Hooghly Jelar Itihas O Bangasamaj. Vol. II. P.-1114.

6. W. W. Hunter - A Statistical Account of Bengal. Vol. III. Districts of Midnapur and Hugli (including Howrah). P.-307 and PP. - 324-328.

7. L. S. S. O'Malley and M. M. Chakrabarty - Bengal District Gazetteers. Hooghly. PP. - 320-323.

8. Ibid. - Bengal District Gazetteers. Hooghly. P.-106.

9. A. K. Banerjee - West Bengal District Gazetteers (Hooghly). P.-574.

10. Krishnachandra Smrititirtha (ed.) - Aryachar Paddhati or Purohit Darpan. 'Parishista Khanda'. Vol. II. PP.-78 and 85.
Also,
Swai Saradananda - Sri Sri Ramakrishna Lila Prasanga. Vol. I. P.-320.

11. Mundancopavasasca sarvatirthesvayam vidhih Varjjayitva Gayam Gangam Visalam Virajam tatha (*Mundan* (tonsure) and *upabasa* (fasting) are to be performed at all the places of pilgrimage excluding Gaya, places in close vicinity to the Ganges, Visala as well as Viraja.)

Krishnachandra Smrititirtha (ed.) - Aryachar Paddhati or Purohit Darpan. Vol. II. P.-131. 'Parishista Khanda'.

12. Koran Shareef - 3(95-97).

13. Niraharau yataharau tanmanaskau samahitou Dadatustau valincaiva nijagatrasrguksitam 'Surathavaisyayorvarapradanam'. 13/11.
(They began to worship the Goddess with rapt attention through sacrifices soaked with blood from wounds on their bodies while remaining in fast or controlled diet.) Sri Sitaramdas Onkarnath (ed.) - Sri Sri Chandi.

14. The Statesman - 2.11.1998 (Photograph with information on P.-2).

15. Herodotus - The Histories. (1/53).

16. J. Precope - Medicine, Magic and Mythology. P.-260.

17. S. K. Mitra - Tarakeswarer Itikatha. P.-11.

18. Ashok Mitra (ed.) - Paschim Banger Puja Parban O Mela. Vol. II. P.-604.

19. H. H. Risley - The Tribes and Castes of Bengal. P.-365.

20. Ashok Mitra (ed.) - Paschim Banger Puja Parban O Mela. 'Prasangiki'.
Also,
A. S. Hornby - Oxford Advanced Learner's Dictionary of Current English. P. - 484.

21. Koran Shareef - Sura Bakarah - Ayat : 183-187.

22. L. P. Vidyarthi, B. N. Saraswati and M. Jha - The Sacred Complex of Kashi, a Microcosom of Indian Civilization. P.-53.

23. 'Caturvidha bhajante mam janah sukrtinorjuna/Arto jijnasurartharthi jnani ca bharatarsabha//"The Gita" - (7/16).

Oh Arjuna! I am usually worshipped by the artas (those striken by inordinate mundane problems), *jijnasus* (those desirous of gaining etarnal knowledge), *artharthis* (those goaded by the lure of wealth) and the *jnanis* (those already overwhelmed by the joy of eternal knowledge or *moksa*).

24. Satishchandra Giri - Tarakeswar Sivatattva. PP. - 81-87.

25. Interview with Monomohoan Chakrabarty, ex-Secretary (1978-83) of the Purohit Mandali (Association of the Priests) at Tarakeswar on 9.6.97.

26. L. S. S. O'Malley and M. M. Chakrabarty - Bengal District Gazetteers. Hooghly. P.-103.

27. A. K. Banerjee - West Bengal District Gazetteers. Hooghly. P.-655.

28. Yattirtham yasya devasya tat tirthasya dvijasya ca Vandaniyasya pujyasya tesam vakyena putata (Yogini Tantra)
The presiding deity of a certain place of pilgrimage and the assoiated sacred specialists deserve due reverence from the pilgrims concerned with firm commitment to the directions of the said community.
Krishnachandra Smrititirtha (ed.) - Aryachar Paddhati or Purohit Darpan. 'Parishista Khanda'. P.-132.

29. A. K. Banerjee (ed.) - West Bengal District Gazetteers. Hooghly. PP. - 665 and 725.

30. P. Chakrabarty - Social Profile of Tarakeswar. P.-24.

31. Ashok Mitra (ed.) - Paschim Banger Puja Parban O Mela. Vol. II. PP. - 604-606. Also, S. K. Mitra - Hooghly Jelar Itihas O Bangasamaj. Vol. II. P.-1125.

32. The Statesman - July, 22; 1996.

33. The Bengalee - 24.08.24; 5(1).
Also,
The Statesman - 26.8.24; 6(3).

34. L. S. S. O'Malley and M. M. Chakrabarty - Bengal District Gazetteers. Hooghly. P.-103.

35. Sivasaktimayani tattvam tattvajnanasya karanam Vahunam janmanamante saktijnanam prajayate Saktijnanam bina devi nirvanam naiva jayate Niruttar Tantra

(Perfect knowledge regarding the existence of Siva and *Sakti* in unison results in the ultimate realisation of the power of *Sakti* as an imperative for emancipation from the cycle of birth and death.) Shibchandra Vidyarnab - Tantratattva. P.-28.

36. Ya asu hrdayagranthini nirjjihirsuh paratmanah/Vidhinopacare-dedevami tantroktena ca kesavam//Srimadbhagabat. Part. - XI. Chap. III. Sloka. -47
(One should worship Lord Kesagba (*Krishna*) through *Vedic* as well as *Tantrik* methods with the view of renouncing the world at the earliest.)
Also,
Vaidikastantrikomisraitimetribidhomakhah Trayanamipsitenaiva vidhina mam samarcayet Ibid. Part.-XI. Chap. XXVII. Sloka - 7.

(One could achieve the cherished goal by virtue of worshipping the Lord through either the *Vedic* or the *Tantrik* method or the admixture of the both.)

37. Evam kriyayogapathaih puman Vaidika - Tantrikaih Arccannubhayatah siddhim matto vindatyabhipsitam Ibid. Part-XI. Chap. XXVII. Sloka-49.

(One could be endowed with the blessing of the Lord in this mortal world as well as in the heaven by virtue of worshipping through the *Vedic* and *Tantrik* methods.)

38. Janata ajanata vapi valipujam tatha krtam Praticchisyamaham pritya vanhihomani tatha krtam Sarat kale mahapuja kriyate ya ca varsiki Tasyam mamaitanmahatmyam srutva bhaktisamanvitah Sri Sri Chandi. Chap. XII. Sloka-XI-XII.

(I remain ever satisfied with him and endow his with my blessing for the fulfilment of ghis worldly desires if he arranges *bali* (animal sacrifice) and *homa* (ritual fire) for worshipping me accordingly or not in the autumn on annual basis along with citation from *Sri Sri Chandi*.)

39. Nihar Ranjan Roy - Bangalir Itihas. PP. - 579-580.

40. Interview with the Sebayet priest of the Goddess Kali on 7.11.98.

41. L. S. S. O'Malley and M. M. Chakrabarty - Bengal District Gazetteers. Hooghly. P.-104.

42. Ananda Bazar Patrika - 20.2.24.
Also,
Amrita Bazar Patrika - 28.2.24.

43. Imperial Gazetteer of India, Provindial Series. Bengal. Vol. I. P.-336.

44. A. K. Banerjee - West Bengal District Gazetteers. Hooghly. P.-207.

45. Imperial Gazetteer of India. Provincial Series. Bengal. Vol. I. P.-336. Also, L. S. S. O'Malley and M. M. Chakrabarty - Bengal District Gazetteers. Hooghly. P.-106.

46. H. H. Wilson - Essays on the Religion of the Hindus. Vol. II. PP.-211-219.

47. A. K. Banerjee (ed.) - West Bengal District Gazetteers. Hooghly. P.-205.

48. W. W. Hunter - A Statistical Account of Bengal. Vol. III. Districts of Midnapur and Hugli (including Howrah). P.-327.

49. Yugantar - 5 March, 1962.

50. A. K. Banerjee - West Bengal District Gazetteers. Hooghly. P.-725.

51. Basumati - 27 Phalgun, 1365 B.S.

52. A. K. Banerjee - West Bengal District Gazetteers. Hooghly. P.-725.

53. S. K. Mitra - Hooghly Jelar Itihas O Bangasamaj. Vol. II. P.-1124.

54. Ashok Mitra (ed.) - Paschim Banger Puja Parban O Mela. Vol. II. P. - 606.

55. Rajsekhar Basu (ed.) - Chalantika : Adhunik Bangabhasar Abhidhan. P.-181.

56. Nihar Ranjan Roy - Bangalir Itihas. PP. 584-586.

57. Benoy ghosh - Paschim Banger Sanskriti. P.-49.

58. A. K. Banerjee - West Bengal District Gazetteers. Hooghly. PP.-198 and 207.

59. Hansa Narayan Bhattacharya - Hinduder Debdebi :Udbhab O Kramabikash. Vol. II. PP. - 65 and 74.

60. A. K. Banerjee - West Bengal District Gazetteers. Hooghly. P.-205.

61. S. K. Mitra - Hooghly Jelar Itihas O Bangasamaj. Vol. II. P.-253.

62. Satishchandra Giri - Tarakeswar Sivatattva. PP.-81-87.

63. Amrita Bazar Patrika - 16.4.24, 6(5).

64. L. S. S. O'Malley and M. M. Chakrabarty - Bengal District Gazetteers. Hooghly. P.-106.

65. A. K. Banerjee - West Bengal District Gazetteers. Hooghly. P.-725.

66. Satishchandra Giri - Tarakeswar Sivatattva. PP.-82.

67. S. K. Mitra - Hooghly Jelar Itihas O Bangasamaj. Vol. II. P.-1123.

68. Satishchandra Giri - Tarakeswar Sivatattva. PP.-85-86.

69. L. S. S. O'Malley and M. M. Chakrabarty - Bengal District Gazetteers. Hooghly. P.-321.

70. Satishchandra Giri - Tarakeswar Sivatattva. P.-83.

71. A. K. Banerjee - West Bengal District Gazetteers. Hooghly. P.-725.

72. S. K. Mitra - Hooghly Jelar Itihas O Bangasamaj. Vol. II. P.-1122.

73. Satishchandra Giri - Tarakeswar Sivatattva. PP.-83-84.

74. S. K. Mitra - Hooghly Jelar Itihas O Bangasamaj. Vol. II. P.-1122.

75. Satishchandra Giri - Tarakeswar Sivatattva. P.-86.

76. A.K. Banerjee - West Bengal District Gazetteers. Hooghly. P.-725.

77. L. S. S. O'Malley and M. M. Chakrabarty - Bengal District Gazetteers. Hooghly. PP.-105 and 321.

78. W. W. Hunter - A Statistical Account of Bengal. Vol. III. Districts of Midnapur and Hugli (including Howrah). PP.-327-328.
Also,
Satishchandra Giri - Tarakeswar Sivatattva. PP.-83-84.

79. Nihar Ranjan Roy - Bangalir Itihas. PP. 585-586.

80. W. W. Hunter - A Statistical Account of Bengal. Vol. III. Districts of Midnapur and Hugli (including Howrah). PP.-327-328.

81. Yugantar - 14 April, 1963.

Chapter - IX

The Economic Interaction

I

The evolution of this place of pilgrimage shows that the cult of Lord *Taraknath* remains all through the sheet-anchor of the economy of this place of pilgrimage. In fact, a considerable number of residents of this place of pilgrimage eke out their livelihood by virtue of the steady inflow of pilgrims throughout the year. This nature of dependence definitely varies with reference to specific caste-groups.

The involvement of the priestly community seems more direct in the socio-economic context because of its exclusive nature of occupation in relation to ritual observances. Therefore, the dependence of *Sebayet* priests on the temple and its presiding deity remains traditionally extra-ordinary despite the lack of recognition of their status by the *Giri Mohantas*. Hence, their existence as a compact community today seems definitely due to the termination of the *Giri* regime.

The *Sebayet* priests, most of whom are *Radi Brahmins*, have lived at Tarakeswar for generations with initial permission from the *Giri Mohantas* to settle around the sacred complex within the network of estate-*zamindari*. Hence, they began to settle in the vicinity of the temple, alongside members of other castes. Even those who live in the adjacent villages, are averse to form their own neighbourhood.[1] In this regard, they differ from their counterparts in other puranic places of pilgrimage like Puri in Orissa or Gaya in Bihar. Therefore, the social existence of the *Sebayet* priests at Tarakeswar somehow or other allows easy interaction between themselves and other local people, as well as the pilgrims on the other.

However, most of these families of *Sebayet* priests or the sacred specialists are not entirely dependent on priesthood as they possess properties in the places of their origin as well as, in some cases, in the places adjacent to this pilgrim centre. Despite this, the *kulabritti* (the allowance in lieu of service to the presiding deity), *daksina* (the remuneration given by the pilgrims for being of help to them in the worship of the deity) as well as the rent paid by the pilgrims for staying in the rest houses-cum-residences of the priests concerned, contribute also to their livelihood.[2] The strengthening of their position in the socio-economic hierarchy around the sacred complex is definitely due to their comparable inclination to gain literacy.

Despite the relative economic ease resulting from *kulabritti*, widespread dissatisfaction prevails as this profession fails generally to provide for long-term financial security. This had resulted earlier from the traditional mode of payment signifying voluntary gifts from the pilgrims in general. This tradition has, subsequently, undergone much change. This in its turn affects the *yajmani* (clientele) relationship between the priests and pilgrims, thereby complicating economic interaction.[3]

Another noticeable development in the context of socio-economic interaction between the *Sebayets* and the pilgrims following the termination of the *Giri* regime, is the intrusion of the *Pandas* or *Dalals* (brokers) into the areas, formerly the reserve of the *Sebayet* priests. Hence, the acceptance of this *kulabritti* has continued mainly due to sheer economic compulsion. This has become more important by virtue of the assumption of a community character by the *Pandas* or *Dalals*, since the nineteen fifties.[4]

II

Besides the priests, there are also persons who depend almost completely on the cult of Lord *Siva* as well as the pilgrims for their sustenance. Of them the barbers, the potters, the florists, the water-carriers, the milkmen are important.

There are both Bengali as well as non-Bengali barbers engaged in the *kamansala* (tonsuring centre) run by the temple office. They are mostly *Napits* by caste. The Bengalis are proud of having lived around the sacred complex for generations while the non-Bengalis are generally native to the districts of Balia and Arrah of Bihar from where they claim to have come during the tenure of Madhabchandra Giri.

Usually, they work under the supervision of a head barber, who takes annual lease of the site from the Tarakeswar estate. Their meagre income is somehow complemented with the perquisites they get in lieu of their involvement in certain rituals organised by the temple authority.

Like the barbers, the potters also belong to two groups – Bengalis and non-Bengalis, members of the *Kumbhakar* and *Kumhar* castes. Both the Bengali and non-Bengali potters claim to be old residents of this pilgrim centre. The only difference is that the non-Bengalis claim to have come here from the same places as the non-Bengali barbers, during the tenure of the last *Giri Mohanta* of the *Tarakeswar Math*.

In fact, the maximum demand for their pottery comes from the dealers of articles used in rituals, florists and from those involved directly or indirectly with the organisation of temple services.

Of the florists, there are a few employed by the estate to supply flowers daily to the temple while the rest of them are self-employed, offering flowers for the worship of the Lord. They are usually from various caste-groups. Unlike those employed by the Tarakeswar estate, the self-employed florists are allowed to carry on their sales only after the payment of a monthly rent to the estate. Of them, the non-Bengalis are mostly from Orissa and have been at Tarakeswar for generations.

Traditionally, the water-carriers eke out their livelihood by supplying the sacred water of the Ganges to the temple of the Lord. They belong to the caste of *Karan*, and they too have been here for generations as appointees of the estate.

Besides them, there are also milkmen belonging to the caste of *Gopas* who, like others, depend greatly on the deity as well as the pilgrims for subsistence. Their close and almost legendary association with Tarakeswar has been related elsewhere.

Thus this place of pilgrimage provides opportunities for sustenance to a considerable number of professional castes who cater to the needs of the pilgrims. This they do alongside their respective roles in the organisation of services in the temple of the Lord for which they receive perquisites accordingly.

III

Apart from those involved directly or indirectly with the organisation of temple services already mentioned, there are also the owners of the rest houses who, indeed, belong to a peripheral group as the beneficiaries of the temple economy. Incidentally, the houses of the *Sebayet* priests are also the traditional rest houses for pilgrims on pilgrimage to Tarakeswar. But in recent years, there has occurred an escalation in the number of rest houses and *dharmasalas*, owned both by Bengali and the non-Bengali communities. This seems to have been a recent phenomenon, when placed against the prevalence of the *Chandina Sattva* during the *Giri* regime. Reference to it has already been made elsewhere.

In recent times, the rest house owners come from various castes and depend largely on rent. The rooms are generally hired out on a daily basis to the pilgrims congregating at Tarakeswar round the year.[5]

The pilgrim component has also had an impact on the extension of business activities in and around the sacred complex. By the end of 1950, three shops for consecrated items necessary for worship of the Lord, run by caste *Modaks*, and two shops for milk and milk-made items, owned by the caste *Gopas*, as well as a few shops for selling pictures of Lord *Taraknath* by a few *Baishnab* families have come into existence. Besides these, two hotels run by caste *Brahmins* from Orissa, two sweetmeat shops owned by a caste *Modak* and a caste *Mahisya*, two grocery shops run by caste *Gandhabaniks*, two garment shops owned by caste *Tilis*, as well as a shop for brass and bronze articles run by a caste *Tamli*, also cater to the needs of the pilgrims in particular and local people in general.[6] However, there has also occurred an escalation in the number of shops and hotels in and around the sacred complex in keeping with gradual increase in the number of pilgrims in recent years.

IV

Over and above, the secular aspect of the twin institutions is conspicuously revealed in the given economic sphere. It has already elsewhere been clarified that the economic evolution of the *Tarakeswar Math* owes much to the devotees of Lord *Taraknath* who, over the years, enriched the estate with donations as well as gifts of various kinds. Besides, the interest from the bank from fixed deposits, the leases of various sites within the estate and rents from establishments owned by the estate, give financial strength to the estate today.

Despite these, the Tarakeswar estate remains short of becoming a profit-oriented enterprise as the income from various sources is spent mostly on daily worship, the maintenance of the twin institutions, arrangements for the benefit of the devotees and on salaries of the employees, among whom the *Brahmins* are predominant. Therefore, the prosperity of the town somehow or other depends much on the visits of the pilgrims, which became very important ever since the extension of the railway line from Sheoraphuli to Tarakeswar in 1884 and its consequent electrification.[7]

V

In fact, the steady development of the communication system since the establishment of railway line connecting this place of pilgrimage with the surrounding areas comprises a major contribution to the needs of the pilgrims. Besides the construction of the railway line, the construction of the metalled roads connecting distant towns, interior villages as well as neighbouring districts not only exposes the influence and extent of the manifold characteristics of Tarakeswar as a place of pilgrimage on thousands of pilgrims round the year but also emphasises its considerable importance as a commercial centre.[8]

Of late, Tarakeswar has become a viable market for the sale of the agricultural products of the surrounding regions. The agricultural products include mainly raw jute, potatoes and other vegetables.[9] In fact, the nodal position of Tarakeswar in connecting the interior of the district contributes to its steady economic development. Noticeably, the craftsmen of the neighbouring villages produce certain articles with an eye to the pilgrims on Tarakeswar pilgrimage. Therefore, the benefits accruing from the inflow of pilgrims, in consequence of the development of the communication system , are reaped not by any particular caste or group but by all those whose livelihood depends on the cult of Lord *Siva* at Tarakeswar.

People living not only in the neighbourhood but also far away from the pilgrim centre derive economic benefit by reason of the all – pervasive influence of the temple of Lord *Taraknath* on the region. No doubt, that the places from where the seasonal pilgrims begin their journey, or rest while on pilgrimage to Tarakeswar, attract those selling articles for rituals and items for light refreshment. Sheoraphuli derives maximum benefit as compared to all the other places, as the seasonal pilgrims from the neighbouring states as well as from Bangladesh congregate here by train, boat and other conveyances to begin their journey from *Nimaitirtha Ghat*. Besides, a large number of people residing along the Tarakeswar-Baidyabati route gain from the inflow of seasonal pilgrims through the sales of aforesaid items.

There is no denying that the cult of Lord *Taraknath* has helped considerably in the development of a number of cottage industries like the manufacture of pottery, the yoke poles (*banks or kanors*), the reticulated slings (*sikas*), incense sticks, hand-woven ritual threads, napkins, coarse clothes and so on in the neighbourhood. Naturally, different groups of people are involved in dealing in different products. These people of different age groups with diverse socio-economic background, are thus found engaged in cottage industries as well as in stalls temporarily erected beside the route through which the seasonal pilgrims are on pilgrimage to Tarakeswar. Incidentally the *Sivaratri* as well as *Gajan* festivals have special attraction for not only the petty businessmen dealing in vegetables, fruits, utensils, stationary goods and so on, but also for those from Gaya and Dumka, with their products of various types made of stone.[10] Therefore, it can be asserted in clear terms that this sacred complex, along with the presiding deity not only soothes the weary souls, but also generates viable economic opportunities for a large number of people belonging to this temple town as well as to the surrounding regions.

Note

1. Interview with the ex-Secretary, Purohit Mandali on 7.10.99.
2. Ibid.
3. Interview with the Secretary, Purohit Mandali on 25.12.99.
4. Ibid.
5. Interview with the Secretary, Tirthayatri Nibas Malik Sangha on 26.12.99.
6. Interview with the ex-Secretary, Purohit Mandali on 9.6.'97.

7. L. S. S. O'Malley and M. M. Chakrabarty – Bengal District Gazetteers. Hooghly, P-321.

8. Ashok Mitra – Paschim Banger Puja Parban O Mela. Vol. II. P.-603.

9. A. K. Banerjee – West Bengal District Gazetteers. Hooghly. P.-664.

10. Ashok Mitra (ed.) – Paschim Banger Puja Parban O Mela. Vol. II. P.-604.

Conclusion

I

This dissertation encompasses the history of the evolution of Tarakeswar as a place of pilgrimage with reference to the cult of Lord *Taraknath* from 1729 to 1952. Hence, it puts forward a profile of the socio-economic and religious perspectives of the pilgrim town alongside the changes that took place over the years.

Primarily, it points to an elucidation of the salient features of *Svayambhulingam* which are obviously related to the presiding cult of this non-puranic place of pilgrimage. It has been propounded that the revelation of Lord *Taraknath* and the consequent emergence of Tarakeswar since 1729 happened initially in association with a member of the *Gopa* caste and the *Chhatri zamindar* of Baligari, not far-off from this pilgrim centre. The subsequent addition to this process was a *Dashnami Giri Sannyasi* who led to the establishment of the monastic system under the patronage of the aforesaid *Chhatri zamindar*, that lasted for over two centuries at Tarakeswar.

II

Tarakeswar has also been studied in retrospect with reference to the historical geography of the region in which this place of pilgrimage is situated. It has been shown that the retarded civic evolution for long owed much to the seasonal floods of the Damodar that told heavily on the growth of cultivation and population as well. Besides the *Kaibarttas* and the *Gopas*, all were found to have been outsiders to this place of pilgrimage.

Noticeably, the age-old rituals and beliefs of the original inhabitants came easily to terms with the *Mohanta* culture resulting in the popular form of *Saivism* with its bearing on fairs and festivals.

Reference has also been made to the possible influence of the *Nathpanthis* on the religious history of Tarakeswar along with the prevailing trend of adherence to popular *Tantrik* rites in and around the religious complex which developed definitely under the patronage of the *Giri Mohantas*.

III

It has been emphasised that the evolution of the pilgrim town owes greatly to the evolution of the monastic system put forward by the *Dashnami Giri Sannyasis* with preceptor-disciple lineage. Hence, the *Tarakeswar Math* was the nucleus, around which the temple-*zamindari* evolved in due course.

The indulgence of the *Giri Mohantas* in commercial transactions including usury has been brought within the purview of discussion in the given context along with their endeavours primarily to extend and consolidate the estate-*zamindari*.

With an overall commitment to keep a good hold on the twin institutions upto the end of the 18th century, the *Giri*

Mohantas overcame the forces of destabilisation that often threatened the *Tarakeswar Math* during this period under review.

IV

The evolution of the monastic system during the 19th century witnessed the same process of extension and consolidation of the temple-*zamindari* by dint of the perseverance of the *Giri Mohantas*. The only noticeable feature in this process was their determined efforts at categorising the properties acquired over the years as *nij* (self) and *debutter* (in the name of the deity). Besides, the tradition of playing the role of *talukdar* that had begun during the preceding century remained unchanged till the end of the *Giri* regime.

Another noteworthy development during this phase of the monastic system was the spread of education on traditional as well as modern lines along with the humanitarian measures that continued remarkably till the end of the *Giri* regime. The gradual development of this pilgrim centre in this phase owed much to the extension of the railway network that happened during the tenures of the last two *Giri Mohantas*. Despite these, the diminishing trend in the monastic system became conspicuous that ultimately led to the overthrow of the said regime.

V

The verdict given by the District Judge on 6.11.29, in connection with the Title Suit 28/1922, brought about the overthrow of the *Giri* regime. Satishchandra Giri, the last *Giri*

Mohanta was made the victim against whom the allegations ranged through moral turpitude, defalcation of funds and damage to religious property.

Despite earnest efforts, the last *Giri Mohanta* failed to adhere to his position at the *Tarakeswar Math* and to control the administration of the *Math* even through his *Chela* (disciple) as was proved by the appointment of *Dandiswami* Jagannath Ashram by order of Mr. Justice S. Mukherjee in the month of *Agrahayan,* 1344 B.S. (1937 A.D.). Thus ended the long-drawn *Giri* regime that helped grow this place of pilgrimage in name over the years.

VI

It has been emphasised in the ensuing discussion that the *Satyagraha* movement facilitated the removal of the *Giri* regime at Tarakeswar. This was resorted to in 1924 to remove the glaring abuses that had crept into the management of the twin institutions.

The *Mahabir Dal* had been organised to fight against the authoritarianism of the last *Giri Mohanta* of the *Tarakeswar Math*. To make the whole project a complete success, the *Dal* solicited help from the President of the Bengal Provincial Congress Committee (B. P. C. C.) for the start of the movement. The B. P. C. C. took the decision to sanction the movement at the behest of Deshbandhu Chittaranjan Das, President of the B. P. C. C. The *Satyagraha* movement, therefore, began on 20 May, 1924 following the failure of the talks for a compromise between the District Magistrate and the Secretary of the B. P. C. C. It has been shown that the Government showed no hesitation to apply its power to suppress the *Satyagrahis*.

Besides the direct involvement of the B. P. C. C., the *Akalis* as well as the Muslims participated in this movement upto a certain extent in order to weed out corruption from the twin institutions. The participation of the female volunteers in this movement has also been taken note of in the ensuing discussion.

This movement had come ultimately to an end following the decision of the incumbent *Mohanta* to abdicate in favour of his *Chela* (disciple), Prabhatchandra Giri, on 22 Sept, 1924. It has been put forward that the *Satyagraha* movement lost much of its thrust simply because of the lack of human as well as material resources in the given context.

VII

It has been propounded that the interregnum between the passing of the *Giri* regime into oblivion and the advent of the *Ashram* order of the *Dashnami Sannyasis* in the administration of the twin institutions witnessed the tenures of two Receivers – Amulya Chandra Bhaduri and Rashbehari Mukherjee.

The appointment of the new *Mohanta* at the *Tarakeswar Math* coincided with the setting up of a new administrative hierarchy in accordance with the order passed on 29.8.34 by the Calcutta High Court. Mention has been made of the endeavours of the new *Mohanta* from a different order of the *Dashnami Sannyasis* to fight boldly against corruption that flourished over the years in the twin institutions along with his determination to initiate remarkable changes into the rituals performed within the temple. The traditional outlook of this *Mohanta* has been made a point, in so far as his interest only in the promotion of the Sanskrit language.

However, his disenchantment with the litigation strengthened his determination to resign in favour of his trusted disciple, Hrishikesh Ashram in 1952 (1358 B.S.). This definitely proves again that the age-old principle of *Guru Sisya Parampara* dies hard at the *Tarakeswar Math*.

VIII

Tarakeswar is a celebrated place of fairs and festivals of different types from the month of *Baisakh* to that of *Chaitra* of the Bengali calendar year. It has been found that casteism plays an important role in almost all the sacred performances except during the time of fairs and festivals which are held at frequent intervals.

Emphasis has been made on the relative similarities of some of these rituals with those performed by the devotees of other religions. The rituals performed by the *Mohantas* as well as by the *Sebayet* priests within the temple conform to sanskritised prescription while the folk rites are mostly found to have been performed during the *Gajan* festival. It has incidentally been noted that the priestcraft that developed during the *Giri* regime was definitely in contrast to its counterpart in the other puranic places of pilgrimage all over India, as it was devoid of professionalism.

Mention has also been made of the festivals organised completely in the local context with incidental reference to the inclination of the *Giri Mohantas* to *Saktipuja* alongside an unwavering commitment to the presiding deity. Moreover, reference has been made to the proof of compromise with the *lokayata* (popular) culture on the part of the upholders of Brahminical religion.

It has also been noted that the pilgrimage to Tarakeswar and its bearing on fairs and festivals over the years emphasise the capacity of this pilgrim town for accommodating people from all castes on the common platform of Hinduism as is proved from the ever increasing flow of pilgrims over the years.

IX

An endeavour has also been made in this dissertation to understand the importance of the cult of Lord *Taraknath* in terms of being the sheet-anchor of the economy of this place of pilgrimage.

The involvement of the priestly community seems more direct in the socio-economic context because of the exclusive nature of its occupation. Besides the *Sebayet* priests, the barbers, potters, florists, water-carriers and the milkmen also depend almost completely on the cult of Lord *Taraknath*. But the owners of the rest houses are found to have been belonging to a peripheral group in so far as the temple economy is concerned. Over and above, the Tarakeswar estate remains short of becoming exclusively a profit oriented enterprise despite its sustenance in the temple economy.

The exposure of this temple town by virtue of the improvement in the communication system resulted in the development of this place of pilgrimage as also a commercial centre. Hence, this study reveals that Tarakeswar always remains like other places of pilgrimage, a refuge for those seeking fulfilment of material and psychological needs as well as spiritual satisfaction in an ever changing socio-economic scenario.

Bibliography

A. Primary Sources

1. Court Records.

i. Plaint Suit No. 4458 of 1790 in the Judge's Court of Burdwan. Parasuram Giri Vs. Fatey Giri.

ii. Title Suit No. 28/1922. D. Sinharoy and others Vs. S. C. Giri. Suit Under Sec. 92 Civil Procedure Code.

iii. The list of properties submitted by the defendant in the Court of the District Judge, Hooghly. Title Suit No. 28/1922. D. Sinhroy and others Vs. S. C. Giri.

iv. Judgement of Mr. Justice K. C. Nag, District Judge of Hooghly, in the Title Suit No. 28/1922. Dated 6 Nov. 929.

v. Appeal from original decree daed 6.11.29, filed in the High Court of Judicature on 25th Nov. 1929, for the stay of further proceedings. D. Sinharoy and others Vs. Satishchandra Giri.

vi. The Security Bonds offered at the behest of Central Bank Limited, Calcutta as well as by a few propertied persons for staying of execution of decree as per order of the Hon'ble High Court dated 20.12.29 in Civil Rule No. 1550 (F) of 1929 in the Court of the District Judge of Hooghly. Title Suit No. 28 of 1922. D. Sinharoy and others Vs. S. C. Giri.

vii. Draft schemes filed in the Court of the District Judge of Hooghly. Title Suit No. 28/1922. D. Sinharoy and others – Plaintiffs Vs. S. C. Giri, defendant. Date – 6.2.30 and 24.2.30.

viii. High Court of Judicature at Fort William in Bengal. Civil Appellate Jurisdiction. F.A. file No. 23427 of 1930. S. C. Giri Vs. D. Sinharoy and others. Date : 5 Sept, 1930.

ix. Petition submitted by the plaintiffs in relation to the Title Suit No. 28 of 1922 in the Court of the District Judge. Hooghly. Date – 18.9.30.

x. High Court of Judicature at Fort William in Bengal. Date of Order – 11.11.30.

xi. Judgement of the Calcutta High Court in F.A. No. I of 1930; 6 July 1934 and 24 August 1934.

xii. Appendix to the Judgement in F.A. No. 255 of 1930. Dated – 1.8.1934.

xiii. In the High Court of Judicature at Fort William in Bengal. Civil Appellate Jurisdiction. Appeals from original decree No. 255 of 1930. Appeals against the decree of Mr. Justice K. C. Nag, District Judge of Hooghly. Satishchandra Giri Vs. D. Sinharoy and others. Dated. – 24.8.34 and 29.8.34.

xiv. In the High Court of Judicature at Fort William in Bengal. Civil Appellate Jurisdiction. 13th January, 1938. Appeal against the order of S. Mukherjee, District Judge of Zillah Hughly in the Title Suit No. 28 of 1922, dated 29th of June 1937; Prabhatchandra Giri Vs. D. Sinharoy.

xv. Petition on behalf of *Dandiswami* Jagannath Ashram under clause XVIII of the scheme framed under Sec. 92, filed on 11 March, 1946. *Dandiswami* Jagannath Ashram Vs. Srijib Nayatirtha and others.

xvi. Petition of objection on behalf of Srijib *Nayatirtha* and others filed on 9 July, 1946. *Dandiswami* Jagannath Ashram Vs. Sri Srijib *Nayatirtha*, Member and Secretary, Committee of Management, Tarakeswar estate and others.

xvii. Judgement of the Court of the District Judge, Hooghly, Misc. Case No. 32 of 1946. Dated 16th Apr. 1947.

xviii. Sl. No. of Orders or Proceedings	Dates.
121	28.3.25.
134	9.7.25.
142	22.2.26.
143	2.3.26.
149	10.3.26.
153	20.3.26.
212	28.4.26.
214	28.4.26.
286	24.6.26.
290	28.6.26.
312	24.7.26.
440	9.12.26.
449	17.12.26.
650	18.1.28.
652	18.1.28.
694	28.2.28.
701	29.2.28.
720	21.3.28.
798	17.7.28.
831	20.8.28.
981	7.11.29.
1000	10.9.34.
1033	2.1.35.
39	3.8.35.
51	2.12.35.
1320	18.5.37.
1328	24.5.37.
40	10.8.38.

2. Resolutions and etc.

i.   Resolution passed at the meeting held on 30 July, 1930 at the behest of *Rai* Satishchandra Mukherjee *Bahadur* B. L.; M. L. C.; Chairman of the District Board. Hooghly.

ii.   Resolution passed at the meeting held at Bahirgarh on 17 August, 1930.

iii.   Resolution passed at the meeting of *Bangiya Brahman Sabha* held on 25 *Bhadra*, 1337 B. S. at the behest of Ramranjan Roy, Assistant Secretary, *Bangiya Brahman Sabha.*

iv.   Notice put up with signature of A. C. Bhaduri M. A., Receiver, Tarakeswar estate, at Receiver's office on 11 *Bhadra*, 1337 B.S.

v.   Advertisement made in the newspapers signed by the District Judge on 20.9.30 at the behest of the Receiver, Tarakeswar estate.

vi.   Letter from A. C. Bhaduri. Esq., Receiver, Tarakeswar estate to the Hon'ble District Judge. Date – 29.3.30.

vii.   Letter from Trilok Chandra Giri, *Mohanta, Bhotbagan Math*, Ghusuri, Howrah to A. C. Bhaduri, Receiver, Tarakeswar estate. Date – 3.9.30.

viii. Letter from A. C. Bhaduri. Esq. M. A. Receiver, Tarakeswar estate to Mr. Justice K. C. Nag, District Judge, Hooghly. Date-11 Sept. 1930.

B. Official Documentary Works

1. The Calcutta Gazettee – 11 Oct. 1787.

2. Hunter, W. W. – The Imperial Gazetteer of India. Vol. IV. London. Trubner and Co. 1881.

3. Imperial Gazetteer of India. Provincial Series. Bengal. Vol. I. Superintendent of Government Printing. Calcutta 1909.

4. O'Malley, L. S. S. and Chakrabarty, Monomohan – Bengal District Gazetteers. Hooghly. Calcutta. The Bengal Secretariat Book Depot. 1912.

5. Bengal District Gazetteers – 'B' Vol. Hooghly District Statistics. 1911-1912 to 1920-1921. Calcutta. Bengal Secretariat Book Depot. 1923.

6. Bengal Administrative Report – 1924-25 (XII-XIII).

7. Bengal District Gazetteers. 'B' Vol. Hooghly District Statistics. 1921-1922 to 1930-1931. Calcutta. Bengal Secretariat Book Depot. 1933.

8. Mitra, Ashok – West Bengal District Hand Books. Hooghly. 1952. Series 10 – Ancient monuments and fairs. Glossary of the better-known ancient monuments in Hooghly District. Superintendent of census operation. W.B.

9. Roy, B.-West Bengal District Census Hand Book. Census -1961. P- XXVII. Calcutta Government Printing Press. W. Bengal.

10. Census of India. Paper No. I of 1962. 1961 Census. Government of India. XXXVII.

11. Banerjee, Amiya Kumar – West Bengal District Gazetteers. Hooghly. Calcutta. Oct. 1972.

C. Books in English

1. Bentley, C. A. – Fairs and Festivals in Bengal. Calcutta. Bengal Secretariat Book Depot. 1929.

2. Bharati, Agehananda – Pilgrimage Sites and Indian Civilisation, in Elder, J. W. (ed.) Indian Civilisation. Madison. Department of Indian Studies, University of Wisconsin. 1967.

3. Bhattacharya, Buddhadeb – Satyagrahas in Bengal. (1921-1939) Calcutta. Minerva Associates (publications) Pvt. Ltd. 1977.

4. Bose, Nirmal Kumar – Culture and Society in India. Calcutta. Asia Publishing House. 1967.

5. Buckland, C.E. – Bengal Under The Lieutenant Governors. 2nd ed. Vol. II. Calcutta. Kedarnath Bose. B. A. 64 Akhil Mistri Lane. 1902.

6. Chakrabarty, Prafulla – Social Profile of Tarakeswar. Calcutta. Firma K. L. M. Pvt. Ltd. 1984.

7. Chakrabarty, Ramakanta – Vaisnavism in Bengal. Calcutta. Sanskrit Pustak Bhandar. 1985.

8. Chandra, A. N. – The Sannyasi Rebellion. Calcutta. Ratna Prakashan. 1977.

9. Cohn, Bernard S. – The Role of the Gosains in the Economy of Eighteenth and Nineteenth Century Upper India. In Vidyarthi, L. P. and Jha, M. (ed.) Symposium on the Sacred Complex in India. Ranchi. Council of Social and Cultural Research. 1974.

    Also, I. E. S. H. R., Vol. I, No. IV, 1964.

10. Crawford, Lt. Col. D. G. – A Brief History of the Hughli District. Calcutta. Bengal Secretariat Press. 1902.

11. Dasgupta, Sashibhusan – Obscure Religious Cults. Calcutta. Firma K. L. M. 1976.

12. De Leury, G.A. – The Cult of Vithoba. Poona. Deccan College. 1960.

13. Dey, Shumbhoo Chandra – Hooghly Past and Present. Hooghly. M. M. Bay. 1906.

14. Diehl, Carl Gustav – Instrument and Purpose : Studies on Rites and Rituals in South India. Lund, C. W. K. Gleerup. 1956.

15. Eschmann. A, Kulke, H and Tripathi G. C. – The Cult of Jagannath and the Regional Tradition of Orissa. South Asia Interdisciplinary Regional Research Programme, Orissa Research Project, South Asia Institute, New Delhi. Monohar Publications. 1978.

16. Farquhar, J. N. – An Outline of the Religious Literature of India. Delhi. Motilal Banarsidas. Reprint. 1967.

17. Firminger, Walter K. – Historical Introduction to the Bengal Portion of the Fifth Report. Calcutta. 1917.

18. Frykenberg, Robert Eric (ed.) – Land Control and Social Structure in Indian History. New Delhi. Monohar Publications. 1979.

19. Ghosh, Jamini Mohon – Sannyasi and Fakir Raiders in Bengal. Calcutta. 1930.

20. Hunter, W. W. – A Statistical Account of Bengal. Vol . III. Districts of Midnapur and Hugli (including Howrah). London. Trubner and Co. 1876.

21. Hunter, W. W. – Annals of Rural Bengal. London. 1897.

22. Mazumdar, Ramesh Chandra – History of the Freedom Movement in India. Vol. III. Calcutta. Firma K. L. M. Pvt. Ltd. 1963.

23. Mitra, Rameschandra – Education in Narendrakrishna Sinha (ed.) The History of Bengal. (1757-1905). Calcutta University. 1967.

24. Mukherjee, Nilmani – A Bengal Zamindar – Joykrishna Mukherjee of Uttarpara and His Times. 1808-1888. Calcutta. Firma K. L. M. Pvt. Ltd. 1975.

25. Precope, J. – Medicine, Magic and Mythology. London. William Heinemann. 1954.

26. Risley, H. H. - The Tribes and Castes of Bengal. 2 Vol. Calcutta. Firma K. L. M. Pvt. Ltd. Reprint. 1981. (Government Printing 1891).

27. Sanyal, Hitesh Ranjan – Social Mobility in Bengal. Calcutta. Papyrus. 1981.

28. Saraswati, Baidyanath – Studying Sacred Complex in Kashi, in Vidyarthi, L. P. and Jha Makhan (ed.) Symposium on the Sacred Complex in India. Ranchi. Council of Social and Cultural Research. 1974.

29. Sarkar, Jadunath – The History of Bengal. Vol. II. (1200-1757). Patna – 6. Academica Asiatica. 1973.

30. Singer, Milton – The Great Tradition in a Metropolitan Centre : Madras. – Singer, M (ed.) Traditional India : Structure and Change. Philadelphia. American Folklore Society. 1959.

31. Sinha, S – Kali Temple at Kalighat and the City of Calcutta. In Sinha, S. (ed.) Cultural Profile of Calcutta. Calcutta. The Anthropological Society. 1972.

32. Sinha, Surajit and Saraswati, Baidyanath – Ascetics of Kashi, Varanasi. N. K. Bose Memorial Foundation. 1978.

33. Swami, Pavitrananda – Pilgrimage and Fairs : Their Bearing on Indian Life, in : Bhattacharya, Haridas (ed.) The Cultural Heritage of India. Calcutta. Ramakrishna Mission 1956.

34. Toynbee, George – A Sketch of the Administration of the Hooghly District from 1795 to 1845. Vol-II. Calcutta. Bengal Secretariat Press. 1888.

35. Vidyarthi, L. P. – Sacred Complex in Hindu Gaya. Bombay. Asia Publishing House. 1961.

36. Vidyarthi, L. P.; Saraswati, Baidyanath and Jha, Makhan – The Sacred Complex of Kashi : A Microcosm of Indian Civilisation. Delhi. Concept Publishing Co. 1979.

37. Wilson, H. H. – The Religious Sects of the Hindus. Calcutta. Sushil Gupta (India) Pvt. Ltd. 1958.

D. Books in Bengali

1. Bandyopadhyaya, Asit Kumar – Bangla Sahityer Itibritta. Vol. III. Calcutta. Modern Book Agency. 1966.

2. Bandyopadhyaya, Asit Kumar (ed.) – Bangalir Dharma O Darshanchinta. Calcutta. Nabapatra Prakashan. 1980.

3. Bandyopadhyaya, Brajendranath – Sambadpatre Sekaler Katha. Vol. I. Fourth edition. Calcutta. Bangiya Sahitya Parishad. 1377. B.S.

4. Bandyopadhyaya, Narendranath – Tarakeswar Satyagraha Sangram. Calcutta. Samar Library. 1949.

5. Bandyopadhyaya, Tarit Kumar – Sri Sri Ma O Dakatbaba. Calcutta. Deb Sahitya Kutir Pvt. Ltd. 1994.

6. Banerjee, Anil Chandra – Madhya Yuge Bangla O Bangali. Calcutta. K. P. Bagchi and Co. 1986.

7. Basak, Gopal – Paryataker Dristite Ei Bangla. Calcutta. Author. 1390 B.S.

8. Basu, Rajshekhar – Chalantika; Adhunik Bangabhasar Abhidhan. Calcutta. M. C. Sarkar and Sons. Pvt. Ltd. 1373 B.S.

9. Bhattacharya, Dinesh Chandra and Bhattacharya, Ashutosh (ed.) – Sivayana by Ramakrishna Kabichandra. Calcutta. Bangiya Sahitya Parishad. 1363 B.S. (1956).

10. Bhattacharya, Hansa Narayan – Hinduder Deb Debi : Udbhab O Kramabikash. Vol. II. Calcutta. Firma K. L. M. Pvt. Ltd. 1978.

11. Bose, Nirmal Kumar – Hindu Samajer Gadan. Calcutta. Visva Bharati Granthalaya. 1949.

12. Brahmachari, Akshoy Chaitanya – Banglar Tirtha. Calcutta. Model Publishing House. 1362 B.S.

13. Chakrabarty, Ramakanta – Bange Vaisnava Dharma. Calcutta. Ananda Publishers Pvt. Ltd. 1996.

14. Das, Bhupati Ranjan – Paschimbanga Bhraman O Darshan. 2 Vols. Calcutta. Sarat Publishing House. 1385. B.S.

15. Dutta, Akshoy Kumar – Bharatbarsiya Upasak Sampradaya. 2 Vols. Calcutta. Pathbhaban. Ashar. 1376 B.S.

16. Giri, Satishchandra – Tarakeswar Sivatattva. Tarakeswar. Tarakeswar Math. 1922.

17. Giri, Swami Vishnusivananda – Tarakeswar Math O Sadhu Bharamalla. Bahirgarh. Author. 1958.

18. Ghoshal, Swarna Kumar – Tarakeswar Satyagraher Itihas. Calcutta. Author. 1934.

19. Ghosh, Benoy – Paschim Banger Sanskriti. Vol. II. Calcutta. Prakash Bhaban. 1978.

20. Ghosh Benoy – Samayik Patre Banglar Samajchitra. Calcutta. Bengal Publishers Pvt. Ltd. 1962.

21. Goswami, Jayanta – Samajchitre Unabingsha Satabdir Bangla prahasan. Calcutta. Sahityasri. 1974 (1381 B.S.).

22. Jnananjan – Acharya Sri Sri Jagannath Ashrampad. Kanko. Sri Shankar Math. 1978.

23. Kabiraj, Gopinath – Tantrik Sadhana O Siddhanta. Vol. I. The University of Burdwan. 1995.

24. Mitra, Ashok (ed.) – Paschim Banger Puja Parban O Mela. Vol. II. Delhi. Govrnment of India. 1968.

25. Mitra, Sudhir Kumar – Hooghly Jelar Itihas O Bangasamaj. 2 Vols. Calcutta. Mondal Book House. 1991.

26. Mitra, Sudhir Kumar – Hooghly Jelar Deb Deul. Calcutta. Aparna. 1991.

27. Roy, Durgacharan – Debganer Martye Agaman. Calcutta. Dey's 1984.

28. Roy, Nihar Ranjan – Bangalir Itihas (Adiparba). Calcutta. Book Emporium. 1356 B.S.

29. Sanyal, Pramathanath – Tarakeswar. Dacca. Author. 1936.

30. Sarkar, Kedarnath – Tarakmangal. Calcutta. Author. 1877.

31. Sen, Pralay – Paschimbanglar Tirtha. Calcutta. Model Publishing House. 1386 B.S.

32. Sen, Sukumar (ed.) – Chandimangal by Kabikankan. New Delhi. Sahitya Academy. 1975.

33. Swami, Saradananda – Sri Sri Ramakrishna Lila Prasanga. Calcutta. Udbodhan Karyalaya. 1358 B.S. Reprinted in Jan. 1994.

34. Vidyarnab, Shibchandra – Tantratattva. Calcutta. Nababharat Publishers. 1380 B.S.

35. Vidyavinod, Sundarananda – Sriksetra. Calcutta. Gaudiya Mission, 2nd ed. 1951.

E. Books in Sanskrit and Arabic

1. Acharya, Sri Ram Sarma (ed.) – Sri Mahasivapuranam. Berily. Sanskriti Samsthan. U.P. 1966.

2. Bhattacharya, Mihir Kiran (ed.) – Mahanirvanatantram. Goalpara. Assam. Aswin – 1368 B.S.

3. Deb, Raja Radhakanta – Savdakalpadrumah. Part-II. Varanasi. The Chowkhamba Sanskrit Series Office. 1961.

4. Mukherjee, Satish Chandra (ed.) – Stavakavacamala. Calcutta. Basumati Sahitya Mandir. 1334. B.S.

5. Onkarnath, Sri Sitaramdas (ed.) – Sri Sri Chandi. Magra. Hooghly. Debjan Karyalaya. 1382. B.S.

6. Smrititirtha, Krishnachandra – Aryachar – Paddhati or Purohit – Darpan. Vol-II. Parishista Khanda. Calcutta. P. M. Bagchi and Co. Pvt. Ltd. 1391 B.S.

7. Swami, Jagadananda (ed.) – The Gita, Calcutta. Udbodhan Karyalaya. Agrahayan – 1400 B.S.

8. Tarkacharya, Kalipada and Nayatirtha, Sri Srijib (ed.) – The Srimadbhagabatam in Aryashastra. Nabam Sankhya (9th issue) Phalgun – 1374 B.S. and Saptabingsha Sankhya (27th issue). Calcutta. Sri Sitaram Vedic Mahavidyalaya. Baisakh. 1375 B.S.

9. Vidyalankar, Ramtosan (ed.) – Prantosani Tantra. Calcutta. Nababharat Publishers. 1991.

10. Moulana Mobarak Karim Jaohar (tr.) – Koran Shareef. Calcutta. Haraf Prakashani. 1974.

F. Journals and Pamphlets in English

1. Marriot, Mckim and Cohn Bernard, S. – Networks and Centres in the Integration of Indian Civilisation. Journal of Social Research. 1(1). 1958.

2. Redfield, Robert – The Social Organisation of Traditions. Far Eastern Quarterly. 15(1). 1955.

3. Redfield, R. and Singer, Milton – The Cultural Role of Cities, Economic Development and Cultural Change. (3). 1954.

4. Roychowdhury, P. C. – The Pandas of Deoghar. Modern Review. 46(2). Calcutta. 1964.

5. Stein, Burton – The Economic Function of a Medieval South Indian Temple. Journal of Asian Studies. 19(2). 1960.

6. Vidyarthi, L. P. – Origin and Development of the Gayawal : A Priestly Community. Journal of Bihar Research Society. XI, Part. II. 1954.

G. Journals and Pamphlets in Bengali

1. Chattopadhyaya, Kamal – Swadhinata Sangrame Hooghly Jela. Paschimbanga. Hooghly Jela Sankhya. West Bengal Government. Department of Information and Culture. 1403 B.S.

2. Dwija, Sahadeb – Tarakeswar Bandana (Punthi). Calcutta. Asiatic Society of Bengal. 1244 B.S. (1837 A.D.)

3. Gangopadhyaya, Sukumar – Sri Sri Tarakeswar. Tarakeswar. Tarakeswar Lila Mahatmya Prakashani. 1961.

4. Masik Basumati – Bhadra. Cal. 1362 B.S.

5. Sripantha – Mohanta – Elokeshi Sambad. Ananda Bazar Patrika. Autumn Special. Calcutta. 1976.

6. Sri Sri Taraknath Jiu Seba Samiti (ed.) – Sri Sri Tarakeswar Lila. Tarakeswar. Hooghly. 1994.

H. English Newspapers

1. Friend of India - July 17, 1873.
2. Hindu Patriot - July 21, 1873.
3. The Statesman - April 29, 1884.
   (Editorial)
4. The Statesman - 07.09.1897.
5. The Statesman - 26.8.24, 6(3).
6. The Statesman - 22.7.1996.
7. The Statesman - 2.11.1998.
8. Forward - 8.4.24, 4(2).
9. Forward - 10.4.24. 3(5).
10. Forward - 25.4.24, 4(2).
11. The Bengalee - 9.4.24, 4(4).
12. The Bengalee - 9.5.24, 4(7).
13. The Bengalee - 9.5.24, 6(3).
14. The Bengalee - 14.5.24, 3(7).
15. The Bengalee - 21.5.24, 4(4).
16. The Bengalee - 31.5.24, 4(7).
17. The Bengalee - 22.6.24, 5(6).
18. The Bengalee - 26.6.24, 5(7).
19. The Bengalee - 20.7.24, 2(3).
20. The Bengalee - 20.7.24, 6(4).
21. The Bengalee - 24.8.24, 5(1).
22. The Bengalee - 26.8.24, 3(4).
23. The Bengalee - 20.9.24, 4(6).
24. The Bengalee - 20.9.24, 4(6-7).
25. The Bengalee - 20.9.24, 6(4).
26. The Bengalee - 25.9.24, 5(7).

27. Amrita Bazar Patrika -   28.2.24, 6(3).

28. Amrita Bazar Patrika -   2.3.24, 7(4).

29. Amrita Bazar Patrika -   16.4.25, 6(5).

30. Amrita Bazar Patrika -   20.4.24, 3(4).

31. Amrita Bazar Patrika -   25.4.24, 8(1).

32. Amrita Bazar Patrika -   4.5.24. 5(6).

33. Amrita Bazar Patrika -   6.5.24, 6(3).

34. Amrita Bazar Patrika -   15.5.24, 6(3).

35. Amrita Bazar Patrika -   16.5.24. 6(2).

36. Amrita Bazar Patrika -   17.5.24, 5(2)

37. Amrita Bazar Patrika -   18.5.24, 5(1-5).

38. Amrita Bazar Patrika -   20.5.24, 5(1-2).

39. Amrita Bazar Patrika -   21.5.24, 5(4).

40. Amrita Bazar Patrika -   31.5.24, 5(4).

41. Amrita Bazar Patrika -   10.6.24, 8(2).

42. Amrita Bazar Patrika -   12.6.24.

43. Amrita Bazar Patrika -   13.6.24.

44. Amrita Bazar Patrika -   5.7.24, 6(1).

45. Amrita Bazar Patrika -   6.7.24, 5(3).

46. Amrita Bazar Patrika -   8.7.24, 6(5).

47. Amrita Bazar Patrika -   9.7.24, 5(6).

48. Amrita Bazar Patrika -   18.7.24, 3(4).

49. Amrita Bazar Patrika -   17.8.24, 6(6).

50. Amrita Bazar Patrika -   31.8.24, 6(1).

51. Amrita Bazar Patrika -   25.9.24, 6(3-4).

52. Amrita Bazar Patrika -   18.2.25, 7(2).

53. Amrita Bazar Patrika -   12.3.25, 3(3).

54. Amrita Bazar Patrika -   10.7.25, 3(4).

I. Bengali Newspapers

1. Bharat Sanskarak -   12.9.1873.
2. Yugantar-   5.3.62.
3. Yugantar -   14.4.63.
4. Yugantar -   23.3.95.
5. Basumati -   27 Phalgun, 1365 B.S.
6. Ananda Bazar Patrika -   20.2.24.
7. Ananda Bazar Patrika -   27.2.24, 3(6).
8. Ananda Bazar Patrika -   6.3.24, 2(3-4).
9. Ananda Bazar Patrika -   20.3.24, 4(2).
10. Ananda Bazar Patrika -   3.4.24.
11. Ananda Bazar Patrika -   13.4.24, 2(5-6).
12. Ananda Bazar Patrika -   19.4.24, 2(6).
13. Ananda Bazar Patrika -   20.4.24, 2(4-5).
14. Ananda Bazar Patrika -   24.4.24, 2(6).
15. Ananda Bazar Patrika -   27.4.24.
16. Ananda Bazar Patrika -   2.5.24, 2(2).
17. Ananda Bazar Patrika -   11.5.24, 2(7).
18. Ananda Bazar Patrika -   17.5.24, 2(1).
19. Ananda Bazar Patrika -   17.5.24. 2(4).
20. Ananda Bazar Patrika -   18.5.24, 2(5-6).
21. Ananda Bazar Patrika -   18.5.24, 2(7).
22. Ananda Bazar Patrika -   22.5.24, 3(1).
23. Ananda Bazar Patrika -'   22.5.24, 3(2).
24. Ananda Bazar Patrika -   23.5.24, 3(1-2).
25. Ananda Bazar Patrika -   5.6.24, 2(7).
26. Ananda Bazar Patrika -   7.6.24, 2(5).
27. Ananda Bazar Patrika -   13.6.24, 3(3-4).
28. Bhananda Bazar Patrika -   30.7.24.

J. Interviews

1. Interview with Monomohan Chakrabarty, ex-Secretary (1978-83) of the Purohit Mandali (Association of the Priests) at Tarakeswar.

2. Interview with the ex-Secretary, Purohit Mandali on 9.6.97.

3. Interview with the Sebayet Priest of the Goddess Kali on 7.11.98.

4. Interview with the ex-Secretary, Purohit Mandali on 7.10.99.

5. Interview with the Secretary, Purohit Mandali on 25.12.99.

6. Interview with the Secretary, Tirtha Yatri Nibas Malik Sangha on 26.12.99.

Glossary

A.

1. *Abir* – coloured powder used during the festival of colour.

2. *Aksay Tritiya* – the third date of the lunar month after the new moon in the first month of the Bengali calendar.

3. *Amabasya* – the lunar date associated with the new moon.

4. *Anadilingam* – self-manifested symbol of the cult of Lord *Siva*.

5. *Annaprasan* – the first time a baby is fed rice.

6. *Artha* – money.

7. *Asvamedha Yajna* – the vedic ritual sacrifice of horse.

8. *Aus* – paddy cultivated during the rainy season.

9. *Ayurveda* – the method of treatment with medicinal plants.

B.

1. *Baishya* – a caste dependent exclusively on business in the Hindu caste hierarchy.

2. *Baki* - the remaining part of the income and expenditure.

3. *Bank* - yokepole.

4. *Bazar* – market.

5. *Bena* – vetiver, a kind of grass.

6. *Benami* - in the name of the other.

7. *Bhandara* – distribution of consecrated food among the ascetics.

8. *Bhogarati* – the ritual feeding ceremony of the Lord.

9. *Bibadi* - contestant.

10. *Bigha* – a type of measurement of land (1/3 acre. App.).

11. *Bijoya Dashami*- the fourth day of the four days' festival relating to the worship of the Goddess *Durga*.

12. *Bilwa* – the wood-apple.

13. *Brahmachari* – a person performing lifelong celibacy.

14. *Brahmacharya* – lifelong celibacy.

15. *Brahmin* – the person belonging to the highest caste in the Hindu caste hierarchy.

C.

1. *Cachari* – the replica of a court.

2. *Chakran* – land given in lieu of salary.

3. *Chanchar* – a festival relating to the burning of an effigy of a demon.

4. *Chandigan* – the song sung in honour of the Goddess *Chandi*.

5. *Chandina Sattva* – a Tenancy Act by which the landlord could impose any amount of land tax on the tenants.

6. *Charanamrita* – water sanctified through the worship.

7. *Charpatra* – title-deed.

8. *Chatuspathi* (*tol, chaubadi and chaupadi*) – the school for learning Sanskrit.

9. *Chaukidari* – service related to ensuring security.

10. *Chaulpatti* – the market for dealing in rice.

11. *Chela* – the disciple.

12. *Chhatri* – a caste in the Hindu caste hierarchy known also as *Kshatriya*.

13. *Chittas* – hand-written accounts.

14. *Cottah* – 1/20 of a *bigha*.

D.

1. *Dakhne* – of the South.

2. *Daksina* – the remuneration given to the priest by the pilgrim for being help to him in the worship of the deity.

3. *Dalal* – broker.

4. *Dandi* – prostration.

5. *Dandiswami* – an ascetic holding sacred stick.

6. *Dangli Sannyasis* – the *Saiva* ascetics who indulged in business.

7. *Darshan* – a look to the God.

8. *Debutter* – in the name of the deity.

9. *Dewan Daftari Cachari* – the office for the collection of land revenue.

10. *Dharmasala* – rest house.

11. *Dharmathakur* – the popular god worshipped mostly by low-caste people.

12. *Dhawja* – flag or banner.

13. *Diksa* – initiation.

14. *Diwali* – the festival of the light.

15. *Dudhpukur* – the sacred tank.

16. *Durwan* – gatekeeper.

G.

1. *Gadighar* – the room specified for the seat of administration.

2. *Ganja* – market for selling crops.

3. *Ghee* – clarified butter.

4. *Golah* – granary.

5. *Gopa* – a caste in the Hindu caste hierarchy dependent mostly on cattle rearing.

6. *Gosain* – an epithet for a *Saiva* as well as *Vaisnavite* ascetic.

7. *Guddee* – seat of administration.

8. *Gurubhrata* – disciple-brother.

9. *Gurupita* – preceptor.

10. *Gurupurnima* – the date specified in the lunar month for the worship of the preceptor.

11. *Guru-Sisya Parampara* – preceptor-disciple lineage.

H.

1. *Habeli Cachari* – court-house.

2. *Hajat* – the lock-up where the prisoners are imprisoned.

3. *Hat* – market.

J.

1. *Jama* – collected rent.

2. *Jamai land* – rented land.

3. *Janmastami* – the birth-date of Lord *Krishna*.

4. *Jiu* – the epithet used in honour of the divinity.

5. *Jote* – cultivable land.

K.

1. *Kabuliyat* – deed of consent.

2. *Kama* – desire.

3. *Kamansala* – tonsuring centre.

4. *Kantajhanp* – jumping into the bed of thorns.

5. *Kaonrias* – those who carry yokepoles.

6. *Kaparpatti* – the market dealing in clothes.

7. *Kathakata* – art of explaining the tales from the *Puranas*.

8. *Khagra* – a kind of grass.

9. *Khatian* – ledger.

10. *Kistibandis* – arrangement for payments in instalments.

11. *Koras* – labourers.

12. *Ksetramahatmya* – fame of the place of pilgrimage.

13. *Kshatriya* – the second important caste in the Hindu caste hierarchy.

14. *Kulabritti* – the allowance given on genealogical basis in lieu of service to the deity.

15. *Kurshinama* – genealogical table.

L.

1. *Lat* – part of an estate.

2. *Lakheraj* – rent-free land.

3. *Langarkhana* – free community kitchen where all dine without any consideration of caste, creed and religion.

4. *Lingam* – symbolic manifestation of Lord *Siva*.

5. *Lokachara* – popular rite.

6. *Lokadharma* – popular religion.

7. *Lokayata* – popular.

M.

1. *Mahal* – part of an estate.

2. *Mahamandalesvar* – the head of the organization of the *Dashnami Sannysis*.

3. *Maiji* – mother.

4. *Malik Sebayet* – worshipper-cum-owner.

5. *Mandali* – an organisation.

6. *Mantra* – incantation.

7. *Math* – the monastery.

8. *Mathdhari* – an ascetic having allegiance to the monastery organised under the shadow of *Advaita* school of *Saivism*.

9. *Mela* – fair.

10. *Mitra Saptami* – the seventh date of the lunar month of *Agrahayan* celebrated in honour of the Sun.

11. *Mohanta* – the head of the monastery.

12. *Mokarari* - the land revenue of which is fixed.

13. *Moksa* – freedom from the cycle of birth and death.

14. *Monoharipatti* – market dealing in toys, pictures and etc.

15. *Mouza* – village.

16. *Mul Sannyasi* – principal ascetic.

17. *Mundan* – tonsure.

N.

1. *Nad* – primordial sound.

2. *Nathpanthis* – the ascetics who believe that Lord *Siva* is the supreme Lord and the source of primordial sound.

3. *Natyamandira* – court-hall.

4. *Nazurat* – the property acquired by way of gifts.

5. *Nij* – self.

6. *Niler bati* – the candle burnt with reference to the marriage anniversary of Lord *Siva*.

7. *Nil utsab* – the marriage anniversary of Lord *Siva*.

8. *Niskar* – rent-free.

9. *Niyampatra* – ordinance.

P.

1. *Paramanna-bhog* – consecrated rice boiled generally with milk and sugar.

2. *Pardanashin* – covered with the veil.

3. *Pergana* – part of a district.

4. *Poila* – the first date of the week, month, year and etc.

5. *Pranami* – money and other things given to the preceptor in obeisance to him.

6. *Prasad* – consecrated food.

7. *Pratyadesh* –divine direction to overcome crisis.

8. *Puja* – worship.

9. *Purbe* – of the east.

10. *Purnima* – the lunar date associated with the full moon.

11. *Putni Mahal* – part of an estate on which stipulated amount of land revenue is fixed.

12. *Putni taluk* – the estate on which stipulated amount of land revenue is claimed.

R.

1. *Radi* – of the Rarh.

2. *Rajbati* – palace.

3. *Rakhipurnima* – the festival of tying embellished thread on the wrist.

4. *Rarh* – the area in Bengal on the west bank of the Ganges.

5. *Rarhi-Khanda-Jangal* – bushy area in Bengal on the west bank of the Ganges.

S.

1. *Sadabrata* – hospitality.

2. *Sadgopas* – the *Gopas* who take to cultivation.

3. *Sakar* – the land which is not rent-free.

4. *Sakta* – the worshipper of *Sakti*, the variform of the consort of Lord *Siva*.

5. *Samadhi Ksetra* – the burial place of an ascetic.

6. *Sambat* – the year concerned.

7. *Samkranti* – last date of the month in the Bengali calendar.

8. *Sankalpa* - vow taken prior to worship.

9. *Sannyasa* – renunciation of the world.

10. *Sannyasi* – an ascetic.

11. *Santi-sastayan* – propitiatory rite.

12. *Sasthi* – the goddess worshipped for ensuring security of the children.

13. *Seba* – service to the god or goddess.

14. *Se-pattani* – a kind of land-settlement which requires the land-holder concerned to pay fixed amount of land revenue after a stipulated period to the higher authority in the given hierarchy.

15. *Sika* – reticulated sling.

16. *Sitala* – the folk-goddess of the diseases.

17. *Sripata* – the sacred place for the devotees of Lord *Vishnu*.

18. *Sudra* – the lower caste in the Hindu caste hierarchy.

19. *Suvamastu Sakabda* – may the *Sakabda* (B.S.+515) herald bliss for all.

20. *Svayambhulingadilaksanam* – the feature by which the symbol of the self-manifested cult of Lord *Siva* is recognised.

T.

1. *Taidad* – the register bearing the description of the boundaries of the landed estates.

2. *Taluk* – the landed estate acquired by virtue of a settlement with big landlord in the given hierarchy.

3. *Tantra* – a branch of Hindu religion that has developed with reference to *Siva* and *Sakti*.

4. *Thak* – classified.

5. *Thakur* – the deity.

6. *Tirtha-Guru* – preceptor of the religious complex.

7. *Tirthasthala* – place of pilgrimage.

8. *Tirthayatra* – pilgrimage.

9. *Tithi* – lunar date of the month.

U.

1. *Upanayan* – the wearing of sacred thread.

2. *Uttariya* – hand-woven cotton threads tied together with a tuft of *Kusha* grass.

W.

1. *Wajeb* – vow.

2. *Wasil* – collection.

Y.

1. *Yajmani* – clientele.

2. *Yogi* – ascetic.

Z.

1. *Zamindari* – the landed estate of a *zamindar*.

Author Biography

The author spent his childhood, adolescence, and part of his youth in Tarakeswar. He started his education in the primary section of the Higher Secondary School in Tarakeswar. After completing his school education in 1970, he pursued a full-time graduate programme at the Ramakrishna Mission Vidyamandira, Belur Math. He then enrolled at Calcutta University in 1973 for his post-graduation. Following the completion of the process, he was subsequently appointed as a part-time lecturer at his alma mater in a specialised academic programme.

After meeting the criteria of the College Service Commission and receiving the necessary approvals, he was then appointed as a full-time lecturer at the end of 1982. He retired in 2013 as an Associated Professor, according to the planned schedule. Thereafter he continued to walk at his own pace and space.